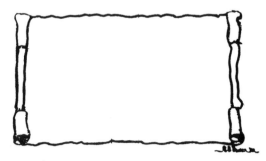

Liberating Voices

LIBERATING VOICES

*Oral Tradition in African
American Literature*

Gayl Jones

HARVARD UNIVERSITY PRESS

Cambridge, Massachusetts, and London, England
1991

Copyright © 1991 by Gayl Jones
All rights reserved
Printed in the United States of America
10 9 8 7 6 5 4 3 2 1

This book is printed on acid-free paper, and its binding materials have been chosen
for strength and durability.

Library of Congress Cataloging-in-Publication Data

Jones, Gayl.
Liberating voices : oral tradition in African American literature
/ Gayl Jones.
p.   cm.
Includes bibliographical references and index.
ISBN 0-674-53024-1 (alk. paper)
1. American literature—Afro-American authors—History and
criticism. 2. American literature—20th century—History and
criticism. 3. Literature and folklore—United States. 4. Afro-
Americans in literature. 5. Oral tradition—United States.
6. Folklore in literature. 7. Music and literature. I. Title.
PS153.N5J66   1991
810.9′896073—dc20   90-45559
CIP

For my mother, Lucille Jones,
and
in memory of my father, Franklin Jones

Contents

Contents

Liberating Voices

Introduction

Modern African American writers began to shape and modify their literature using models not only from European and European American traditions, but also from their own distinctive oral and aural forms. This book explores the technical effects of this alternative tradition. When the African American creative writers began to trust the literary possibilities of their own verbal and musical creations and to employ self-inspired techniques, they began to transform the European and European American models and to gain greater artistic sovereignty. Contemporary African American writers often recognize no boundaries. The territories of so-called "art forms" and "folk forms" interpenetrate. Along with the African writer Geormbeeyi Adali-Mortly, most would assert, "It is out of these forms that modern creative writing can be built."[1]

The poems, short stories, and novels discussed in this book represent such creative writing. Each writer has redefined Western literature and literary influence either by incorporating (subordinating, not merging) folktales, spirituals, blues, within the traditional framework (as in Charles Waddell Chesnutt's and Paul Laurence Dunbar's stories), or by drawing dramatic and lyrical counterpoints from a whole spectrum of oral referents, as in Langston Hughes's poetic use of blues to redefine stanzas, reorganize development, and liberate meter, or in Amiri Baraka's (LeRoi Jones) recreation of the short story as a jazz composition. The various oral forms, like the literary ones, not only hold forth artistic possibilities, but also imply aesthetic, thematic, and social dimensions.

Oral stories, seen merely as the "first stories" of a pre-literate culture, are often dismissed as crude rather than appreciated as the continuing, complex, inventive heritage of African, African American, Native American, and other Third World literatures. Many of the writers within these traditions draw upon their oral heritage for the power and diversity of its narrative forms and storytelling techniques; for them it indeed confers, as the narrator declares in N. Scott Momaday's *House Made of Dawn*, "whole and consummate being."[2] Certainly, in these cultures, oral heritage in both its verbal and musical renderings stays vital in observation, experience, and imagination.

This book begins with the writers of the turn-of-the-century. It is here that the literary uses of oral tradition actually started to flourish. From 1773, when Phillis Wheatley published her book of poetry (and became the first African American to do so), to the nineteenth-century slave narrative novels of William Wells Brown and Martin Delany, African American writers worked in strict and formal adherence to Western literary forms, as in Wheatley's use of the neoclassical style of Alexander Pope. And when orality does manifest itself, it is the restricted, subordinate orality of Brown's and Delany's prefacing songs and slaves' conversations. Oral tradition in Brown and Delany was moreover only incidental to the authors' main intention; it did not represent the deliberate correlation of form and content that is found in the twentieth century's use of oral technique. Yet to make their novels they utilized the slave narrative forms and impulses, if not speech-linked devices and oral modes. And, indeed, the slave narratives might be the only continuous pre-twentieth-century examples of oral tradition in action. Because of its narrative procedures and episodic structure, some critics have even hailed the slave memoir as a new American literary form, indeed the only authentic one, although its "life forms" in many instances resemble the Spanish picaresque in the uses of speech, sequence of events, migratory impulses, character types and character introductions, ironic attitude, and social morality. But while the slave narratives serve as a precedent for African American writers in the New World and have in fact inspired many, I have chosen to concentrate on imaginative literature, because it deliberately derives its themes, language, design, and vision from oral literature.

Although this book focuses on technique, it does nevertheless stress social, political, historical, and human implications when these techniques imply a corresponding moral or social vision. In many of the works there are indeed important correlations between, in Ralph Ellison's words, "society, morality, and the novel" (or other work of art). Like many of their Latin American counterparts, African American writers frequently combine aesthetics with social motive, so that art almost always conjoins humanity and society; thus, "kinetic art"[3] is mostly championed.

In the chapters that follow I outline the differences in the ways short stories, novels, and poetry make use of the oral continuum and point to certain similarities between forms and motives in each genre. Literary generations differ in their approach, though each generation and individual within it are in concert regarding their interest in problems of African American identity and self-definition in the New World, and the ways in which both form and content merge to solve or complicate the questions of language, art, reality, morality, and human value. Thus, in this central concern, the many voices in this book cohere as one voice.

Not every literature admits the influence and validity of its folklores and oral tradition in its literary criticism, yet all literatures have an essential connection with orality; indeed one might say that the foundation of every literary tradition is oral, whether it is visible or invisible in the text. For example, the oral principles in Chaucer's *The Canterbury Tales, Troilus and Criseyda, The Book of the Duchess,* and *The House of Fame,* are evident in the modes of discourse, tales, repetitions, rhetorical parallelisms, exclamations, interposed remarks to reader (audience), abrupt transitions, stories within stories, and the texts' affinity for recitation. At a time when French was the language of the literate classes, the prestige language of the nobility, Chaucer helped to extend the literary resources and scope of the vernacular English, its greater diversity and vigor. His use of his native speech, however, was not done with ease or without pondering circumspection. In fact, in his envoy for *Troilus and Criseyda,* Chaucer worries that its "gret diversite" might lead others to "myswrite, mysmeter" and mis-"understonde."

Likewise Miguel de Cervantes Saavedra, in his *Don Quijote* (1605–1615), maximized the sphere of the novel through oral traditions of interpolated stories, folktales, proverbs, orations, recollections, and dreams. In Cervantes's time too there were literary purists (who did "myswrite" and mis-"understonde") whom he challenged by these "intrusions" and by mingling forms and genres, poetry and prose, breaking rules to create a truly multiple and expansive novel of many voices. The "composite novel" *Don Quijote* also incorporates medieval ballads *(romances viejos)* and uses the rich vocabulary of Spain's oral traditions. Don Quijote recites some of these ballads (some plotlines of the frame-stories take their form and subject matter from the medieval ballads); otherwise his speech parodies the flamboyant, convoluted language of the chivalric romances, or when he is mad, refined and elevated oratory, in such speeches as "The Golden Age" and "Arms and Letters."

Cervantes's use of Sancho Panza as a counterpoint to Don Quijote also challenged the literary purists. Though Sancho represents everything that is "lower" thematically, linguistically, and socially, his language broadens the novel's territory simply because Cervantes allows it in and because Sancho is a foregrounded, major character. Sancho's vernacular—even with its vigor, inventiveness, and color—was considered vulgar, as American, Canadian, and other colonial Englishes were considered vulgar by the Old World English speakers, yet it paved the way for indigenous and independent literary traditions. Sancho's vernacular too usually did not have literary uses. It was inappropriate. By admitting Sancho as a main character speaking in his own voice, Cervantes further breaks rules to admit experiences, free imagination, add new perceptions, and tell a whole story. Toward the end of the book, when Don Quijote and Sancho exchange voices, reality and language, like the magical knight himself, become enchanted.

The modern Spanish poet Federico García Lorca also mined oral resources. He acknowledged that his metaphorical techniques had been greatly influenced by the strengths of "images created by the people" in their oral literatures: for example, "heaven's bacon" and "nun's sigh" for kinds of sweetmeats; "half-orange" for cupola; the Andalusian "an ox of water" for a deep, slow watercourse. And Lorca once heard a Granada farmer say, "The rushes love to grow on the tongue of the river."

Besides such popular imagery in his poetry, Lorca also made use of the Spanish *romance* (ballad) and the *cante jondo* ("deep song") or sung lyric in Andalusian tradition. In form, melody, and repetitions, one sees the oral imprint in his poetry and drama. In fact, the epic tradition and the *romance* have influenced not only Lorca but whole traditions of Spanish literature: "The ballad *(romance)* is a *type* of epico-lyric poem, which derives ultimately from the Spanish national epic. The old, traditional, anonymous, and popular ballad has grown with the spread of the language and has been nourished wherever Spanish was spoken . . . Exceptionally versatile, it is the poem of open fields and village squares, equally adaptable to the most exquisite baroque refinements, sung at times with simple, ancient, nostalgic melodies, or to the delicate measures of court music. Lope de Vega and Gongora used the romance in the seventeenth century, as did the Duque de Rivas and Zorrilla in the romantic period, and many modern poets."[4]

In non-European literary traditions there were similar "openings out" with the vernacular language as the literary extensor. In early Japan, prose was written in Chinese, the language of the Japanese court; to write in the Japanese vernacular was thought vulgar. Only women, untrained in Chinese, wrote novels in Japanese; thus the first intrusions of Japanese oral culture into the novel were made by women. The people's own language then contributed to an early masterpiece of Japanese fiction, Lady Murasaki's *Tale of Genji,* which was also "the first psychological novel in world literature." Imaginative literature flourished in Japan when the colloquial novel came into its own, no longer "frozen by a literary elite." In China, however, because there were many forms of the vernacular, the writer was often plagued by what form to use. In Arabic-speaking cultures special problems occur because no language can compete with the language of the Koran, and any deviation from this classical Arabic is considered undesirable; yet creative writers in the Arab world use modern dialects in literature because it is "argued by some that it [classical Arabic] is not suited for the modern world." In India Sanscrit was the language of the scholastic and priestly caste and the language of literary traditions. Only now do modern [spoken] Indian languages such as Hindi and Bengali have a literature of their own.[5]

Of course the problems and resolutions of these Asian literatures may be different from those of the West; nevertheless it is interesting again to parallel world literatures that are "opening out" to afford access to the oral, and to see that rather than reducing literary standards of excellence, this process extends requirements and possibilities.

James Joyce, the most far-ranging, multifarious, and influential European linguistic innovator of this century, felt that one should actually hear his tremendous literary experiment *Finnegans Wake* to get the full richness of its music, its Dublin brogue, and its multiple meanings (and he recorded some of the text himself). Though Joyce's "made words" make the visual reading of *Finnegans Wake* difficult, when they are heard or read aloud the meanings often resolve themselves through spoken syntax and sounds. What is initially impenetrable is then recognized as rich and energetic Dublin brogue. Though the words are changed (meanings jammed, augmented lexicon), the fundamental rules of speech are maintained, together with the sound if not the appearance of native speech. Thus a spoken "hospodch" easily resolves itself into "hodgepodge" and "hopscotch"; "crossmess parzel" phonologically resolves its dual content of "Christmas parcel" and "crossword puzzle"; "shaulders" is "shawl," "shoulders," and "shoals"; "falskin" is both "fall" and "foreskin"—the thematic significance is also revealed in the suggestion that Adam's (one of Finnegan's–H. C. Earwicker's multiple mythological and historical identities) fall might also have been a sexual one; perhaps Finnegan's fall and resurrection will be both.

Reading *Finnegans Wake* aloud, listening to its being read, resolves many of the tensions that visual reading creates—the conversational rhythms, Irish brogue, and humor succeed despite the orthographic changes, mixture of many languages, the puns, suggestions, the portmanteau, telescoping, association: "How good you are in explosion! How farflung is your fokloire and how velktingeling your volupkabulary!"[6]

Oral tradition, then, transforms these works. But we see even more clearly the relationship between oral tradition and national aesthetic identity in the work of the contemporary Canadian writer Margaret Laurence. In her foreword to *The Manawaka World of Margaret Laurence,* Clara Thomas states: "Margaret Laurence is a Canadian writer, solidly rooted in southwestern Manitoba, the setting of Neepawa, her home town, and of Manawaka, her fictional one. Her characters 'talk Canadian'; in their idiom and turns of speech we hear 'Canadian' as distinct from 'American' English."[7]

Laurence's Canadian is heard in *A Jest of God, The Stone Angel,* and *The Diviners,* three fine examples of her first-person novels that "involve the reader immediately into the sound of the characters' voices," dimensions of their imagination, their obsessions, repetitions, questionings and reevaluations of motive; and in the case of Rachel in *A Jest of God,* their colloquial grace. Not only the dialogue and thought processes, but even the descriptive beginning of *The Diviners* show the oral motif: "The river flowed both ways. The current moved from north to south, but the wind usually came from the south, rippling the bronze-green water in the opposite direction. This apparently impossible contradiction, made apparent and possible, still fascinated Morag, even after years of river watching."[8]

Often, Laurence's writing steps off the page with the immediacy of voice and recognition, with a compelling resonance; one hears her storytellers; her Canadian voices are broad and ranging, rich in personality and history. Yet Laurence's language perfectly illustrates one of the great problems of orality as spoken voice in literature: it sounds too easy; it sounds not complicated enough. As a result it is easily dismissed (especially by rival traditions) as literature of little artistic effort or consequence. Because one can so easily hear the prose, because it sounds too natural, because it suggests the voice so authentically, it seems "artless." Apparently simple, its speech-linked structures seem to lack artistic ingenuity or complex range, the full display of linguistic skill and virtuosity that one *notices* in the more self-conscious literary stylist. It seems more lightweight, a toy, rather than immediately valuable, an intricate jewel. Yet there is both art and wisdom in Laurence's prose, in her fully realized landscapes and personalities. And there is virtuosity, but it is similar to the virtuosity of certain seemingly "natural" actors. In this, the most egregious example of this sort of literary persona, one doesn't notice the art; one either assumes the author is "playing herself" (writing in the only style she can write) or is assured there is no effort involved, no process of study or development; it seems too simple, it must be quite easy. An occasional critic will tell the ingenuous or doubtful reader (or listener; though most true listeners know this) that such simplicity or colloquial ease took years to acquire, but the very need to make such assurances—to "protest too much"—itself proves the point. There are actors and writers who acquire that ease early—who seem to act without acting or to write without writing—but they are generally the exception.

But whether or not the art is noticed, it is the telling that is important here. In telling her own story, *A Jest of God*, Rachel names herself, both individually and nationally. She tells us who she is. In Margaret Laurence's prose and Clara Thomas's description of it, we see the need for asserting identity through language. This applies to a nation's need to name its own songs, themes, and character in its own distinct language, and to a person's need to say, this is who I am (or in collective oral traditions, as are most by implication, "this is who we are"). And by discussing the Canadian writer Margaret Laurence we move closer to the motives of the African American writer and many other minority and Third World writers in their usually more manifest and deliberate use of oral traditions and folklore to achieve and assert a distinctive aesthetic and literary voice. Joyce acknowledges in *A Portrait of the Artist as a Young Man* the aesthetic tension between Ireland's rich linguistic modifications and Ben Jonson's English: "The language in which we are speaking is his before it is mine. How different are the words . . . on his lips and mine! I cannot speak or write these words without unrest of spirit." Perhaps it is the revelation of this language, "so familiar and so foreign," which made *Finnegans Wake* possible. In this respect African writers even more closely parallel the African Americans by the deliberate connectives between oratory, story-telling, and written literature, informing works which combine African language idioms, folklore and oral literary forms, proverbs, songs, conceptions of time and space, mythologies, in the works of such writers as Gabriel Okara, Chinua Achebe, Buchi Emecheta, Ama Ata Aidoo, and Amos Tutuola, certainly among many.

In Tutuola's *The Palm-Wine Drinkard*, for example, the style is "so closely related to talk, and his content compounded of fantasy and variations of African-religious-Heroic myth": "there we saw the creature that we called 'Drum, Song and Dance' personally and these creatures were living creatures." And Gabriel Okara, the Nigerian poet and novelist, proceeds this way: "In order to capture the vivid images of African speech, I had to eschew the habit of expressing my thoughts first in English. I had to study each Ijaw expression I used and to discover the probable situation in which it was used in order to bring out the nearest meaning in English."[9]

Not only in the narrative and thematic dimension, in this valorization of identity, but also in symbols and images are the literary consequences of indigenous oral traditions evident. One finds this recreation of sustaining mythologies and culture heroes through oral tradition in Ralph Ellison's *Invisible Man,* N. Scott Momaday's *House Made of Dawn,* Carlos Fuentes's *Where the Air Is Clear,* Gabriel García Márquez's *One Hundred Years of Solitude,* as well as Amos Tutuola's *The Palm-Wine Drinkard,* again among many writers of the Third World.

However, it is also important to place African American writers into the context and contours of *American language* and literature, to consider and understand that standard American English and (standard) American literature as well are modified by oral traditions, and that American literature came into its own when it consciously recognized, employed, and explored the techniques of American orality and landscape as distinct from the European models. In descriptions of American English we see this. For instance, in Thrall, Hibbard, and Holman's *A Handbook of Literature,* under "American language," one finds:

> A term used to designate idioms and forms peculiar to English speech in America. As pointed out in the *Encyclopedia Americana,* these differences usually arise in one of three ways: some forms originate in America independent of English speech ("gerrymander" is an example); some expressions which were once native to England have been brought here and have lived after they had died out in England ("fall" for "autumn"); and certain English forms have taken on modified meanings in America (as we use "store" for "shop"). Besides these matters of vocabulary, H. L. Mencken points out six other respects in which American expression differs from English: syntax, intonation, slang, idiom, grammar, and pronunciation.[10]

The *Handbook* reveals something which also has important implications in regard to problems that African American writers have in making literary use of their oral traditions: "Although for many years the sensitiveness of Americans made them deny the existence of anything like an American language, its existence has been recognized and its nature applauded for over a quarter of a century. It is a unique language of American literary art, impressively present in the work of writers like Mark Twain, Ring Lardner, Ernest Hemingway, and J. D. Salinger. Scholars have given it serious attention."[11]

In African American literary tradition, it was during the period known as the Harlem Renaissance of the 1920s, with its manifestos of artistic self-assertion (Hughes's "We intend to express our individual dark-skinned selves without fear or shame") and its celebrations of black heritage and aesthetic, that a similar attitude and abandonment of literary double-consciousness occurred: an applauding of African American modifications of American language. African American writers whose tradition serves as a parallel to that of Twain, Lardner, Hemingway, and Salinger began to make a serious literary use of that other "unique language of American literary art." Among the fiction writers in this tradition were Zora Neale Hurston, Jean Toomer, Rudolph Fisher, John Matheus, Eric Waldrond, Bruce Nugent; among the poets were Langston Hughes, Sterling Brown, and James Weldon Johnson; among the dramatists Langston Hughes, Jean Toomer, and Willis Richardson. This unique language was no longer seen as quaint, or as having only two stops, as James Weldon Johnson described them, of "humor and pathos." The range of sensibility broadened beyond the traditional literary dialect of Paul Laurence Dunbar, Charles Waddell Chesnutt, and William Wells Brown. This shift in attitude made possible a new seriousness and range in subject matter, experiences, and concerns, as well as deeper, more complex characterizations.

In an interview in *Chant of Saints,* Ralph Ellison comments on folklore, acknowledging its often invisible resources: "Folklore has been such a vital part of American literature that it is amazing that more people (and especially writers) aren't aware of it. Constance Rourke points out that there are folk motives even in the work of Henry James. I guess one of the difficulties here is that people think of folklore as 'quaint,' as something that is projected in dialect, when in fact it is its style and wisdom that count. The same problem arises when you speak of *American* folklore in the general sense and overlook the complex influence of vernacular idioms, the mixture of vernacular styles, that operate in American culture."[12]

During the Harlem Renaissance, then, folklore or oral tradition was no longer considered quaint and restrictive, but as the ore for complex literary influence. This new attitude provided the base for contemporary African American writers, who make use of folklore cognizant of its multiple and complex linguistic, social, historical, intellectual, and political functions.

Even with the recognition of the importance of oral traditions and techniques in resolving the problems of aesthetic identity, a tension usually continues to exist between the oral modes and the literary ones. This tension is suggested in Thomas's celebration of Margaret Laurence's Canadian English and, as we saw, voiced by Joyce as Stephen Daedalus's thoughts in *Portrait*. Such tension becomes problematic when it affects critical reception. It has always existed between African American and European American literatures and has been aggravated by social relationships, but is not unique; it parallels the aesthetic tension between the American and the European models. For instance, Mark Twain's initial uses of Western lore and American colloquialisms were thought crude and unpolished by the writers of the Eastern establishment devoted to a more genteel and imitative tradition, such as Henry Wadsworth Longfellow and Oliver Wendell Holmes. Certainly Henry James found nothing in the American models, language, and landscape. He went off to Europe because America lacked the institutions and cultural complexity necessary for the development of the artist, and it held nothing which could be culled for style or literary technique. And James felt Twain "amused only primitive persons, was the Philistines' laureate"; others called him "the wild man from the West." [13] Twain, on the other hand, used the materials in the American environment, registered them, recognized that the rich and varied American oral traditions could also be a base for style, range of content, literary procedures, and that they could be artistically developed and renewed. It is this attitude that makes for the difference between the artificial and stylized and the open and innovative: the sense of flexibility and integrity of American landscape and personality. It is the basis for the "Americanness" of many Southern writers such as Eudora Welty, as it is reflected in her intricate orality.

Yet it is important to note here the paradox of James's "folk motives." One is reminded again of the exiled Joyce whose texts are still ebullient with Irish brogue and humor and constellation of Dublin characters. That is, James's later style became more conversational in rhythm and vocabulary, more idiomatic, lending some support to the idea that the seemingly easy, conversational style can be artistically and artfully developed or won after long apprenticeship; James's earlier style, although it drew more attention, seemed more difficult (to read and write); it was more convoluted and "overjangled," to use James's word. Remaining highly periodic and self-conscious, his later style nevertheless moved in the direction of speech: James's mannerly and observant speech at any rate. Even in novels such as *The Portrait of a Lady,* however, one might find evidences of oral mode in the indirect speech of Isabel Archer's numerous meditations, the long telescoped speeches, addresses to reader, the intrusive "I," the place of conversation in the Osmonds' well-mannered entertainments, and perhaps even more profoundly in the structure of revelations—the major revelations of the text come through "talk," are spoken as Isabel "learns to hear," in dialogue exchanges between Isabel and Madame Merle and others. (Again, oral tradition does not always mean "vernacular" and, as Ellison points out, it need not be "projected in dialect." And in James's letters one finds an even greater raciness and sublime conversational rhythm.)

Twain's early orality was of course less mannerly than James's, but not less attentive to nuances of style and voice—his own and others. However, and this must be noted for its implications regarding the critical reception of oral-based African American writers, Twain himself, in an attempt to win deeper approval and higher recognition, came to "distrust himself and his own tastes"[14] and abandoned his earlier intrusions (and intuitions) of American lore. He defended himself as an artist by giving into the genteel traditions of New England (whose models were in essence European); in order to prove himself he found it necessary to move in the opposite direction of James. It must be noted that some critics say his art became richer—although I trust Twain's earlier tastes. Indeed, the two tastes could have coexisted in one work, as Cervantes's *Don Quijote* proves. Actually, *Don Quijote* is a novel of multiple tastes, maximizing the artist's territory. The writer allows himself to roam and graze in many areas, even in many areas at once, exploring, growing, and showing what he can do.

Repeatedly, in order to infuse literature with new life and creativity, contemporary American writers turn to the oral procedures; this may not only produce linguistic and stylistic innovations but often modernize the text, siting it in the writers' contemporary world. Still, this modernization can be resisted, as Ishmael Reed points out in his introduction to *19 Necromancers from Now*:

> I suspect that the inability of some students to "understand" works written by Afro-American authors is traceable to an inability to understand the American experience as rooted in slang, dialect, vernacular, argot, and all the other putdown terms the faculty uses for those who have the gall to deviate from the true and proper way of English.
>
> Slang and colloquial speech have rarely been so creative. It is as if the common man (or his anonymous spokesman) would in his speech assert his humanity against the powers that be, as if the rejection and revolt subdued in the political sphere would burst out in a vocabulary that calls things by their names: "head-shrinker" and "egghead," "boob tube," "think tank" and "beat it," "dig it" and "gone man gone," Herbert Marcuse wrote in *The One-Dimensional Man*.

And it may turn out that the great restive underground language rising from the American slums and fringe communities is the real American poetry and prose, that can tell you the way things are happening now. If this is not the case, then it is mighty strange that a whole new generation exploits this language, in what White racist critics call "folk rock lyrics."[15]

Reed reiterates this subject in John O'Brien's *Interviews with Black Writers:*

I think that there's so much of American literature that we don't know. It's been hidden and suppressed. I was reading a dandy book called *Caleb Catlum's America* (1936) by Vincent McHugh. It's better than Melville but since it's written in vernacular and slang, and since it has something to do with what's going on here instead of the eternal verities of Europe, and since it doesn't have a style reminiscent of Shakespeare or Moby Dick, it's been cast aside. It's like a great fantasy, a science fiction book based on *American* folklore. Its style is absolutely fascinating and innovative . . . Most Americans aren't educated to American culture; that's why they don't know themselves and are confused.[16]

To "seize the territory" (Steptoe's phrase)[17] with oral tradition, for the writers discussed in this text, is a way of knowing themselves.

In oral as well as (written) literary techniques there are both limitations and possibilities in recognizing the grace and power of the African American oral traditions. James Weldon Johnson expressed the limits of the incipient dialect style, its restrictions in range and subject matter. One sees this in the poems of Dunbar. And as the critic George Kent recognized, a number of Langston Hughes's poems merely repeat classical blues structure without creatively developing and enhancing it to compete with the imagery, imagination, range of the folk creators themselves. Sherley Williams's blues poetry, in contrast, starts with the premise of the blues, then amplifies the context into the multilayered, multivoiced, and recreative poem "Someone Sweet Angel Chile." It takes its impetus, its discursive raciness, its manner, motives, experiential context from the blues, but it is not bound by the perimeter of the blues form. The blues offers a point of contact and departure, the poet's imagination and her own "modal improvisations" and craft broaden and deepen that point, realizing greater potentialities, moving out and into new and newer directions.

Oral tradition, like written tradition, provides techniques and suggests new structures for the writer. In reinventing oral tradition for use in writing, it is often necessary, however, to combine the flexibility and fluidity of voice found in oral tradition with the extended character development, descriptive continuity, and more elaborate dramatic scene-making necessary in written presentations. One must often balance and counterbalance techniques from oral tradition with those indispensable to writing in handling the dynamics of character, time and space, pacing and transition, and of making the words work visibly on the printed page. Such literature often reads better than it appears on the page; it must therefore oblige itself to visual as well as auditory magic. Even then, the most effective reading is the reading that "hears" it, rather than the strictly silent one. As in a dramatic text or music, such literature must be "played" to yield its fullest art. But there is not always a sturdy bridge between imitation and rejection of Western literary form and its discoveries, many of which are certainly vital and valid. Toni Morrison, for instance, balances the strengths from each tradition by organizing the elements of the novel around "tales of how come and why"; speeding up time with oral tradition; refocusing it; introducing elements of song into the dramatic structure and narrative voicings, and conflict in the manner of the *cante fable;* employing open-ended resolutions like those of the dilemma tale, but maintaining the leisurely, richly detailed, and explicit character development and narrative analysis requisite of the written literary (Western novelistic) tradition. For this reason her writing, like that of Ernest Gaines, appears more conventional (on the printed page; perhaps less so when read aloud) than its experiments with oral modes attest. Other literary experimentalists exhibit more complexity and perplexity, for instance Leon Forrest, Clarence Major, Steve Cannon, and Ishmael Reed, whose works are even less bound by the West's prerequisites. But Gaines's and Morrison's less obvious experiments with orality (the principal reason I have chosen them rather than the more noticeable adventures in the oral mode), also illustrate the "catch-22" of the African American writer, trapped between proving he can write traditionally and meeting the inventive demands of modernity. To write in the oral tradition, yet to be taken seriously, like Twain, such writers are often led to some form of the composite novel or the composite poem, multilinguistic writings that admix both vernacular and literary styles.

Finally, oral literature, like written, offers points of technical discovery for the individual writer. Techniques from oral literature can be as viable and engaging as those of the written tradition. Oral forms can likewise be examined and studied for their dramatic structure, conflict patterns, actions, verbal play and interplay, points of view, characterization, transitions, tone and vigor, visual and auditory imagery, conceptions of time and value.

I

Poetry

I

From Dialect to Blues and Spirituals:
Paul L. Dunbar
and Langston Hughes

Paul Laurence Dunbar, "When Malindy Sings"

African American poetry from the turn-of-the-century to the present shows a movement toward the freeing of African American character and voice in literature. "I have recently speculated upon what Dunbar might have done with Negro dialect if it had come to him fresh and plastic," James Weldon Johnson wrote in his preface to *The Book of American Negro Poetry*.[1] Because dialect did not come to Dunbar "fresh and plastic" but through the conventions of the Plantation Tradition and the local colorists, this restricted his emotional range to "humor and pathos" (Johnson), and reduced for him the possibilities of African American character. Consequently, in Dunbar's short story "The Lynching of Jube Benson," which will be discussed in a later chapter, the black character Jube remains a reductive background figure revealed only through the perspective of white Dr. Melville, a perspective which says more about the character and "psychic reality" of Melville than it does of Jube. In Dunbar's poem "When Malindy Sings," the perspective appears restored insofar as the voice of the poem has a broader knowledge of Malindy than Melville did of Jube; nevertheless, some properties of plantation dialect tradition remain. But although Dunbar shares many of the surface methods of that tradition, he takes a fundamentally different attitude toward his characters, as Dickson D. Bruce acknowledges in his essay "Jingle in a Broken Tongue": "It is true that Dunbar's dialect poems were not far removed from the Plantation Tradition in which some critics have placed them . . . Chicken stealing was a stock-and-trade theme for racist proponents of the plantation school, just as it was the subject of Dunbar's poem. But the difference between the plantation-writers' treatment of that theme and Dunbar's was great. Whereas the plantation-writers' attempt was to ridicule the freedman so that their audience would laugh at black Americans, Dunbar was successful at getting the reader to laugh with."[2]

Houston Baker agrees with this transformation of attitude in Dunbar's "When Malindy Sings": "While it is true that in a poem like "Chrismus [sic] on the Plantation" Dunbar showed black southerners preferring the plantation to the world, it is also true that in poems like "The Party," "The Spelling Bee," and "When the Colored Band Comes Marching Down the Street" Dunbar managed to capture the communal love, humor, strength, and devotion that unite black people . . . Moreover, in "When Malindy Sings" the poet raises the black American's gift of song to a cosmic and etherealized plane; Malindy's singing and the voice of God, or that which is ultimately spiritual, become one."[3] This is an important distinction. However, though Dunbar's evaluation of the rural folk character was different from that of the plantation writers, the linguistic forms for narrative, description, and analysis of that character continued to enable only generalized character portraits instead of individual features. Dunbar's portrayal therefore shared the *consequences* if not the *intentions* of the Plantation Tradition and its inversion of perspective to the "outsider." This inversion makes the surface (if not superficial) portrait possible, but not the inner reality. In his introduction to Sterling Brown's *Collected Poems,* Sterling Stuckey discussed the alternative to this portrayal: "Brown realized the need to explore the life of the Southern Negro below the surface in order to reveal unseen aspects of his being . . . Brown's creation of folk characters presents individualized portraits revelatory of interior lives."[4] Within the perceptual framework of Dunbar's poem, however, the reader might detect the need to "justify" or "prove" Malindy to an outside audience, already personified in the poem as Miss Lucy. Complementing the individualized portraits of later writers might also be Malindy's music, taken for granted as *raal right singin'* without the accompanying defense of character or creation.

"When Malindy Sings," then, makes an important claim regarding African American perspective and matured attitude toward character. But Dunbar's lack of plasticity carries beyond the impulses of the language itself to the potential of character revelation; the interior landscape of character is not yet visible. The poet remains subtly outside of character; character is a convincing metaphor which does not break out of background into the foreground of the poetry.

The first stanza of Dunbar's "When Malindy Sings" is addressed to "Miss Lucy" by the poem's persona, a dialect speaker; the poem itself will become a comparison of the possibilities of Malindy's voice with those of Miss Lucy's. We are introduced to the subject of the comparison in the active, dramatic way of oral traditional verse. Immediately, the audience is addressed, in this case a particular one, while the general audience (the reader) overhears.

> G'way an' quit dat noise, Miss Lucy—
>   Put dat music book away;
> What's de use to keep on tryin'?
>   If you practise twell you're gray,
> You can't sta't no notes a-flyin'
>   Lake de ones dat rants and rings
> From de kitchen to de big woods
>   When Malindy sings.[5]

This stanza functions also as dialogue, for at the same time that Miss Lucy is being addressed, the narrator's talk has other functions: it introduces the comparison between Malindy's music and Miss Lucy's "noise"; it establishes the plantation setting; and it clarifies the relationship between Miss Lucy, the young mistress, and Malindy, the kitchen slave.

The second stanza continues to address Miss Lucy; as the narrator tells her what she can't do, he is telling her (and us) what Malindy can and does do.

> You ain't got de nachel o'gans
>   Fu' to make de soun' come right,
> You ain't got de tu'ns and twistin's
>   Fu' to make it sweet an' light.
> Tell you one thing now, Miss Lucy,
>   An' I'm tellin' you fu' true,
> When hit comes to raal right singin',
>   Tain't no easy thing to do.

The next stanza further delineates the differences between the two singers, and enables us to gauge more boldly the two traditions:

> Easy 'nough fu' folks to hollah,
>   Lookin' at de lines an' dots,
> When dey ain't no one kin sence it,
>   An' de chune comes in, in spots;
> But fu' real melojous music,
>   Dat jes' strikes yo' hea't and clings,
> Jes' you stan' an listen wif me
>   When Malindy sings.

We know from this that Miss Lucy reads music ("de lines an' dots"), but it is sound without feeling or "sense." Malindy's singing, however, strikes the heart and clings. In John O'Brien's *Interviews with Black Writers* the poet Michael S. Harper says, "I think too that articulation is all that we have in certain situations. But a man's deepest feelings are really inarticulate. Feelings don't go unexpressed, it's just that they don't translate very well."[6] It is this translation that Malindy has accomplished in song, and the cause for the narrator's celebration, which will anticipate bolder celebrations of this extraordinary, self-authenticating music, transforming the "lines and dots" of African American poetry as well. Yet this poem cannot in its manner of presentation serve to explore the range or complexity of that hearing, not even through the self-asserting confrontation of the language itself, as Nikki Giovanni, of a later literary generation, will do. In her poem "My House," people must learn to speak *through* English in order to express emotional complexities.[7] Here, in Dunbar's poem, the narrator invites Miss Lucy to stand and listen with him while Malindy sings. The third stanza concludes the introductory movement of the poem and establishes the theme and contrapuntal relationships.

Stanza four, in the middle of the poem, continues the address and the exclamations to Miss Lucy as she and the witness both listen:

> Ain't you nevah hyeahd Malindy?
>> Blessed soul, tek up de cross!
> Look hyeah, ain't you jokin', honey?
>> Well, you don't know whut you los'.
> Y'ought to hyeah dat gal a-wa-blin',
>> Robins, la'ks, an' all dem things,
> Heish dey moufs an' hides dey faces
>> When Malindy sings.

The fifth stanza continues to enumerate the comparisons: the fiddling man stops and lays down his fiddle; the mockingbird quits trying to whistle, ashamed of himself; banjo players drop their fingers on the strings and forget to move them. Malindy's voice is heard indirectly, through the reactions of musical others; nevertheless, this mode of presentation amplifies our sense of her voice, authenticates it, and prepares us for the further claims the narrator will make for it. Because Malindy is always the subject of these comparisons, she can contain all those tremendous qualities as well. In addition, the use of active images of comparison moves the center (and meaning) of the poem forward. This is not merely hyperbole but a reflection—if not rendering—of the voice's true effect. Yet Dunbar's descriptions too have their effect, and the speaker brightly celebrates Malindy's song.

Stanza seven begins the conclusion and summing up of this poem. With each new stanza the effect of the voice has been heightened and this is the ultimate effect of her spirituals:

> Floatin' by de hills an' valleys,
> Way avove dis buryin' sod,
> Ez hit makes its way in glory
> To de very gates of God!

The eighth stanza reiterates comparisons, reaffirms the music by comparing it again with "edicated bands" and contrasting it with battle hymns. It is sweeter than these and "holier than evenin'" (in contrast to what we shall see as Dr. Melville's demonic vision of Jube!). Again the narrator places himself as listener/witness to Malindy: "I . . . I sit an' ca'mly listen / While Malindy sings."

The last (ninth) stanza—like many orally defined structures—is circular (nonoral traditions tend toward linearity) and returns to address the "young mistress," the "child" Miss Lucy with even greater assurance of voice and viewpoint.

The sixth stanza brings us directly to the description of Malindy's voice:

> She jes' spreads huh mouf and hollas,
> "Come to Jesus," twell you hyeah
> Sinnahs' tremblin' steps and voices,
> Timid-lak a-drawin' neah;
> Den she tu'ns to "Rock of Ages,"
> Simply to de cross she clings,
> An' you fin' yo' teahs a-drappin'
> When Malindy sings.

Though Malindy "hollahs" too here, the effect of her "Come to Jesus" is transcendental, the effect is emotive; listeners are moved beyond listening to an activity of the spirit. It is this activity that later poets will seek not merely to describe but to recreate in poetry as revealed song: "the notion that black language leads *toward* music, that it passes into music when it attains the maximal pitch of its being"[8] or when it attempts to become "singing that is strange souls . . . raised . . . voices in celebration."[9] Though we know Malindy's voice is glorious and though her voice (and character through her voice) is glorified, she nevertheless exists, paradoxically, in the background of the work. We never *really* see her as a complex intricate foreground personality; and there is a tension between the seen and unseen territory, to use Ellison's metaphors for being. The dialect mode in the African American poetic tradition will need to be stretched and bent to move into the interior landscape and discover the true complexities of the African American voice in a manner similar to Walt Whitman's handling of the European American voice in poetry: "Desirous of writing a poem that engaged experience in a way that was both inclusive and democratic, Whitman abandoned meter and rhyme in favor of more fluid and capacious kinds of parallelism; and he abandoned the distinction between vernacular expressions [such] as 'so long' (i.e., 'good-bye') [and] literary words like 'circumambient,' together with assorted foreign words."[10] With African American writers as well a new language culled from their own oral traditions and folk creators would be "essential to the task of exploring its [the black experience's] full range and complexity."[11]

Malindy we recognize as a generalized character, almost a metaphor herself rather than an actual woman, though the narrator does his best and is an attentive listener. It will not be until such later poems as Sterling Brown's "Uncle Joe" and Sherley Williams's multiple poem "Someone Sweet Angel Chile" that flexibility of voice and revelation of character (individual features) coalesce. This is when the African American poet attains the blending of possibility found in Whitman, and such characters as Malindy speak their own stories, allowing us into their interior worlds as they themselves enter seen and scene territory; or in another mode, as in the poetry of Michael S. Harper, where transformations of technique bridged to oral tradition through the "perceptual mode" (Harper) and intricate modulations of jazz, enhance character revelation and engage experience and moral and conceptual vision. Yet Dunbar's reinterpretation of the Plantation Tradition in his characterization of Malindy was a necessary beginning for these later writers' extensions of territory and freeings of poetic voice.

Langston Hughes's "Blues at Dawn" and "Mystery"

One way that early poets first attempted to break away from the restrictive conventions of literary dialect and extend the territory of language and character was to look to the language, forms, and subjects of the folk creators. James Weldon Johnson, again, was the first to recognize the distinctive motives and therefore possibilities of these two traditions:

"Negro dialect poetry had its origin in the minstrel traditions, and a persisting pattern was set. When the individual writer attempted to get away from that pattern, the fixed conventions allowed him only to slip over into a slough of sentimentality. These conventions were not broken for the simple reason that the individual writers wrote chiefly to entertain an outside audience, and in concord with its stereotyped ideas about the Negro. And herein lies the vital distinction between them and the folk creators, who wrote solely to please and express themselves." [12]

Johnson, in his own works, attempted to break away from the strictures of dialect by turning to the more flexible dynamics of folk creations for the overall form and language of his poetry. His use of the folk sermon form, language, and metaphor in such poems as "The Creation" (1927) is a primary example of this. These poems are not written in traditional literary dialect with elisions and orthographical changes but reflect the imaginative imagery, wisdom, syntax, and characterizations of the folk creators. Therefore all the narrative modes of the folk creators, the metaphors and dramatic procedures, stay intact without the attendant linguistic and character distortions. Just the first few stanzas of "The Creation" serve to illustrate this point:

> And God stepped out on space,
> And He looked around and said,
> "I'm lonely
> I'll make me a world."
>
> And as far as the eye of God could see
> Darkness covered everything,
> Blacker than a hundred midnights
> Down in a cypress swamp.
>
> Then God smiled,
> And the light broke,
> And the darkness rolled up on one side,
> And the light stood shining on the other,
> And God said, "That's good!"
>
> Then God reached out and took the light in His hands,
> And God rolled the light around in His hands
> Until He made the sun;
> And He set that sun a-blazing in the heavens.
> And the light that was left from making the sun
> God gathered it up in a shining ball

And flung it against the darkness,
Spangling the night with the moon and stars.
Then down between
The darkness and the light
He hurled the world;
And God said, "That's good."[13]

This is not mere translation of dialect into standard English as some critics, misled by the absence of orthographic changes, have thought. Johnson maintains the syntax and expressive language and rhythms of the folk orators and seems to presage more contemporary ways of transcribing dialect or folk speech as a self-authenticating language.

Langston Hughes also looked to the methods of the folk creators. Two additional folk genres employed by Hughes were blues and spirituals. His poem "Blues at Dawn"[14] uses the classic blues form to order the verse. There is little to say about this poem except that it has the best qualities of the blues: the concrete, straightforward language, the incremental repetition. Like Johnson's use of the sermon, Hughes's use of the blues as poetic model enables him to break from dialect, to maintain a sense of the syntax, vocabulary, imagery, metaphors, and expressive rhythms of a different vernacular and linguistic tradition, but without the caricature. The grammatical systems are maintained without pathos or comedy. The character tells his own story, and with the sense of an interior we are moved further toward the realization of the whole personality in the poem. Indeed, many of Hughes's poems are not to be taken as the author's voice in confessional revelations but as interesting, individuated personalities speaking.

Perhaps it was Hughes's interest in the texture of oral tradition and folklore in his own poems that led him to include, along with his literary experiments in African American oral genre, translations of Federico García Lorca's ballads. Hughes renders Lorca's ballads in English, retaining the melodies in English oral equivalents. In one such ballad "mountain, mountain, mountain" echoes. We hear of "mules and the shadows of mules." A load of sunflowers, "vasty night" and "salted dawn" blur and crackle in one surrealistic image, illuminating oral tradition in its literary excellence, in the concrete magnetic images, "clean" language, and rhythmic music of Spanish balladry.[15]

This kinship of oral tradition and folkloric metaphor also explains Hughes's attraction to translating Nicolás Guillén's poetry. In his article on these translations, John F. Matheus says that Hughes transforms the

Cuban Negro dialect to American Negro dialect to suggest Guillén's welding of Afro-Cuban oral tradition (slang and Negrismo) into the idiom and poetic strategies that transformed the traditional Spanish-Cuban form. Here's Hughes's version of Guillén's poem "Blade":

> Knife-toting, sweet-man
> become a knife himself:
> whittling chips of the moon
> until the moon runs out,
> whittling chips of shadow
> until the shadows run out,
> whittling chips of song
> until the song runs out—
> and then,
> sliver by sliver, the dark body
> of his no-good gal.[16]

Here is the stark, unambiguous language of the blues linked—as the blues links seeming contrapuntal language—with the compelling metaphors of surreality. Again, one finds the balanced repetition, the exacting imagery. Hughes's attachment to the poetic devices of the oral modes as they apply to African American poetry, and certainly to his own poems, initiates the "vasty" possibilities present in transforming poetic strategies through oral modes: "By going back to that original use of language they have contributed a new energy to contemporary poetic expression."[17]

"Blues at Dawn," though it seems slight, is important in its break from literary dialect and its use of oral tradition as an artistic source for the whole poem. However, stylistically, metaphorically, and thematically it merely duplicates oral tradition. Its importance is in what it *opens up* and where it *directs* the poet. Hughes also demonstrates, along with Johnson, that the poets turned to oral tradition for the "whole form" of the work long before the fiction writers, who continued (except for the slave narrative impulse) to "frame" their fictions. But for the poets the entire poem was often "oral in its sequence."[18]

In his essay "Langston Hughes and Afro-American Folk and Cultural Tradition," George E. Kent speaks of the poet's rather pedestrian adherence to blues structure without the complementary imaginative interplay and complexity that generally attend the work of the real folk creators. First, however, Kent assures us that Hughes's introduction of blues forms and attitudes into poetry is an "obvious and original innovation."

"Blues at Dawn" also shows the literary possibilities of the form and embodies the "essential folk spirit." It contains the "wit and irony of attitude . . . closely associated with the blues."[19] Though Kent's examples—"Midwinter Blues," "Young Gal's Blues," and "Down and Out"—are perhaps more imaginative poems, "Blues at Dawn" can also illustrate both the problems and possibilities of the form. Kent notes that in the folk blues poem the "black audiences hold assumptions in common with the singer—a fact that permits him to impose a unity not based upon simple logical structure but upon his total performance . . . the conscious literary artist runs the risk of appearing second-rate when he is compared with the blues artist at his best, if he simply tries to mine exactly the same ore."[20] On these terms, Hughes's "Blues at Dawn" cannot compete with the true folk blues poem. It does not have the range of implications, imagery, character, mood, wonder, or surprise.

Not all of his poems, however, are mere duplications of folk forms, without imaginative input and spirit. "Mystery," for example, using the spiritual as impulse and structural model, challenges the folk creator's model and shows greater creativity in the use of the spiritual as genre than does "Blues at Dawn" with the blues as genre. The poem has the complementary imaginative intensity and complexity that a creative writer should have when making literary use of any folk or traditional literary form—"Mystery" does not laboriously adhere to the spiritual motif. Perhaps the adaptation was easier to accomplish because the spiritual itself does not have the set form and stanzaic patterns of the classical blues; the lines are "looser," more "unpredictable," the "improvising imagination seems freer"[21] and can work more fully with a variety of materials and styles. The poem also catches the reader's imagination more completely than does "Blues at Dawn." Through fragments of description, spoken word, exclamation, meditation, "other language," naming, "signifying," song and statement, Hughes creates a mosaic here. It has a greater "effect of complexity," of play and "interplay"[22] than does "Blues at Dawn," which adheres to the stricter form of its genre. And following this we hear other poems, perhaps influenced by Hughes's voicing of a new flexibility, such as Aimé Cesaire's "Return to My Native Land," the poems of Leon Damas and other African and Caribbean poets of the Negritude movement. Hughes, like Johnson, points the direction but "the work has only begun."

Because there is no singer in these poems of Hughes to use the *forms* of blues and spirituals, there is no way to achieve variations in stress and style; more imaginative procedures are necessary on the part of the poet.

By creating a variety of styles, images, imaginative flexibility through dramatic shifts, sharp juxtapositions and thematic improvisations, special patterns of sounds and rhythms, multivalent meanings than the folk structure itself may provide, the African American poets gain the wherewithal to experiment with traditional structure by introducing folk forms and attitudes, or they may, as Hughes did in "Mystery," explore the folk forms themselves in the *whole* poem.

With the entrance of the character speaking his own story in the manner of the blues, and the greater flexibility of imaginative and experiential territory derived from the spiritual, we now have a base—indeed, a foundation—for much of the poetry that will follow and the achievement of the "full ranging voices"[23] of whole characters.

2

Folk Speech and Character Revelation: Sterling Brown's "Uncle Joe"

In her introduction to Sterling Brown's poetry, Ruth Miller discusses Brown's modifications of the literary dialect tradition: "His dialect seems to be the language spoken just outside his door, in the very present . . . He used the folk idiom, fragments from blues and work songs, rhythms from jazz; he knows the tall tales and the folk sermons and above all he knows how the people are getting through their days."[1]

Sterling Brown's poetry complements Hughes's transition from the dialect tradition by creating a language which takes authority and knows itself capable of anything—in narrative, thought, conversation, judgment and metaphor. The change from the assumptions and distortions of the early dialect tradition also required a new attitude toward the folk character—the speaker of the language—himself.

James Weldon Johnson's narrator in *The Autobiography of an Ex-Coloured Man* expresses the old pre-Harlem Renaissance attitude toward the folk character and his language: "The unkempt appearance, the shambling, slouching gait and loud talk and laughter of these people aroused in me a feeling of almost repulsion. Only one thing about them awoke a feeling of interest; that was their dialect."[2]

Since the Harlem Renaissance period of the 1920s it has often been the folk character who contains the wisdom of the work, who is the revelatory or key character. Some examples are Toni Morrison's Pilate; Alice Walker's Grange Copeland (when he becomes "reborn"); Ellison's grandfather, "old slave," and Jefferson; Baraka's Lynn Hope; Robert Boles's caterer's daughter. In Jean Toomer's *Cane*, Kabnis must return to the folk South before he can emerge as a true artist. In such literature, it is usually the middle class character who experiences or symbolizes the moral dilemma and ambiguity: Hanby in "Kabnis," Bledsoe in *Invisible Man*, Macon in *Song of Solomon*. These portrayals are the exact opposite of the "bourgeois realists" and "uplift writers," whose attitudes mirrored that of Johnson's ex-colored man in their repulsion at the lower class and their desire to show only "the best elements of the race," approving of them (as Brown has noted in *The Negro in American Fiction*) only when they resemble the white middle class. Their impulse, like Jesse Fauset's in *The Chinaberry Tree* and *Plum Bun,* was to show how alike "the best elements" of the races were in order to eliminate discrimination.

These are values apart from the values of fiction and not ones on which to build a literature. As Brown has noted, one does not build a literature exclusively on "plaster of Paris saints." The Harlem Renaissance writers rejected this approach and instead began to celebrate differences between the races; they did not judge their humanity on resemblance to whites, middle-class or others. In fact, like the Black Revolutionary writers of the 1960s, they often exaggerated differences, though on cultural rather than political grounds. At any rate they brought to the forefront, without embarrassment, characteristics which a previous literary generation had repudiated. Each generation had instances of ambivalence and confusion of virtues and vices—what could or could not be seen or heard. The generation after slavery, for instance, rejected the spirituals, and a later generation rejected jazz for the popular song. This generational antithesis is a theme in Amiri Baraka's "The Screamers"[3] and Brown's own "Children's Children."

The black writers' celebration of folk characters is connected to the emergence of the Marxist social-justice proletarian heroes of the 1930s, the heroes of James T. Farrell, Erskine Caldwell, John Steinbeck. Although this American literary shift of a heroic ideal reinforced a direction already begun by African American writers in the 1920s, in the 1930s many black writers and intellectuals were in turn influenced by that renewed focus and the Marxist literary critique. (It is interesting that during the 1930s anthologists of American literature tended to be more democratic, including literature from Native Americans and Blacks with examples from both folk and oral tradition as part of the American literary heritage; only in later decades did the anthologies "whiten" again with the advent of the New Critics and the Southern Agrarians. It awaited the 1960s for a renewed broadening and democratizing of the canon, a process still in progress for the needed inclusion of Chicano, Asian-American, and other American voices.) Because of the Depression, both black and white writers found themselves paddling a similar canoe. Many publishing houses were going bankrupt; first novelists (and certainly poets) of either color were commercial risks. Both black and white writers were attracted to the Communist party and its ideals as a solution to economic and social problems, and joined the John Reed clubs as an outlet for their creative energies.[4] But though African American literature shared many of the surface concerns of proletarian literary theory and practice, African American creativity seemed also at cross purposes with Communist doctrine and many of the writers, like many of their white counterparts, turned anti-Communist—indeed, felt betrayed by it—and revived their own definitions of art, as Richard Wright finally did: "I was already afraid that the stories I had written would not fit into the new, official mood. Must I discard my plot ideas and seek new ones? No, I could not. My writing was my way of seeing, my way of living, my way of feeling; and who could change his sight, his sense of direction, his senses?"[5] Ironically, certain African American writers would, decades later, respond in a similar rebellious fashion to Black Aesthetic doctrine, a literary critique and new official mood prescribed by their own theorists.

However, African American writers mostly continued to reject the norms for middle-class values and acceptability, their convictions reminiscent of Frederick Douglass' rejection of the master's values. And, as with Baraka's initial involvement with the Beat Generation, one often sees modern African American writers drawn to American and European movements of literary upheaval and rejection of "old order" (as the "uplift" and "bourgeois realist" generation were conversely drawn to the established, approved, and proved models) that seem to reinforce their own battles with the status quo from their position as outsiders/strangers/rebels in American culture. Similarly, white literary insiders seeking their own myths of the artist as "outsider in search of wholeness" (Aronson) are often drawn to the "natural creations" of outsiders—beat, bop, and blues. Sometimes, in misjudgment, these insider/outsiders again recreate outsider codes (black codes?) for "the other," as when the Beat Generation reinvented or resurrected stereotypes and caricatures for Blacks, especially in their rambling Jazz novels' "agrammatism" and "bursts of inspiration," as cover for their own hedonism. The black artist's outsider status in America was not a matter of choice or will like that of the "wild men of the West." But like Ellison's Invisible Man, the black artist in music and literature attempts to use his exclusion to create and recreate himself—to "make music out of invisibility." As one critic said of Richard Wright, he has had to be a born existentialist. This is perhaps one motive for the Renaissance writer's choosing the previously rejected folk character—the outsider's outsider—to be not only celebrated but often to contain, as does his art, a Jungian/Joycean "collective consciousness of the race." Nevertheless, we can see legitimacy in writers' avoidance of the folk character before the Harlem Renaissance. *The Autobiography of an Ex-Coloured Man* offers an explanation, in the narrator's description of the rural folk: "log-cabins and plantations and dialect-speaking 'darkies' are perhaps better known in American literature than any other single picture of our national life . . . so I shall endeavor to avoid giving the reader any already overworked and hackneyed descriptions. This generally accepted literary ideal of the American Negro constitutes what is really an obstacle in the way of the thoughtful and progressive element of the race . . . However, this very fact constitutes the opportunity of the future Negro novelist and poet to give the country something new and unknown, in depicting the life, the ambitions, the struggles and the passions of those of their race who are striving to break the narrow limits of traditions."[6]

Poetry too needed a reappraisal of the folk as serious, complex, and multidimensional. This is what Brown offered, though some critics have been unable to distinguish realistic dialect from that ridiculous dialect of the minstrel tradition, where form is mistaken for substance. For instance, Nathan Huggins in *The Harlem Renaissance* fails to differentiate Brown's folk characters from those in Johnson's description, who form the whites' "ideal and exclusive literary concept."[7] Similarly, Richard Wright accused Zora Neale Hurston of perpetuating minstrel humor. However, even with their misjudgments, these critics point out the problematic nature of literary intention with regard to the folk, and especially the language of the folk. True, the new attitude reverses the uplift writers' riveting devotion to the middle class and offers a welcome new description. Yet through the Harlem Renaissance of the twenties and the proletarian literature of the thirties, the middle class, though no longer used as "window display" by the Jessie Fausets or satire by the Wallace Thurmans and George Schuylers, continued to be set apart from "the values of fiction,"[8] and we see such middle-class characters as Robert Boles's astronautical engineer caught in a social, moral, and ideological dilemma, while the folk character exists as a potential or real moral savior, or at least one who offers clarity; the complex human potential of neither class is explored in its own right. The treatment of the folk and the middle class in African American literature is a subject for a whole new study, but here it is sufficient to say that Brown's folk characters, like those of Hurston and Gaines in prose, have gained complex substance. The transition to the full humanity of the folk hero and heroine was vital.

The dichotomous presentation of the folk/middle class in African American literature shares a practice found not only in proletarian literature but also in European literature in general. It was only in the great Russian novels of the nineteenth century that the levels of society were treated with equanimity, and the peasant classes considered with complexity and seriousness and not used merely as "folk comedians."[9] These novels could perhaps provide the tangible key to how African American writers might bring variety and depth to the treatment of both lower- and middle-class black personalities in one work, with rich and individualized portraits of characters that do not stand for some private or political mythological figures but for real people in "living multiplicity." Yet one must admit that the often violent resolution of dilemmas of identity as they manifest themselves in class distinctions can make for apt and effective poetic tension, as in two poems by French Guianan writer Leon Damas, one of the founders of Negritude: "Hiccup" and "Bargain." This effect is especially evident in the abrupt transition in the last stanza of "Bargain."[10]

Pre-Brown and pre-Hughes literature had problems even when a particular author held no restricting attitude toward dialect or the folk. Dunbar's poems, such as "When Malindy Sings," for instance, certainly do not repudiate folk characters or folk language, but the conventions of the dialect tradition with its truncated range did not generally allow for surprises or explorations of subject matter and character. Brown's dialect innovations do show such areas of possibility. Aimé Cesaire is speaking principally of the innovations of Brown when he says: "The ordinary Black man, the everyday Black man whom a world literature has sought to portray as grotesque and exotic, the American Negro poet makes this man a hero. He depicts him seriously, with passion, and, by a miracle of love, the understated power of his art, succeeds where greater means fail: at suggesting the deep forces which shape destiny. Is it a small thing to create a world?"[11] With Brown, folk character and folk speech, as he prefers to call dialect, become whole; there is more of the inner life; and because Brown's poems are "revelatory of interior lives"[12] as well as society, history, landscape, and language, we have even greater extension of the human territory.

The transitional leap from Dunbar to Brown has an interesting parallel in Spanish oral tradition that might also serve to emphasize the significance of Brown's modification of literary dialect. In his study of the Spanish *romance* (ballad), Menéndez Pidal speaks of the movement from *épico* to *épico-lírico* to *dramático-lírico* in the development of the genre.[13] This is the same progression as from Dunbar to Brown, in the movement from subjective and sentimental elements, through objective images and narration, to a scenic style in which dialogued elements predominate in dramatic situations. Dialogue in Brown's poetry has these scenic and dramatic functions—of revealing character, emotional and intellectual states, and strengthening the sense of reality both inside and outside the character. And to be able to listen to the poetic character has deeper implications in our tradition. The monologues and dialogues in the African American tradition also relate to Robert Steptoe's ideal of the black narrator's controlling his own story where literary technique and character revelation combine. Because outsiders have attempted to control and define African American character through "narrow and restrictive terms," this seizing of story (Caliban's seizing of the word) becomes vital not just for its literary or technical effort and effect. Literary metamorphosis is linked to social struggle in Blacks' attempts to "paint their own picture of themselves"[14]—a self-authenticating endeavor from the slave-narrative period on; it is the reason realism and naturalism persisted in the African American literary tradition for so long (the need to paint the clear image and the "well-lighted" one). Not until Ellison, Reed, Young, and others ("stepping outside of history") was naturalism seen as compounding the confinement and distortion of art and personality, in that it still followed the whites' definition of African American social reality. Later, the African American writer discovered this clear image could also be achieved through new psychic and literary "conceptual voyages" beyond the parameters of social realism: "The Third World writer no longer relies on the photographic rendering of reality, of the things he sees and perceives around himself. He imposes order on the objects around him, rather than accepting the order established by the objects . . . The concerns of the Third World writer have moved from protest and description to the many levels of abstraction."[15]

A representative poem of Sterling Brown's that is even more magnificent when heard is "Uncle Joe." In this poem the human story and language receives full value and we move to the *dramático-lírico* in African American oral-literary tradition.

"Hot dawg it, but it's hot-hot dis mawnin,"[16] the poem begins, after the poet/narrator's description: "Unc' Joe, c'est drole." We are drawn into the poem immediately through speech—the quick, rhythmic, dramatic pace of Uncle Joe's talk. The first line and the whole stanza put us into landscape, mood, atmosphere, and feeling. Though Brown shares some of the transcription techniques with the turn-of-the-century poets, his text has more authority and flexibility. It is an open-ended folkspeech capable of any reflection, any sort of expository and narrative strategy.

33
▾

Brown does not make easy assumptions about the speech or the speakers. His conception of Uncle Joe is broad yet particular. The speech leaps beyond the page. "Hot-hot" is exact in rhythm, alliterative intensity, and meaning. Uncle Joe is not an inept speaker, nor is the poet/narrator/schoolteacher. He speaks a different language with different cadences from Uncle Joe's, but one has a sense of the linguistic integrity of both speakers. Uncle Joe controls his story [17] as he reveals his own character (and the poet's introductory assertion)—as complete a character as we might see in any literature—through speech and recalled dramatic action.

And we have an interest in this *particular* man from the beginning and through his own voice:

> I wouldn't pick a pon' uh cotton to day.
> Not fuh all de money in de Opelousas Bank.

Introduction of setting and personality is completed in explicit dialogue. "How you feel yosef, son?" The listener is acknowledged as in any oral genre—there is the recognition and easy correspondence between the storyteller (tale teller and bearer) and listener—the active listener in the poem and the equally attentive listener/reader outside of it. The identity of the listener is first implied in the fact that he has "store bought" tobacco. Both storyteller and listener are introduced in the first stanza and contrasting values are indicated through selective detail. Uncle Joe could be merely the plantation tradition stereotype in the description of his "corncob" and "grinning," but as he conducts his story he will be revealed as more than that, his personality will not be restricted to anybody's narrow conception. This strategy reminds me of Ellison, who in the beginning of characterizations often suggests the stereotypes and then proceeds to explode them. Uncle Joe's story helps us to discover him and offers a new range, evolving a heroic dimension. We learn the listener is a schoolteacher, but one who doesn't talk "de teacher's talk." That is, Uncle Joe can understand him.

There is humor in their banter, there is a joking relationship, but Uncle Joe "changes the joke and slips the yoke." [18] This is not the grotesque humor of the minstrel tradition nor parody of Uncle Joe; he is not minimized by it or made ridiculous. Neither does one stand back from him and laugh; it is no burlesque. This is a spirited and shared joke; we laugh with him as we grow to know him (and ourselves?) better. Uncle Joe continually addresses the listener as "you," a "you" the reader shares. We learn that Uncle Joe reads "printing but not writing," that he speaks Creole and "Americain." With its continuous references to the listener, this is a playful, reciprocal story where the storyteller always refers to those present: "A good speaker . . . makes sure of the participation of the audience in a way analogous to story-telling; he expects murmurs of support and agreement, muttered rejoinders of his rhetorical questions, laughter when he purposely brings in something amusing or exaggerated, and thanks and acknowledgment when he has ended."[19]

The apparent monologue is raised to the level of dialogue even before the actual verbal exchange, because the acknowledgment creates a space for the sense, if not the reality, of reciprocation. The storytelling nature of the monologue also prevents it and the poem from being static. The action within the monologue is both physical—the conflicts and dramatic suspensions "in the world"—and reflective; in addition, the character's developed thought, analysis of the past, and his shrewd, blues-humor perspective on the events add to the dynamism of the poetry in familiar, coherent, idiomatic phrasing. There is creative energy and interest here. And when the schoolteacher's voice does come in, it enters without verbal hierarchy (Wideman). Certainly differences in voice and educational background are evident, but the narrator's language has its own versatility in intonation; it too is an interesting and vibrant voice, in contrast to other "educated" narrators whose voices were often too stylized and formal, such as Martin Delany's *Blake* (in spite of his virtues) and even Hughes's narrator interrogating Simple. Uncle Joe's voice, in keeping with the folk character as the key figure, is more fluid and has more tonal intensity than the narrator's; it is more immediate, more vibrant, reproducing real emotions and varieties of them in a small space. Again, energy and interest unite in an act of humanizing imagination, in which Uncle Joe is allowed both emotion and intellect, both spirited and active, without the brooding quality of Kabnis in Jean Toomer's *Cane,* or the black intellectuals portrayed in Wallace Thurman's or Claude McKay's works.

Uncle Joe controls the humor as well as the story. The listener's participation is wordless for most of Uncle Joe's story, but it is there in his attention and ours, as we are placed, through dialogue, into the human landscape—the violent social and historical relationships which do not have to be explained. Old Thibodeaux's insistence that Joe not send his children to school is reminiscent of the slave narrative tradition, when learning to read was a crime. Joe pays Thibodeaux no mind. Says Joe:

> Me, I doan pay nobody no mind. Not too much mind.
> I 'member when de sheriff and dem others,
> Git hot after de boy from de penitentiary . . .

A new kind of "hot" is introduced, a variation on the initial usage, which then shows itself as a foreshadowing of this one. Joe, in a heroic spirit of defiance, refuses to tell sheriff Thibodeaux the whereabouts of the "game-leg boy." "Dey axe me 'Where he?' and I say 'Who he?'" When Didee Lebon wants to "rawhide it outa' him," Uncle Joe tells sheriff Thibodeaux he'll have two men to hunt if Didee lays a rawhide on him, "or a finger too." They back down. Retelling the story he gives "objective testimony" about himself and his actions as "Uncle Joe," then he describes another incident, where courage is also needed. On their way back from Catholic Church at Villeplatte, he and his mother are surrounded by Cajans:

> And at Papa Lastrape's gate dey put up a rail.
> And gimme de dare to take it down.
> Dey had dey shotguns across dey saddles,
> But dey had to have some good reason to mob us up,
> Cause dey hadn't so long left Father Antoine.
> Well, I ain't scared, an' my ma she don't scare.
> I didn't say nottin'. She didn't say nottin'!
> But I had heart enough to take de rail down.

In this parallel scene, the Cajans too back down, like Thibodeaux and Didee. The repetition increases the drama, the music, and the poetic tautness of the conflict. Joe has heart enough and humor enough. There is the feisty double-edged and daring wit of African American folklore; the complex vision, the intelligence, and the heroic dimension of Uncle Joe have brought us through the decisive moments to the resolved action.

The listener responds like one worthy of such a story and such storyteller, who does what he "gots to do": "Uncle Joe is all right by me." Here, as in Dunbar's poem, we have the witness/listener commenting on the subject of the poem, but now the subject of the poem—heralded by a new attitude toward the folk character ("Uncle Joe is all right by me")—is brought forward as a full personality, a great voice, telling his own story in his own intelligent and articulate poetry.

Though Brown still shares some transcription techniques with the writers of Dunbar's generation, the language is more accurately heard, its conceptual range is more complex, backed by expanded character and wider experiential detail. Perhaps there was more such articulate poetry of the folk present in the Depression years of the 1930s. We do not know of it, except for the voices that remained of the folk creators themselves. The literary range of the 1920s was not simply brought on by the economic determinants and audiences of the Jazz Age, nor did it simply end with the economics of the Depression. The spirit and talent were there before and after the 1920s, and inspired by such poems as Brown's, more voices with broad range and conceptual complexity were waiting to be heard.

3

Multiple-Voiced Blues:
Sherley A. Williams's
"Someone Sweet Angel Chile"

Sherley Williams described Langston Hughes's use of the classic blues
structure in his poem "Young Gal's Blues" as "an example of an oral form
moving unchanged into literary tradition."[1] Her own poem, "Someone
Sweet Angel Chile," resolves this limitation and takes us steps further
from an earlier literary generation. Because Williams stretches and bends
the blues tradition, her poem has greater elasticity through poetic improvisation; it is not limited to one blues form but suggests limitless possibilities in a free-verse blues which informs the metaphor, narrative, and
spirit of the poem.

"Someone Sweet Angel Chile" is a poem about Bessie Smith. It is a
poetic biography and collective blues dialogue containing fragments of
experience (event and speech), abrupt changes (thematic and structural),
shifts in perspective (first to third), hesitations, repetitions, worrying the
line. All this enables the poem to function within and beyond the strictness
of the blues form. Much of Williams's innovative expansion of blues form
is also achieved by perspective shifts: "The shift from first to third person
perspective provides both an inner and outer view . . . and creates an
atmosphere which encourages one to enter into and understand the experiences presented in the poems at both an emotional and analytic level."[2]

Williams mingles photographic descriptions with narrated stages of
Bessie's life from age fifteen to thirty-nine, the poet becoming simultaneously storyteller and audience (as the blues singer becomes one with the
audience):

> Bessie on my wall: the thick triangular
>   nose wedged
>   in the deep brown
>   face nostrils
>   flared on a last
>   long hummmmmmmmm.

38

> Bessie singing
> just behind the beat
> that sweet sweet
> voice throwing
> its light on me.[3]

The music enters the description in run-on syntax, repetition, assonance, words as blues notes, shifts in accents (syncopation)—"Bessie singing just behind the beat." The blues connection between singer and audience is reinforced as "Voice throwing its light on me." Perhaps this is the same light which is the principal metaphor in Ralph Ellison's *Invisible Man,* giving form and visibility through the illumination of experience. The experience encompasses us as well: "The particularized, individual experience rooted in a common reality is the primary thematic characteristic of all blues songs no matter what their structure. The classic song form itself internalizes and echoes, through the statement/response pattern, the thematic relationship between individual and group experience which is implied in these evocations of social and political reality."[4]

Self-definition is defining self in recognized kinship with others. In this way Ma Rainey becomes a prophecy for Bessie's own womanhood and simultaneously leaps backward and forward in time, restoring communal integrity:

> fifteen: I looked in her face
> and seed the woman
> I'd become. A big
> boned face already
> lined and the first line
> in her fo'head was
> black and the next line
> was sex cept I didn't
> know to call it that
> then and the brackets
> round her mouth stood fo
> the chi'ren she teared
> from out her womb. And
> yo name Bessie; huh.
> she say. (Every one
> call her Ma o' Ol
> Lady) Bessie; well
> le'me hear you sang.

She was looking in
my mouth and I knowed
no matter what words
come to my mind the
song'd be her'n jes as
well as it be mine.

The principal narrators are the poet/persona, Bessie, Ma Rainey, and Bessie's man Blue. The poet creates multiple dramatic dialogues in which her voice connects with the voices in the poem in "diction (that) hovers marvelously between the standard and the black dialects (and thus embodies both)."[5]

The poem's monologues contain concrete visual metaphors and energetic details. Many voices are witnesses to Bessie, adding dimension to her character and complicating her relationships while extending the expressive range of the poem with conjunctions of subject/object and seer/seen. Voices comment on Bessie's personality from the outside, but each provides an inside look at the commentator through a blending of objective testimony and what Janheinz Jahn terms the subjective territory of the blues.

recollections: Man, first time she come to the
studio with Blue—that was
something. She was fine as fine
could be. A dark blue suit and
orange feather boa a
little cloche with a feather
that curled down around her cheek,
all woman—even after
she got heavy, which she wasn't
that day. Blue was tellin folks—
that's everyone what to do.
I mean he'd say Miss Smith—last
time we'd recorded they'd said
Bessie, not Miss, not Ma'm—don't
like the piano so loud
Miss Smith want horns right here
lookin at the arrangements
sayin Mister sayin please
and steady pickin his teeth
It was years before I knowed
the man couldn't read no music
that's how strong his talk was.

> The white mens didn't know how to
> take it. They flash a look at
> Bessie and she just sittin
> there with them fine legs crossed, one
> shoe dangling off the end of
> her toe Aw, man, Bessie was
> just natchally what her
> song say: some sweet angel chile.

In her article on blues and African American poetry, Williams comments on the function of collective dialogue that may be applied to her own poetry: "the evocation of certain first person experiences and the extensive use of multiple voices in Afro-American poetry may be, at least in part, an outgrowth from this characteristic of the blues. Nikki Giovanni's "The Great Pax Whitey" which seems a rather pedestrian and undigested patchwork of folk and personal legend and black nationalist philosophy becomes, when viewed (or better yet, read) as a poem in which a congregation of voices speaks, a brilliant literary approximation of the kind of collective dialogue which has been going on underground in the black community at least since the nineteenth century and of which the blues in its various forms was an important part."[6] The "patchwork of folk and personal legend," historical prophecy, and "congregation of voices" makes Williams's own multiple blues, creates a new literary voice in the tradition, one which ascertains the parameters of the classic blues, then explores and explodes them with expressive dexterity:

> hear it? what's out there
> knowin is what the
> world don't get enough of
> meanin love meaning love.

But because classic blues is the base for the experiments in this poem, we finally reach fragments that reproduce the classic form, acknowledging it as supreme foundation:

> fragments: Aw just move toward me
> baby, like you did
> in the woods that day
>
> Aw move close to me
> honey; be the light
> that show me my way

> Ahhh come down on me
> baby; see me like
> you saw me that day.

The poem ends "down torry pine road," the road on which Bessie was allowed to bleed to death because a local white hospital would not admit Blacks. It is a description by a central consciousness that merges voices and perspectives—the poet's and Bessie's and the other voices—in the same "I":

> This could be that road
> in Mississippi
> though this one winds up
> the hill from the sea
>
> The way the moonlight washes
> out all colors and
> the high beams bounce shadows off
> the overhanging
> trees, the way cars come round the
> curves gathering speed
> for the climb up the road to
> the canyon rim is
> something like Mississippi
> that stretch of highway
> outside Coahoma close by
> Clarksdale and the Jim
> Crow ward in the hospital
> that used to be there.
>
> I dare each curve to
> surprise me as I
> round it show me as I
> rear-end of some truck
> before I can stop.

This merging of the poet's voice and history with the other voices has moral-aesthetic implications similar to Carlos Fuentes's *Where the Air Is Clear (La Región Más Transparente)*.[7] It also informs us of an essential connection among all Third World voices, for at the end of the novel the main character's voice becomes all the voices of the people we have encountered in the novel. The novel begins with "Mi nombre es Ixca Cienfuegos," the character naming himself, saying "I am," but ends with Ixca affirming all the other characters, their personalities, their contradictions, their voices in one multitudinous voice. Fuentes reiterates bits and pieces of conversations that we've heard throughout until all the city, all the voices are integrated finally into the one speech of Ixca. This is the sense of integration that we have in Williams's poem—the unity of personal and collective consciousness—the poet-persona becoming at one time, like Fuentes's "notarized witness," the hearer, teller, questioner and tradition bearer.

Williams has also done what Dunbar did not do—that is, she makes the character/singer also speak for and identify herself, take authority over her own story, and recreate her song. In the multitude of other voices we have listeners/witnesses become storytellers and storytellers become listener/witnesses. Williams's poem is still in the tradition and spirit of the poem by Sterling Brown, but it extends the great voice of Uncle Joe to a multitude of great voices, liberated and visible.

"Someone Sweet Angel Chile," then, is a significant poem in the tradition, an oral biography of fragments of speech, memory, imagination, nightmare. The senses of wholeness and complex possibilities continue to evolve beyond both the early dialect uses and the uses of blues in theme and structure result in an expansive, articulate, imaginative rendering. The poet succeeds in creating a wilder, freer form than any of those previously discussed, building a sense of communal wholeness out of multiple fragments and juxtapositions of voices. She has shown how an individual talent, prepared for and spurred on by the discoveries of earlier literary generations and the resources of classic oral tradition, can give a new vitality to poetic language as speech and music, transfiguring a developing tradition.

4

Jazz Modalities: Michael S. Harper's "Uplift from a Dark Tower"

On the jacket of one of John Coltrane's albums Michael S. Harper states, "Black musicians have always melded the private and the historical into the aesthetics of human speech and music, the blues and jazz." This could well be a comment on Harper's own motives and procedures in poetry. Other key words and phrases he applies to music might equally apply to himself: "testamental process," "incantation," "prophecy," "internal . . . external journey," "synthesis of personal history and overtones of American," "open-ended forms." [1]

"Uplift from a Dark Tower" offers the simultaneous compressing and magnifying of personal and historical experience, a sense of the paradox and modal possibilities of jazz and blues. "Uplift" is complex in its narrative texture and pluralistic visions. Clearly in the jazz tradition, the poem is defined by its metaphoric variations, its sense of the poet as articulator or articulate hero, its simultaneity and multiple thought contexts as it breaks out of the traditional confinements of landscape, personality, and history; the poet, like the jazz musician, "seizes . . . the territory" (Steptoe).

As in Ellison's *Invisible Man,* the prologue of Harper's poem introduces the basic motifs; and here we also anticipate expansion and transformation. The poet, like the storyteller, establishes the perspective of the poem, and like the jazz musician, he will "have control of his history" (Steptoe).

> Just when I think I've got you nailed
> to your cross of uplift
> I see your name in the private printing
> of a history of *Yaddo,*
> meaning *shadow* or *shimmering,*
> its 500-acre testimonial to lakes
> over gardens, trees

buried with *lost* children
whose memory donated this tower
studio to my writing of you.

Outside the door might lie *Etienne,*
the cannibal brought by missionaries
from Africa to be trained for service
in the experimental summer of 1881.
He would be St. Patrick to Yaddo's Ireland
handling snakes, woodland spiders,
as simple playthings, his station
outside this room asleep at threshold,
his carving knife, guarding me safely from exit.
Such loyalty, devotion might lie in
pure strain of his cannibal ancestry:
"my body may be black but my soul is white."
He went back to Africa as a trader.[2]

Booker T. Washington is the "you" of the poem who appears in the history of Yaddo, the artist's colony located in Saratoga Springs, New York. Because the landscape is psychological as well as historical, stanza two offers a contrasting identity and personality, that of Etienne, referred to in an understatement as "the cannibal brought by missionaries from Africa to be trained for service." This feared image—an impugning of African/African American character—establishes a basis for ambivalence and contradiction, for in the sense of self-defined manhood, Etienne is nevertheless a counterpoint to Washington. His appearance sets up the poetic tension in the first stanza where the poet places himself as witness; like Jean Toomer's "true artist," he is both critic and creator of values and meanings. Etienne guards him "safely from exit" in a metaphor of heightened paradox and irony.

The author, in the artist colony's tower studio, views the territory while reading the history of Yaddo, or recollecting it. The poet still does not call Washington by name, but speaks to him keenly in "signifying phrases":

At the dinner table where you sat with Peabody,
stirred by the shrewd handicap of scholars and savants,
you opened your certain ginger face
"I was born a slave," rolling jordanized,
accomplished in freedom of all pride
of all bitterness of a handicapped race

made really safe from Democracy,
the *Trask* check slipped in loamed black
cloth in many dinner wallets of conversation.

The poet later *names* other black personalities who appear in the
Yaddo history, Thom Campbell and his wife Nancy, slaves

quartered in clear pieces of Bear Swampground
southeast of the Rose Garden, conjuring amused
comic tales of Tom Camel's unselfish episodes
of tree-climbing and masquerade.
Told to saw off a limb on Mr. White's place
he sat on the limb vigorously sawing the obstructing
branch; dazed after a loud crack on the ground
Tom cried to Mr. White: "Oh, noSah! I had the good
fortune to land on mah head";
dressed up in carriage, in women's clothes,
Camel posed as Burr's Mistress in Stone's
"Reminiscences of Saratoga," as Madame Jumel on one of her
visits in 1849, in criminal intimacy, at US Hotel,
threatened, bribed, as she followed her counterfeit
double, Tom Camel, fanning himself, curtseying
to crowds on every side to the lakefront with Burr.

In Yaddo's history Etienne's is a "savage memory," while Thom Campbell
(changed to Tom Camel) and Nancy exist as "comic tales" in episodes of
masquerade. They have merely anecdotal, comedic importance in that
"broader history." Minstrel humor appears in the masquerade and the
cavorting, but the language in which this humor is conveyed and the
scenes from the anecdotal history are redescribed and renamed in the
double-entendre metaphors of the blues. In being *identified,* Thom and
Nancy come to occupy the center rather than the periphery or background. The poet gains ascendency when his version of the story rescues
these unrealized personalities and brings them to the foreground despite
the anecdotal reference. Harper has spoken of this type of restoration: "I
did not see many voices from my own ancestors ably represented in our
literature, and I wanted to do my part, to testify to their efforts and
achievements, and the values implicit in the making of this country and
its character."[3]

This is an act of reclamation such as Robert Hayden made in his tremendous poem "Aunt Jemima of the Ocean Waves." In this restored
image, the woman in the poem reveals a greater sphere of action, interest,

and ambiguous human complexity than the Aunt Jemima stereotype would allow.[4] In an interview in John O'Brien's *Interviews with Black Writers,* Harper speaks of this freeing of territory in the open-ended myth as truth: Myths "are open-ended *when they are true* in that they suggest new arrangements of human essentials based on contingent human experience, not on historical, systematic experience . . . one ought to be careful about myth as lie, when it's stereotyped, when it's reductive, when it freezes experience and denies freedom."[5]

These are the nonreductive levels on which African American music as "modal" and "holistic" functions; "singing in dimensions"[6] Harper calls it in another interview. And because the African American artist hears the multiple possibilities and levels of jazz, his response is different from the typical European and European American perception. Westerners only perceive the colors they have names for, only hear the notes that conform to their own harmonic scale; the vast and resonant polyrhythms outside of their harmonic tradition go unnoted. We know, for instance, that the richness of African music, the antecedent of jazz music, cannot even be transcribed, much of its sounds lying outside the West's notation system.

This difference in perception will become evident in our discussion of Imamu Amiri Baraka's short fiction. We can also see it articulated in Hermann Hesse's novel *Steppenwolf,* and the Steppenwolf's reductive way of hearing jazz music, much like Westerners' way of "hearing" other oral traditions in general. Though he is drawn to it by his "wild longing for strong emotions and sensations," his "rage against" the "toneless, flat, normal and sterile" middle-class life (similar to Baraka's rage, we will discover)—this "brood of mediocrity" (again parallels)—he is nevertheless repulsed by it; there is no "refuge" for him in it. Given Kimberly Benston's assertion that jazz music engages European-American culture in a revolt and "a nearly total negation of Western history and civilization,"[7] perhaps this is the only way the Western artist *should* legitimately hear and respond to the music—as Sandburg does; as a battle. Hesse's description however, even more fully than Sandburg's poetic rendering, serves to crystallize the "agonistic relationship" (Benston) of two different artistic and musical traditions—where one artist's spiritual sustainer in such an antithetical context can easily be another's spiritual insult. This becomes even more poignantly evident when we think of aesthetics on the purely material plane: for an African to attempt to meet the European "beauty standard" would be absurd and self-destructive—a recurring trope in African and African American and other non-European writings.

(It would be equally absurd in this purely material aesthetic to speak of "lowering the [European] standard" to accommodate great Oriental or African beauty.) In Hesse, however, we must first note the unifying effect of Harry Haller's—the Steppenwolf's—own music: "It was at a concert of lovely old music. After two or three notes of the piano the door was opened of a sudden to the other world. I sped through heaven and saw God at work. I suffered holy pains. I dropped all my defenses and was afraid of nothing in the world. I accepted all things and to all things I gave up my heart. It did not last long, a quarter of an hour perhaps; but it returned to me in a dream at night, and since, through all the barren days, I caught a glimpse of it now and then." After this exhilaration, Hesse (or his narrator) counterpoises jazz music: "From a dance hall there met me as I passed by the strains of lively jazz music, hot and raw as the stream of raw flesh. I stopped a moment. This kind of music, much as I detested it, had always had a secret charm for me. It was repugnant to me, and yet ten times preferable to all the academic music of the day. For me too, its raw and savage gaiety reached an underworld of instinct and breathed a simple honest sensuality."[8]

There can be no more violent or vigorous dismissal of this music: the Steppenwolf's contention, finally, that it is not even real music. Yet there is ambivalence—the West's own ambivalence—here in the conditional praise the narrator gives it. Within his "compartmentalized" hearing, it nevertheless, like the "beat, bop, and blues" of the Beat Generation, represents an aesthetic alternative to the "flat and sterile." But it is not real music as Bach and Mozart are real. It is "dangerous and savage" music. The music, or his response to it, represents the duality of Haller's nature, the mythology that he has invented for himself, and the West's own dualistic compartmentalization(s) of its own reality. This is the antithesis of "modality"—in Harper's usage holistic, a continuum—the "both/and" one finds in African American music, rather than an "either/or"—for instance, the jazz soloist works with and against the group at the same time. In Western tradition, this would be the absurdity, the nonlogic, the paradox.

Mozart and Bach are the sources of Haller's human being, of sublime "thoughts and feelings, of culture and tamed and sublimated nature," while jazz represents the "wolf, that is to say, a dark world of instinct, of savagery and cruelty, of unsublimated or raw nature." Ironically or paradoxically, though, it is the jazz that reconciles Harry's personal "division into wolf and man" (his own brand of double-consciousness) and the Western duality; jazz has "thousands and thousands" of possibilities rather than the either/or polarity Harry (and the West) have invented and that is the foundation of Western ontology. At least the African American writer sees such complexity in the music: its "potentialities and possibilities," an aesthetic philosophy and "theory of being," and certainly the exposition of self that African American heroes and heroines try to achieve.

Section III of Harper's poem contains personal historical references to the poet's own ancestors. The "I" narrator again becomes mobile in space and time:

> Meeting in secret, with my great
> grandfather AME bishop in Philadelphia,
> just before his debarking the ship
> from South Africa, I see the choices
> for education and literacy of a *downtrodden* people
> flushed down the outlet of the ocean
> liner, where my earmarked greatgrand
> fluxed precious diamonds from the Zulu
> chiefs, before stolen by customs.
>
> What tongues did the diamond speak?
> To be educated by black spiritual linguists
> from runaway Canada
> or the pontifs of paternity
> in the plazas of Saratoga,
> I remind myself with a visit to harnessed
> racing, no single black jockey present,
> for this is even betting handicapped
> at fifty dollars and my best thoroughbred
> in August, where the Indian spirits
> praise a five-hundred-year-old tree
> nourished by sacred spring water,
> its radioactivity signs ignored,
> the freed slave runaways
> paddling down the Hudson to Catskill
> to the dayline my grandfather ran
> before the bride to Kingston
> took his house, his children, to Brooklyn.

Time past and time present continue to have tangency. This is not chaos but a "jamming" session: by forcing the personalities, images, time periods, references, situations, events into this stanzaic space, by jamming them, the poet actually extends their "possibility, combination, and diversity"—their territory, "suggesting new arrangements of human essentials"; they break the "narrow borders" of time, space, and definition through the poet's memory and creative investment. The personal and historical are magnificently superimposed.

Section IV, entitled "Psycho-photos of Hampton," like the title of Section II, "Dining from a Treed Condition," pulls us forward in this new poetic sequence but also reverberates with references to Harper's previous poetic sequences in "Photographs/Negatives" of *Song: I Want a Witness,* a sequence of nine poems which speak of "human photo graphs," "negative images," and "treed conditions." The same process of image-making and "metaphoric variation" is seen in these poems. Robert Steptoe, whom I have quoted liberally in the last paragraph, discusses this process in his article "After Modernism": "In these poems, the narrative situation to be invested with metaphorical properties is always that of the solitary poet, as articulate or self-conscious (as opposed to "double-conscious") hero, traversing what Octavio Paz would term a labyrinth of solitude. This labyrinth is simultaneously a literal landscape rich in lore and history . . . and a figurative landscape of racial memory. In each poem, the landscapes link and appear as concentrated images . . . the poet . . . a potential human image—searches for the process by which he will "imagine" himself."[9] In his new sequence the poet "binds the exterior and interior landscapes," "unravels the mysteries of personal history bound to public history," and reclaims dimensions of history as well as personality or metamorphosed human possibility, restoring what N. Scott Momaday would call "consummate human being."

Section IV provides the open-ended resolution of the poetic series as we return to the poet-narrator's jazz perspective in which chronological order no longer holds:

> Dining at 8 and 6:30
> with a lunchpail for noon,
> I type out the echoes of artist
> in the high studio of the tower,
> blackened in the image of Etienne,
> his cannibal ancestry sharpened
> by the sloped Adirondacks toward Montreal
> where French/Indian alliances of beaver pelts
> end in burrows of buffalo in open plains,
> another mountain range to cross, the salt lick
> of lake claiming runaway bigamists,
> and the great Sioux herds on the run to Cody,

named for the diseased man who died in Denver,
his widow offered forty grand to be buried near his name.

On a ride down 9W to Esopus, New York
where Wiltwyck boys from five boroughs
came to the Roosevelt mansion-estate, the volunteers
driving buses with Mennonite alms, to home visits
of abandoned projects, each welfare roll breaking
in fired windows, I take the granite sites
of General Armstrong in view, his great twin
burial rocks, Vermont granite, Sandwich lava
entracing the mausoleum of the great divide
of history, of railroad lands, of the *Dakotah,*
Sandwich missions, the uplift of schoolmarms
tuning the pens of the Freedmen's Bureau toward
the thin line of traintrack near Emancipation Tree.

In his Coltrane album notes Harper speaks of "synthesis of personal history and overtones of American." Section IV, then, reclaims a new historical perspective of an America that would "forget" its total ancestry and therefore its own personality. He attempts to restore both personality and history, to mend "the great divide of history," bringing the whole America into view. (The all-inclusive jazz perspective?) American history and character from the European American perspective have often been viewed in narrow and restrictive terms rather than, to borrow James Baldwin's phrase, as a "continuing, complex reality" made up of its multiple histories and characters. From the jazz perspective one can encompass what Ellison would call all the historical "nodes," acknowledging and restoring them all. "American history" has never been simply white American history, nor when one speaks of an American should one only speak in white-face. Native American history, as the first essential great divided history, is brought to the foreground along with African-American in recalling the landscape from the "Black Hills to mosquitoed swamp near Fort Monroe," in the calling of Native American names in history integrated. Echoes of the beginning return in fragments; histories, personalities, metaphors, landscapes, heroes, American overtones are jammed in a single stanza:

Separate as the limed hand
the five great Indian nations
disappear along the trail
of tears, the common man of Andrew

Jackson looking moonstruck in black regiments
for the Seminoles of Florida,
each Catholic outpost
St. Paul's reservation of Little Crow
waiting for rations,
the St. Louis Fair
where Geronimo breathed the gas
from the Ford caught in the mud
gatewayed in his western eyes
to New Orleans, where the musicians
stomp all night to Buster's for breakfast,
the building boarded up with slave anklets,
the militia protecting the war ships
of Toussaint in Napoleon's gift to Jefferson.
Your simplest image was the crab-barrel,
each black hand pulled the escaping soul
back into the pit where the turpentine
gangs sang, cutting their way through each
wilderness, each Indian amulet dropping
in cross-fires of settlers,
your great dining hall opening:
"I was born a slave,"
countered by Aristotle's
"some men are natural born slaves,"
in the board of Wall Street,
where Melville wrote the dark glimmerings
scrimshaw tales, attacked by the whale,
his bludgeoned knife raised in combat,
his sweat in the oiled battle with self
where the nation stormed in fish beds
as laughing men and women dove
in triangular trade winds.

Many "histories" coalesce here, the historical American forgetfulness remembered by the poet. States Harper in another interview: "As I see it, blacks have always influenced the formation of American character, in every meaningful way . . . The colonial lesson is, finally, that this is not a white country, no matter what the propaganda, in metaphor and in fact. It's a country that gives an opportunity to assert one's beliefs; we blacks always took the sacred documents more resolutely than those obsessed with power and violence—that's a fine gift we tender, a furrow to sow and harvest."[10]

The poet confronts the dilemma of American identity in a poem that represents the process of documenting the full composition or at least a fuller one of all the music in America (the full composition would include the dynamics of the Chicano, the Asian American, and other presences, but all these multiplicities are implied here if not presented directly: all these are in the American nodes, even while we still await the complete American jazz composition playing all of these essential notes). "Composition is structuring and orchestrating, revealing the hidden texts implicit in human experience." Harper brings forward the hidden human texts in language that, like Ellison's, is capable of viewing the contradictions and is "large with elegance and with word invention as an improvisational attitude."[II]

Once more the poet speaks to Washington, recalls and integrates his metaphor with other American aesthetic possibilities and "battles with self." Then the cyclical poem concludes (or opens) with juxtaposed resolutions and coexistences:

> The last view is the best,
> from the terrace overhang,
> with a toothbrush,
> seeing rock gardens and roses
> pool in cascading fountains:
> the Renaissance built on slave trading,
> Etienne proud of his lineage,
> Booker T's bookings humbling his beginnings,
> the abstract masks giving off power,
> its conjured being dynamized in my skin,
> reminiscing at the founder's table
> where the talk was of politics,
> rhetoric, and the literature of the great
> rainbowed swamp from the vision of the black tower.

In Harper's poetry, jazz is not a metaphor for battles and dilemmas of self but for the resolution in journeys of the spirit. The African American's own music has a unifying effect, which brings a sense of wholeness to the individual, not in solitude as Hermann Hesse's *Steppenwolf* or James Joyce's *Artist,* but in communion (or if solitude, then communing solitude). One also sees the potential of the jazz perspective for reintegrating the whole of American experience in a "rainbowed" text. For the African American artists the music is universal, complex, and multileveled in its identities. They claim for their music the "thousands and thousands" of possibilities that the Steppenwolf would claim for his own. It is music that renders visible the "spirit of a people" and can also have cosmic dimensions, music that "strengths and confirms."

The poet's vision from the dark tower, then, like the jazz musician's, "conjures being," reclaims the whole. It is a modal perception. As defined by Harper, "The African Continuum is a *modal* concept which views the cosmos as a totally integrated environment where all spiritual forces interact . . . the music that provides images strong enough to give back that power that renews."[12] His own "Uplift from the Dark Tower" is such music.

Like the other poets in this section, Harper sought to explore the resources of oral tradition in order to restore a sense of wholeness to African American character in literature, even in the midst of contradictions and contradictory realities. African American consciousness and perspective in a general and communal—not monolithic—sense, as the poet's, in particular, can also be moved to the center of the work. (We see from the jazz perspective that to do this is not limiting or limited but can provide resources for true universality.) In addition to restoration of personality, Harper's concern has been with the restoration of landscape and history. Through jazz as a modal concept he has also brought a sense of continuity of tradition. Not all poetry using oral tradition chooses dialect; it may choose the formal orchestrations, values, and tonal contexts. Harper has used these to move the literature to a greater conceptual integrity, contingent with African American tradition, and extended the vocabulary of African American and American landscape through a rendering of the jazz perspective.

"Music . . . is poetry," said Walter Pater.[13] Poetry is also music in our tradition, and more clearly, song. Concrete poetry, a development in Western experimental literary tradition of the purely visual poem divorced from the aural—the human voice or voice extended through musical instrument—does not seem to exist, or is not the vanguard of the African American tradition. There experimentation mostly runs in the direction of the heard, and how best the poem can be heard, and heard, as Harper would say, "in dimensions." Our poetry, because of the oral nature of poetry itself in most world traditions, seems more obviously connected with oral modes and motives. But fiction writers too have drawn from oral traditions' sounds and forms to modify traditional fiction, to destroy and recreate it, and to make and remake whole images.

II

Short Fiction

5

Breaking out of the Conventions of Dialect: Paul L. Dunbar and Zora Neale Hurston

Minstrelsy and Early Literary Dialect

The history of African American fiction, along with poetry, reveals a tension between oral and literary forms. In his book *Neo-African Literature,* Janheinz Jahn speaks of "Afro-American folklore making its breakthrough to literature" in the works of Paul Laurence Dunbar and Charles Waddell Chesnutt; but he also refers to Dunbar as a "black nigger minstrel."[1] This points to a dual problem in African American literary history. First, African American folklore existed in viable and complex literary forms, and African American writers, certainly from the turn-of-the-century, made deliberate artistic use of these forms in their literary creations. Second, the distortions—human and linguistic—of minstrelsy also existed as literary models in the language and character of the three stock characters: the interlocutor, Mr. Bones, and Mr. Tambo. The interlocutor was usually white and spoke in formal, standard, "intelligent" and serious language (the beginning of the "straight man" in American comedy), while Mr. Bones and Mr. Tambo spoke in dialect and their subject matter was limited to clownish discourse.[2] Hence not only was there tension between the "pure" oral and literary models as complex forms, but the uses of oral tradition and "black speech" were further complicated by the intrusion of the "artistic models" (and one may say this) of the minstrel show, and its reduction of the artistic possibilities of the African-American oral tradition—speech and folklore—through distortion and caricature. It is curious that American comedic teams still continue this pattern, which is also the precedent for the American musical comedy. Even the first American talking movie, the 1927 *Jazz Singer,* was without question in the minstrel tradition.

Minstrelsy, then, contributed to the ambivalence of the early African American writers toward "the dialect" and fastened their attitudes toward this language as distortion, compounding, molding, and securing apparent distortions of character and the relationship between language and character. Because audiences were used to hearing "dialect" only in comic contexts, even the writers who used the dialect for other purposes or with different intentions were often accused, as Richard Wright accused Zora Neale Hurston, of "perpetuating the minstrel tradition,"[3] although Hurston's meticulous rendering of dialect was necessary for the serious purpose of authentic representation of the speech of her characters, while it also contributed to broadening the range of dialect in literature.

Paul Laurence Dunbar's short story "The Lynching of Jube Benson" brings together all of the early problems of dialect and demonstrates early attempts at breaking through folklore into literature. James Weldon Johnson, an African American writer whose own works, such as *God's Trombones: Seven Negro Sermons in Verse* (1927), showed efforts to resolve the tensions of literary dialect, clarifies the problems in his introduction to *The Book of American Negro Poetry* (1931):

> almost all poetry in the conventionalized dialect is either based upon the minstrel traditions of Negro life, traditions that had but slight relation—often no relation at all—to actual Negro life, or is permeated with artificial sentiment. It is now realized both by the poets and by their public that as an instrument for poetry the dialect has only two main stops, humor and pathos.
>
> That this is not a shortcoming inherent in the dialect as dialect is demonstrated by the wide compass it displays in its use in the folk creations. The limitation is due to conventions that have been fixed upon the dialect and the conformity to them by individual writers. Negro dialect poetry had its origin in the minstrel traditions, and a persisting pattern was set. When the individual writer attempted to get away from that pattern, the fixed conventions allowed him only to slip over into a slough of sentimentality.[4]

Elsewhere in the introduction, Johnson suggests that if African American writers had been the first to "fix" their dialect as literature, perhaps these conventions of distortion and caricature for the benefit of outsiders could have been superseded. He cites Robert Burns's use of the Scottish dialect as an example of what might have been done. Readers of the poetry of Burns apprehend its elegance, variety of subjects, and range of humanity; it is not the language solely of burlesque or pathos, though even Burns was once "hailed by the literati of Edinburgh as an instance of the natural genius . . . whose poems were the *spontaneous overflow* of his *native feelings*" (my italics).[5] Of course, this accusation of artlessness, as observed in the work of the Canadian Margaret Laurence, continues to be the bane of writers writing outside of standard literary conventions despite the "intelligence and sensibility" their efforts bring to or cull from their indigenous speech and their "deliberate craft." But "the Scottish oral tradition of folklore and folk song, and the highly developed Scottish literary tradition" were jointly parts of Burns's artistic heritage. Perhaps it is this sense of security in both a literary and oral tradition that provided Burns's "sure fix" on intricate poetry in Scottish dialect. But, for the slaves in America, literacy was a criminal act. Not only were they denied legal access to the literary heritage of the West, but they suffered a loss of clear continuity with the African oral literatures, as an aesthetic alternative in a "highly developed African oral tradition" (Finnegan) that included ritual dramas and great epics. The only outlet for their visions, concerns, and struggles in the New World were the oral forms developed here: the blues, spirituals, worksongs. Later African American writers drew upon these forms to insure a new connection with tradition, but they did not hold the same currency or status in a literary culture that had been alien and denied to their ancestors.

Social history, as well then, compounded the problems of the early African American writers who incorporated African American dialect and folklore into their literatures. The two to be considered here are Paul Laurence Dunbar and Zora Neale Hurston; the first a turn-of-the-century writer and the second a representative of the Harlem Renaissance period. The questions that may be raised in reviewing the works of these writers are: How does one use in literature a dialect that has already been codified into burlesque? How does one employ the language in order to return it to the elasticity, viability, and indeed complexity, "intelligence and sensibility," that it often has when not divorced from the oral modes and folk creators?

Paul Laurence Dunbar

Paul Laurence Dunbar's "The Lynching of Jube Benson" illustrates the codification of literary dialect in turn-of-the-century African American fiction, and the links between dialect, perspective, character, and audience.

In the beginning of the story three white men are seated with Gordon Fairfax in his library, and Dunbar uses not only Dr. Melville's viewpoint but indirection to initiate the story. First, through the dialogue of the four, Dunbar sets up the popular feeling of the time of Jim Crow codes and legislation at home, and encroachments abroad in the Pacific and Caribbean extending the convolvulus of white supremacy—a time when lynchings were advertised in newspapers under "amusements." In the conversation, Gay rather callously says, "I would like to see a real lynching." And if a real lynching were to come his way, Fairfax admits, "I should not avoid it." "I should," Dr. Melville speaks up "from the depths of his chair, where he had been puffing in moody silence"; and thus begins "The Lynching of Jube Benson."

This restriction of perspective to Dr. Melville's viewpoint and the use of him as the storyteller is of course related to the audience of this turn-of-the-century fiction. Addressed to white readers, it admonishes them to change their social attitudes and put an end to lynching. Similarly, the nineteenth-century slave narrators addressed such audiences to change them to abolitionist sentiments. As in most literature in that tradition of protest, it is a fellow white man who argues and authenticates the case of Jube and who comes to consciousness and realization, thus giving the lynching story its authenticity.

But there are problems. Jube Benson remains essentially invisible. Revealed solely in a frame-story told by Dr. Melville, he must be seen only through the stereotypes and clichéd metaphors of Melville. The "perfect Cerberus," he is "black but gentle." And as Melville describes Jube, he reveals more of himself than he does of Jube Benson. In addition, the descriptions of Jube allow for dramatic ironies, for instance, when Melville recognizes his "false education" yet persists in being circumscribed by it. "I saw his black face glooming there in the half light, and I could only think of him as a monster. It's tradition. At first I was told that the black man would catch me, and when I got over that, they taught me that the devil was black, and when I recovered from the sickness of that belief, here were Jube and his fellows with faces of menacing blackness. There was only one conclusion: This black man stood for all the powers of evil, the result of whose machinations had been gathering in my mind from childhood up. But this has nothing to do with what happened."[6] Dr. Melville recognizes but ironically continues to be guided by this false education in his symbolic, linguistic, and metaphorical systems. Dunbar compounds the irony, for what happens—the false judgment and its consequence, the lynching of Jube Benson—has everything to do with these machinations.

Dr. Melville is in love with Jube's mistress, Ann. When she is sick Jube takes care of her: "He was a fellow whom everybody trusted—an apparently steady-going, grinning sort, as we used to call him . . . faithful servitor." Jube not only nurses Annie when she falls victim to the typhoid outbreak, but he also nurses the doctor "as if I were a sick kitten and he my mother . . . a black but gentle demon" he sees in his delirium, a "chimerical vision."

These appreciations notwithstanding, when Annie was attacked and murdered by a white fellow masked with soot on his face to resemble a black, and before dying she exclaimed, "that black," Jube is the first to be suspected. The "black rascal" identification, psychosexual myths, and "the diabolical reason of his slyness" insure the white mob's ability to see Jube only as a "human tiger" and judge him guilty of the crime without evidence or trial. The white men pursue Jube—"he gave a scream like an animal's"; they lynched him.

Later, when Jube's brother Ben and another black man come up with the real culprit, his face "blackened to imitate a Negro's," it is too late. Jube's brother Ben accuses fiercely, "you he'ped murder my brothah, you dat was his frien'; go 'way, go 'way! I'll take him home myse'f."

It is Dr. Melville, however, who delivers the final judgment for the story, calling himself and the others in the mob "blood guilty" and telling the "gentlemen" gathered in Gordon Fairfax's library that that was his last lynching.

Because everything is seen from the perspective of Dr. Melville and much of Jube's dialect is contained within this framed story, we may surmise that many of the restrictions and conventions of literary dialect, like the metaphorical restrictions on Jube's humanity, could be ascribed equally to Melville and to the author's concern with the truth and consistency of the narrator's personality. Whether or not this is true, Dunbar's use of dialect in the story clinches the problems in the turn-of-the-century use of the conventions of literary dialect.

First, the emotional range, as James Weldon Johnson argues, is restricted to pathos. We do not rise above pathos to the tragic potential of the story, and are only allowed to glimpse its possibility near the conclusion, when Jube's brother and another black man briefly enter the scene and brother Ben gives his strong accusation. But Dr. Melville's rendering of Jube's language, gestures, and mannerisms has elements of minstrel parody, though Melville doesn't recognize this in what he considers his affective and serious rendering of Jube and genuine sentiment. In his article on Booker T. Washington's *Up From Slavery*, Robert Steptoe noted a "real life" example of this kind of description: James Creelman's *New York World* account of Washington's Atlanta address.

The most offensive passage occurs when Creelman attempts to add a little sentiment and "color" to his story: "A ragged ebony giant, squatted on the floor in one of the aisles, watched the orator with burning eyes and tremulous face until the supreme burst of applause came, and then the tears ran down his face. Most of the Negroes in the audience were crying, perhaps without knowing just why." We needn't labor over Creelman's opinion of the Negroes in the audience, or strain to mine his attitude toward (or anxiety over) the responses of the white women: "The fairest women of Georgia stood up and cheered. . . . It was as if the orator [Washington] had bewitched them." Of Washington, Creelman writes that he is a "Negro Moses," a "tall tawny Negro" with "heavy jaws, and strong, determined mouth, with big white teeth, piercing eyes . . . bronzed neck . . . muscular right arm . . . clenched brown fist . . . big feet . . . and dusky hand."[7]

As in Melville's account of Jube, the language is more apt to tell us about the teller's psychology and attitudes than to give an accurate portraiture.

The second problem concerning dialect in Dunbar's story is that the transcription techniques depend on easy mutilations of spelling and grammar, as well as the use of "eye dialect"—unnecessary orthographic changes such as "tuk" for "took," "a laffin'" for "laughing." Such words do not depend on pronunciation for their changes but add to the visual distortion, increasing the sense of the language as humorous or pathetic aberration.

Finally, literary formulas are used in the place of heard speech. However, again, the character of Dr. Melville accounts for much of the formula in his retelling of Jube's language. Since everyone's rehearing is somehow distorted by imagination, memory, or judgment, and compounded with his "false education," Dr. Melville does not surprise us here. Nevertheless, the problems of literary dialect delineated by James Weldon Johnson are finely illuminated by this story: the restricted emotional range, and the limited range of subject matter, experience, and perception.

Although it is not clear in "The Lynching of Jube Benson" how much of the conventions of dialect are due to persona/perspective/audience or world view, it is important to reiterate and clarify that the limitations of literary dialect are not just limitations of language and not just a literary or artistic dilemma, but that language is inseparable from our comprehension and sense of character. Because of the restrictions on the emotional experiential ranges, as well as the distractions brought about by transcription techniques, a fully realized complex character is impossible. But let us suppose Jube's brother Ben had told the story. Would the range of emotions have been extended beyond pathos and parody? What other aspects of Jube's character, hidden to Melville, might have been revealed? Would a broader range and context of subjects and concerns have entered the story? Would African American characters have been moved from the background to the foreground in dramatic scenes? Even if the "eye dialect" and other transcription devices shared by all the writers of the turn-of-the-century had been used, could the dialect have been made to do more and had more to do? How might it have been stretched? These questions lead us again to the problem of audience, and it was taken for granted at the time that the audience with the "broader perspective" was always white, and the significant relationships were always interracial ones of unambiguous conflict and dangerous confrontation. Only later, when the folklore tradition gained more of its own authority in literature, did it become possible to answer such questions and to have character, audience, point of view and language gain more elasticity.

Zora Neale Hurston

Zora Neale Hurston's short story "The Gilded Six-Bits" (1933)[8] takes us out of the conventional restrictions observed in the literary dialect of Paul Laurence Dunbar. This transformation is partly due to the shift in perspective—inside rather than outside the black community—and the storyteller does not share Dunbar's double-conscious concern with an exclusive, white audience. Because her theme is not part of the protest literature tradition as such, Hurston can be concerned with the relationship between a man and woman in a Negro settlement. She can expand the range beyond humor and pathos to a crisis-of-love story; there can be development and recognition, dilemma and resolution, delineated personality. George Kent has called this a "simple story." In an interview with Roseann P. Bell in *Sturdy Black Bridges: Visions of Black Women in Literature* he says "That one (the story) suggests that really simple people could suddenly resolve all problems by suddenly forgiving each other very easily . . . I . . . recall that incident being very tediously resolved. I don't recall a really imposing short story by her."[9]

Although the story is about simple people whose relationship seems to be apparently simply resolved, in view of the dialect tradition and particularly those problems manifest in Dunbar's turn-of-the-century story, Hurston's simple short story might be reviewed in a more complex light. Its shift in perspective (what Ellison would term "restoring of perspective"), its lack of preoccupation with audience, its sense that Southern rural black speech as dialect may contain any emotion in literature add degrees of complexity not easily acknowledged or perceived in a cursory reading. And although there is humor certainly in places, as in all of Hurston's work, it is the spontaneous good humor of fully realized characters in interaction, not the one-dimensional minstrel humor. We laugh along *with* the characters in their happy moments; we go down into the depths with them during the crisis of love, we come out with them. We are brought beyond humor and pathos.

The focus of the whole story is on relationships, interpersonal conflict, and conflict of values. There are some elements of sophistication in the story—particularly in the many reversals. But the question for Hurston—and this perhaps accounts for George Kent's reaction—is how to write of ordinary people without making the writer's concerns and the story itself seem ordinary, even trivial. The subject of Dunbar's story is perhaps a more "significant event"[10] in sociohistorical reality, nevertheless in rendering that significance his African American characters remain in the background in physical presence and psychological reality. In contrast, Hurston's characters are pulled to the foreground in both these respects. Like most literary transitions, this one doesn't appear to be of great note these days. Contemporary African American writers automatically pull their African American characters to the foreground, and notwithstanding certain persistent (nay, recalcitrant) white critics who may still be asking black writers whether they write about "black people or human beings," consider the African American character's perspective "the broader perspective" and the significant one. However, it was an important transition and should be read as an initial link between a literary technique—viewpoint—and its broader humanistic implications in the depiction of black humanity in literature.

We first meet Missie May and Joe in a ritual scene they enact every Saturday morning, when Joe throws nine silver dollars in the door "for her to pick up and pile beside her plate at dinner." He also brings her candy kisses. The beginning is full of happiness, "joyful mischief," "mock anger," and the "play fight."

Otis Slemmons, introduced shortly after this playful scene, becomes the center of a conflict of values (this, the subject of much of Hurston's fiction, should be considered a worthy subject, even what E. M. Forster would call a noble one). We learn Otis is from Chicago and "spots and places." In the initial dialogue between the husband and wife we see what things interest the couple about him: he has been places, he has gold teeth, he wears "up to date" clothes, his "puzzlegutted" build makes him "look like a rich white man," he has the attention of many women (including white ones up North), and he has gold pieces. These are the things that Joe notices and talks about. Initially, Missie May seems to have no material concerns, and her love for Joe is uppermost; she loves him as he is. Joe, however, feels he "can't hold no light to Otis D. Slemmons" because he "ain't never been nowhere" and "ain't got nothing but you."

At first Missie May is not taken in by Otis and what he represents. But in a reversal, the next time we hear the husband and wife talking together, after they have returned from seeing Otis Slemmons at the local ice-cream parlor, Joe is expressing Missie May's earlier values and she is expressing his. We see then all the things Missie May wants for Joe. There is some blending of values because she wants these things for him "because she loves him," but nevertheless she wants them. Joe's response now is: "Joe laughed and hugged her, 'Don't be so wishful 'bout me. Ah'm satisfied de way Ah is. So long as Ah be yo' husband, Ah don't keer 'bout nothin' else.'"

However, to get the things she wants—the gilded six-bits which the gold coins turn out to be—Missie May betrays Joe with Otis Slemmons. Joe comes home early from work and finds them together. There is a fine handling of emotional reactions here. Joe sees them and "opens his mouth and laughs." Because this is not the expected response—it seems to contradict the occasion—it deepens our sense of the emotion which, like "a howling wind raced through his heart," and he "kept on feeling so much." He fights Slemmons, drives him away, and the crisis of love begins. There is no more laughter or banter.

George Kent calls the resolution easy. I think that it appears easy because here Hurston handles all the emotional reversals and complications in narrative summary rather than active dramatic scenes. One reads over them quickly and so it seems that they are done quickly, but really there are subtle and difficult changes. Once Joe makes love to Missie May, then leaves a piece of Slemmon's "gold" "with the bit of chain attached" under her pillow. She discovers then it was no gold piece. "It was a gilded half dollar." After the love making she had thought "they were man and wife again. Then another thought came clawing at her. He had come home to buy from her as if she were any woman in the long house. Fifty cents for her love." She dresses and leaves the house, but she encounters her husband's mother, and so as not to "admit defeat to that woman" she returns home. Joe discovers she is pregnant and when she has the child he knows it is his (his mother even confirms that the baby looks like him—so it must be his!) and they reconcile. The story is perhaps resolved too simply at that point, the "baby chile" a kind of deus ex machina; nevertheless Hurston's handling of their complications and reversals of emotion before that point is superb, and certainly adds more shadings of emotions than were easily revealed in earlier dialect stories. The dialect itself is more complex and shows more literary sophistication. The links with the interior of characters, the processes of emotional transformation, as well as the foreground presentation carry it away from the "simple story" though it deals with ordinary folks.

Yet this story challenges by containing everything that was considered not the stuff of important fiction—it is regional, it focuses on the relationship between a black man and woman, and it does not make interracial conflict its reason for being. The problem of the "stuff of important fiction" of course transcends racial lines. The white American woman writer Mary Gordon speaks of "bad specters" that she must work to banish. "Let us pretend these specters are two men, two famous poets, saying, 'Your experience is an embarrassment; your experience is insignificant.' . . . it was all right for the young men I knew, according to my specters, to write about the hymens they had broken, the diner waitresses they had seduced. Those experiences were significant. But we were not to write about our broken hearts, about the married men we loved disastrously, about our mothers or our children. Men could write about their fears of dying by exposure in the forest; we could not write about our fears of being suffocated in the kitchen. Our desire to write about these experiences only revealed our shallowness." [11] Most female writers—black and white—have experienced this from male critics. Black writers—male and female—have experienced it from (white) male critics—and ironically—given Gordon's remarks—from (white) female critics. For writers dominated by others' literary standards of "significant events"—national, sexual, racial—the problem is not only finding one's voice but of trusting it when one does find it; then finding the voice or voices that one most values—avoiding destructions of the creative spirit and discovering how one can best, as George Kent would term it, "assert one's existence" and the existences of all one's characters. Kent himself feels that black women writers fail to explore real depth—"Often, the problem is that you don't get a deep enough definition of all the things that the woman encounters which are her responses to power . . . I would say that Black women writers that I've read don't seem to get much into subtle possibilities . . . I don't see much possibility, and I'm not sure that there is always depth."

Yet, unlike most critics, Kent acknowledges that "It might be that male thing you were talking about."[12] It could be "elliptical details" in the work for which a male critic would need more "analytical commentary."[13] Conversely, as the Wife of Bath might put it, "if wommen hadde juged stories," had had the dominant voices in the "juggementz"—well, Gordon's comments suggest the direction.

But regardless of the subtleties—"subtle possibilities" (of society, history, gender?)—that critics confuse with aesthetics, for Hurston, dialect as regional vernacular can do and contain anything: subject, experience, emotion, revelation. Two biographical reasons for this new attitude and sense of possibility in character and dialect might be that Hurston was born in the first incorporated all-black town of Eatonville, Florida, and she was a folklorist with an exact as well as creative ear. In her foreword to the University of Illinois Press edition of *Their Eyes Were Watching God,* Sherley Anne Williams speaks of her "command": "She had at her command a large store of stories, songs, incidents, idiomatic phrases, and metaphors; her ear for speech rhythms must have been remarkable. Most importantly, she had the literary intelligence and developed the literary skill to convey the power and beauty of this heard speech and lived experience on the printed page . . . In the speech of her characters, black voices—whether rural or urban, northern or southern—come alive. Her fidelity to diction, metaphor, and syntax—whether in direct quotations or in paraphrases of characters' thoughts—rings, even across forty years, with an arching familiarity that is a testament to Hurston's skill and to the durability of black speech."

In "The Gilded Six-Bits" one sees the folklorist in the metaphors, images, descriptions in the dialogue: "He ain't puzzlegutted, honey"; "God took pattern after a pine tree and built you noble"; "You can make 'miration at it, but don't tetch it"; "Ah reckon dey done made him vast-rich." Certainly there is a difference between the metaphors here and those in Dr. Melville's descriptive evaluation of Jube or James Creelman's of Booker T. Washington; here there is individuality, range, and elegance.

Oral tradition enters, complements, and complicates character, in the use of storytelling or reported scenes to reinforce the dramatic ones. After Missie and Joe see Otis at the ice-cream parlor, Joe retells the encounter on the way back:

On the way home that night Joe was exultant. "Didn't Ah say ole Otis was swell? Cain't he talk Chicago talk? Wuzn't dat funny whut he said when great big fat ole Ida Armstrong come in? He asted me, 'Who is dat broad wid de forte shake?' Dat's a new word. Us always thought forty was a set of figgers but he showed us where it means a whole heap of things. Sometimes he don't say forty, he jes' say thirty-eight and two, and dat mean de same thing. Know whut he told me when Ah wuz payin' for our ice cream? He say, 'Ah have to hand it to you, Joe. Dat wife of yours is jes' thirty-eight and two. Yessuh, she's forte!' Ain't he killin'?"

Joe's description of the scene is important. Hurston does not take us to the ice-cream parlor directly and dramatically; she skips the scene and lets Joe's storytelling serve as a flashback. Joe does the telling and the story advances through the characters' reactions to the moment. The psychology of relationships is explored as complicating reversals and confusions of value give way to renewed and stronger affection.

Besides the use of dialect in the storytelling dialogue, Hurston also moves the folk expressions into the narrative, while in most early fiction, and certainly the turn-of-the-century fiction of both Dunbar and Chesnutt, it was confined to dialogue: "Way after while," "make his market," "mess of honey flowers." Here the syntax, lexicon, and expressive techniques of oral tradition break through to the narrative and alter it; this enlarges the scope of dialect to the modes of exposition. It is possible for this extensible language to tell a story too.

Hurston breaks new ground here. The novelist John Wideman speaks of this important evolution: "From the point of view of American literature then, the fact of black speech (and the oral roots of a distinct literary tradition—ultimately the tradition itself) existed only when it was properly 'framed,' within works which had status in the dominant literary system. For black speech the frame was the means of entering the literate culture and the frame also defined the purposes or ends for which black speech could be employed."[14] Hurston, in her use of dialect, was one of the first to initiate this breaking out of the frame, an important step for writers committed to such linguistic explorations in fiction.

In "The Gilded Six-Bits" the dialect acquires more functions and is used in a story of greater complexity of character, greater thematic range and literary sophistication. Though the people themselves are "simple" in the sense of ordinary folks, their emotional range extends beyond the sentimental or comic. Because Hurston gives the dialect a fuller value and use, she moves a step further toward a fuller exploration of black personalities in fiction. But not until Hurston's novel *Their Eyes Were Watching God* did language, thought, experience, emotion, and imagination break through and add to the text like an apical bud increasing the length of the stem, or to use Hurston's own image, a peartree bud coming to flower. Hurston actualizes the possibility of what dialect might do when moved beyond the literary conventions and allowed more of the magic and flexibility of authentic folk creation.

6

Blues Ballad:
Jean Toomer's "Karintha"

Not all stories affected by oral tradition are written in dialect or folk-speech, though most of these stories have what E. M. Forster calls "a connection with voice," a connection which extends to "characters . . . plot and comments on life . . . fantasies . . . views of the universe."[1] In this sense the narration, dramatic structure, and presentation of character in Jean Toomer's short story "Karintha"[2] reveal the effects of orality and the motives of oral tradition.

"Karintha" is the first story in a magnificent collection of prose fiction, poetry, and drama published in 1923 by Jean Toomer, a forerunner of the Harlem Renaissance period. His seminal volume *Cane* continues to influence contemporary African American writers concerned with non-traditional forms and the connection between linguistic innovation, psychological reality, and social-historical context. Here is Robert A. Bone's famous quote from the jacket of the 1969 Harper and Row edition: "Stein and Hemingway in prose, Pound and Eliot in poetry, were threshing and winnowing, testing and experimenting with words, stretching them and refocusing them, until they became the pliant instruments of a new idiom. The only Negro writer of the 1920's who participated on equal terms in the creation of the modern idiom was a young poet-novelist named Jean Toomer." Bone goes on to classify *Cane* as "an important American novel." It is often classified as a novel because of its architectonic structure—the recurring themes, metaphors, images; the bridges between histories, personalities, geographical and dramatic spaces and scenes; and because the whole book attempts to answer a question posed by the first story which speaks mysteriously of "sins against the soul." Toomer's "creation of the modern idiom," like that of Langston Hughes (whom Bone fails to acknowledge in his critical vista), is influenced by the pliant instruments of oral tradition: the blues and ballad.

"Karintha" as Blues

Although "Karintha" is not written in dialect, it nevertheless has the resonance of oral tradition. One not only *reads* Toomer, one *hears* him; his
words live beyond the page, full of rhythm and metaphor, sight and
sound, lyrical drama. His work has the dynamics, the spring and season-
ing of speech and music.

Blues repetition weaves the sentences and amplifies the texture of the
story. In fact, "Karintha" is introduced by a verse:

> Her skin is like dusk on the eastern horizon,
> O cant you see it, O cant you see it,
> Her skin is like dusk on the eastern horizon
> . . . When the sun goes down.

The lines sing through repetition, but we puzzle at their meaning and
we wait to discover it, and to discover the woman, to hear her blues. And
when we complete Karintha's story the same verse is repeated at the end,
the chorus is magnified, gains new dimension, once the whole ritual blues
story is told. If the introductory verse raises a question, the repeated last
verse does not answer it completely, but makes the question more complex in light of the whole experience. In her article "Blues Roots of
Poetry," Sherley A. Williams speaks of this internal strategy of the blues:
"Unlike sacred music, the blues deals with a world where the inability to
solve a problem does not necessarily mean that one can, or ought to,
transcend it. The internal strategy of the blues is action, rather than contemplation."[3] "Karintha" is such an open-ended blues, and Karintha the
character is as double-edged and contradictory as any blues.

Karintha's story begins, like a blues song, with a lyrical summary of
her circumstances, which provides the background for her dilemma, motives, actions, and values: "Men had always wanted her, this Karintha,
even as a child, Karintha carrying beauty, perfect as dusk when the sun
goes down. Old men rode her hobby-horse upon their knees. Young
men danced with her at frolics when they should have been dancing with
their grownup girls. God grant us youth, secretly prayed the old men.
The young fellows counted the time to pass before she would be old
enough to mate with them. This interest of the male, who wishes to
ripen a growing thing too soon, could mean no good to her." Men want
to hurry her along to womanhood while she is still a girl. Perhaps she
too is trying to be a woman. Karintha is action, full of cruelty and beauty,

paradoxes of repetition and variation that link her childhood to her womanhood. "She stoned the cows, and beat her dog, and fought the other children . . . Even the preacher, who caught her at mischief, told himself she was as innocently lovely as a November cotton flower. But Karintha is a woman, and she has had a child. A child fell out of her womb onto a bed of pine-needles in the forest. Pine-needles are smooth and sweet. They are elastic to the feet of rabbits . . . A sawmill was nearby. Its pyramidal sawdust pile smouldered. It is a year before one completely burns. Meanwhile, the smoke curls up and hangs in odd wraiths about the trees, curls up, and spreads itself out over the valley . . . Weeks after Karintha returned home the smoke was so heavy you tasted it in water." Toomer does not tell us directly here what cruelty Karintha has done to her child, but the elisions and the juxtapositions tell us. Her full humanity resides in the contradictions of her character; her adult behavior springs from a deeper, more complex cruelty, but it parallels and grows out of her childhood behavior. Her character fits George Kent's assertion regarding the blues: "While I admire a good deal of the blues tradition, it seems to me to contain a good deal of instability and disorder." Blues form also "might enable people to deal with formlessness." Like Karintha's character, it is a mixture of limitations and possibilities. But, according to Kent, blues contains "a whole lot of precariousness."[4] Karintha, then, in this nonromanticized definition of the blues, is a blues person. However, the blues form, which penetrates the prose, also orders her precarious experience.

Repetition, as part of the thematic and verbal architecture of the story, sets off the lyrical beginning (the problem introduced), middle (its complications and consequences), and end/beginning (the open end of blues ritual). The experiences of sexual dilemma and tyranny, plus Karintha's own involvement in acts of cruelty, reinforce the blues theme. "Karintha is a woman" is part of the internal repetitive structure and always moves the reader to the next level of character recognition: "Karintha is a woman. She who carries beauty, perfect as dusk when the sun goes down. She has been married many times. Old men remind her that a few years back they rode her hobby-horse upon their knees. Karintha smiles, and indulges them when she is in the mood for it. She has contempt for them. Karintha is a woman. Young men go to the big cities and run on the road. Young men go away to college. They all want to bring her money. These are the young men who thought that all they had to do was to count time. Karintha is a woman. Men do not know that the soul of her was a growing thing ripened too soon."

The repetition in traditional blues often has a similar function. Repetition in this tradition does not mean stasis, but change/new recognition; a turning point or carrying forward of experience follows each repeated line. In "Dink's Blues,"[5] for instance, each stanza crystallizes the next level of experience and meaning. Poetry in the blues tradition also suggests this active repetition. Thus in the Peruvian poet Cesar Vallejo's "The anger that breaks the man into children," each "the anger of the poor" resolves one stanza and pushes it into the next:

> The anger that breaks the man into children,
> that breaks the child, into equal birds,
> and the bird, afterwards, into little eggs;
> the anger of the poor
> has one oil against two vinegars.
>
> The anger that breaks the tree into leaves,
> the leaf into unequal buds
> and the bud, into telescopic grooves;
> the anger of the poor
> has two rivers against many seas.
>
> The anger that breaks the good into doubts,
> the doubt, into three similar arcs
> and the arc, later on, into unforeseeable tombs;
> the anger of the poor
> has one steel against two daggers.
>
> The anger that breaks the soul into bodies,
> the body into dissimilar organs
> and the organ, into octave thoughts;
> the anger of the poor
> has one central fire against two craters.[6]

Native American writer N. Scott Momaday's *Angel of Geese and Other Poems* (1974) also demonstrates the power of this incremental repetition, which contains energy and sustains movement; and which enlarges the parameters of experience and implication.

There are many kinds of dynamic repetitions in "Karintha." The line repetitions and parallelisms discussed above match internal repetition and variation of internal rhyme: see, feet, sweet, mischief, past, flashes, thought, fought, caught; of consonance: few, feet, front, dart, bit, black, bird, dusk, during, supper, songs, stop, stoned; of assonance: smoke, over, hugged, sudden, running, dust, dusk, hush, bit, vivid. Many of these examples—internal rhyme/assonance/consonance—occur simultaneously. This also contributes to the lyricism and lyrical transformations of the story and its connection with voice and song.

Finally, and most importantly, blues repetition enhances the moral recognition of the story: "Karintha is a woman. Men do not know that the soul of her was a growing thing ripened too soon." This is the initial metaphor that will be reiterated and modified throughout, providing further accounts of moral dilemma and character transformation.

"Karintha" as Ballad

The repetitive rhythms and elements of blues structure also characterize the ballad, and it is often the rhythmical clues—the rhyme, repetition, and variation—that, like the blues and blues vocabulary, link the personality described with the strategies of remembrance as oral transmission. The first stanza of the John Henry ballad is an example of this:

> Some say he's from Georgia
> Some say he's from Alabam
> But it is wrote on the rock at the Big Ten Tunnel,
> John Henry's a East Virginia Man,
> John Henry's a East Virginia Man.[7]

In the ballad tradition it is the line that concludes the stanza rather than the one that introduces it which is repeated; it is the key to character and what Gertrude Stein has called "the rhythm of personality." The repetitive structure of the ballad connects it with the blues, but its perspective distinguishes it from the blues tradition, and it is the perspective of "Karintha" linked with the blues experience that propels it into the ballad tradition. Another modern example is Gertrude Stein's "Melanctha" and *Portraits and Prayers,* suggesting the possibility of a complex link between her inventions and the inventions of African American idiom in making words and describing events.[8] As the West Indian poet and dramatist Derek Walcott has said, "the tone of the language in America was Black,"[9] perhaps hearing it with greater clarity than any American could. Here is how Stein's language shows an improvisational attitude and "sense of dynamism and change"[10] that one finds in African American linguistic innovations inspired by oral tradition:

Juan Gris is a Spaniard. He says that his pictures remind him of the school of Fontainebleau. The school of Fontainebleau is a nice school Diana and others. In this he makes no mistake but he never does make a mistake. He might and he is he is and he might, he is right and he might be right, he is a perfect painter and he might be right. He is a perfect painter, all right he might be right.

Juan Gris is a Spaniard. He says that his last pictures he says that they are as alike as the school of Fontainebleau he says that they are like the pictures of the school of Fontainebleau if he can be like, if he can be like, if he can be like the school of Fontainebleau and not alike. And as not alike.

Juan Gris is a Spaniard.

Juan Gris is a Spaniard and his pictures.[11]

This excerpt and variant of stream-of-consciousness is certainly influenced by the cubists—Gris himself, Braque, Picasso, and others (she also did a cubist word portrait of Picasso)—in the fragmentations and juxtapositions, but one wonders again whether there might not also be the incremental repetition and syntactical details of blues balladry, and in the fragmentations and juxtapositions the effect of African American jazz as well. Surely there is some of it in her fictional prose portrait of the black woman Melanctha. If this interpretation is correct, it would point to an important aspect of the evolution of the American voice in literature—and what critics have called Stein's "echoes of Midwestern talk"[12] may also be patterned on echoes of Black America. In turn, Stein's cadences influenced the native styles of both Hemingway and Fitzgerald, especially the intricate repetitions in Hemingway's style.

Janheinz Jahn makes a distinction between the techniques of blues and those of the ballad. He notes the blues' references to social background, its double meanings. But more important is that the blues offer "subjective testimony,"[13] whereas the ballad describes a third-person experience.[14] In Toomer's story we are fascinated with the rhythms of Karintha's personality, her reported experiences, the tension and suspense in the repetition, but we never move into the interior landscape of the woman—her personal ironies, frustrations, contradictions. We stay on the outside of her personality. "Karintha is a woman," we know, and we know what she does, but we don't know the conscience and consciousness of that from inside her. The narrative reports actions, physical descriptions, imagery. The ballad, Jahn says, is "not . . . a first person song, has no justification or confrontation."[15] (This is certainly "Karintha.") Jahn is examining a specific ballad, which has repetitive lines of blues and blues experiences and metaphors, but is never a part of the subjective territory of the blues:

Old man Ben, he's so bent 'n' lame;
Old man Ben, he's so bent 'n' lame,
He loves his baby 'n' he ain't got a job to his name.

She's got a head like a monkey, feet like a bear,
Mouth full of tobacco, squirting it everywhere,
But she's his baby, he loves her just the same;
She's his Garbo 'n' he's her big he-man.[16]

Of course, this is not to say that the method is a shortcoming in Toomer's writing; it is simply to establish that the first story in *Cane*, rendered lyrically rather than dramatically, is blues/ballad rather than either blues singly or ballad alone. "Karintha" introduces both the metaphorical and concrete substances of the stories that follow in *Cane*, from the blues ballad of "Becky" "who had two Negro sons," through the tensions of personality and conflict in "Carma," to John in "Theater," who seeks to rid his mind of passion, to the dilemma of identity in the final story, "Kabnis." The main aspects of this blues balladry are repeated, but later in the book we move from third person to enter the true territory of the blues' interior conflicts of conscience and consciousness, through the "I"-witnessed stories and stream-of-consciousness, shifting dramatic focus. In "Kabnis" we are in the blues mode from the beginning, as we explore Kabnis's interior landscape and personality through snatches of speech and rumination:

Near me. Now. Whoever you are, my warm glowing sweetheart, do not think that the face that rests beside you is the real Kabnis. Ralph Kabnis is a dream. And dreams are faces with large eyes and weak chins and broad brows that get smashed by the fists of square faces. The body of the world is bull-necked. A dream is a soft face that fits uncertainly upon it . . . God, if I could develop that in words. Give what I know a bull-neck and a heaving body, all would go well with me, wouldn't it, sweetheart? If I could feel that I came to the South to face it. If I, the dream (not what is weak and afraid in me) could become the face of the South. How my lips would sing for it, my songs being the lips of its soul. Soul. Soul hell. There aint no such thing. What in hell was that?

Kabnis is talking to himself here, but he speaks of what his creator has done, is doing: singing, his stories like songs. He has returned South after the urbanization—a psychic consequence of the "great migration" of the central stories of the book, from "Seventh Street" to "Bona and Paul." Kabnis is one of the so-called "talented tenth" (Du Bois) in search

▼

of direction and wholeness—his self-conscious manhood complements the feminine portraits in the first cycle of the book. (Like Karintha he too is built of contradictions, but we see the inner life of his contradictory landscape as we saw the exterior consequences of hers.) In addition to these Kabnis is in search of the "spiritual emancipation" which Alain Locke called the Harlem Renaissance period itself. The inner life that we explore in "Kabnis" of course continues the important transition from the turn-of-the-century stories. For these our focus was always on descriptions of exterior reality rather than the possibilities of the psychological realm, whereas the movement of *Cane* reflects the movement inward that one sees in African American literary history—a movement that does not negate the social reality that influences the psychological reality. But it is Toomer that initiated for the African American writer the "conceptual voyage," the concern with "the forces existing in . . . human behavior."[17] Kabnis's return to the South parallels the author's return for the same essential purposes. Toomer spoke of the spiritual and artistic consequences of his return: "A visit to Georgia last fall was the starting point of almost everything of worth that I have done. I heard folk-songs come from the lips of Negro peasants. I saw the rich dusk beauty that I had heard many false accents about, and of which till then, I was somewhat skeptical. And a deep part of my nature, a part that I had repressed, sprang suddenly to life and responded to them. Now, I cannot conceive of myself as aloof and separated."[18] With regard to our earlier assertions concerning viewpoint, it is significant that such contact caused Toomer to deepen and widen as it "stimulated and fertilized" his creative talent.

Jean Toomer's "Karintha" suggests another direction for exploring how African American fiction writers have made use of oral tradition in transitions of form and content. Though some of the stories in *Cane* contain dialect and "ready" dialect, the oral traditional impulses lie mainly in the narrative motives and modes, the orality and tonal atmosphere of the language; and the insistence of overall structural imperatives from oral idiom. Toomer, too, presages later African American "fictioneers" (Kostelanetz) who will wholly redefine form from oral perception: Ishmael Reed, Henry Dumas, Alexis Deveaux, Leon Forrest, Steve Cannon, Ntozake Shange, and others. He uses the incremental repetitions that one finds in both the blues and ballad traditions for structure, emphasis, character progression, and intensified moments; he achieves the combined force—when the whole book is viewed—of subjective and objective territory. Assertions of identity and self-definition in the "I am" of the blues represent the subjective territory, while the objective territory has its counterpart in the third person pronouns (s/he) of the ballad tradition. Direct actions, as in the blues tradition, enable the reader/listener to pay heed to what a character feels and does rather than what is proper to feel and do. The ambivalence, ambiguities, and contradictions of public and private behavior complicate character (the blues can often be "embarrassing" and criticize meaning and values, balancing "strong contrasts . . . and opposing forms and forces in significant unity,"[15] in this way clarifying how people actually think and feel and act in their adjustment to self and will to be human).

Repetitions reveal situations and advance story interest, give a flexible sense of time that may be contracted, stretched, bent in successive changes. Blues repetition finally expands and broadens meaning as it makes character visible by emphasis and recurring presence. The last line of the story does not therefore merely repeat the words of the beginning, but strengthens and reinforces sense of character, context, and meaning:

> Her skin is like dusk on the eastern horizon,
> O cant you see it, O cant you see it,
> Her skin is like dusk on the eastern horizon
> . . . When the sun goes down.

> Goes down . . .

The oral dynamics of blues and ballad contribute, then, to Toomer's creation of the modern idiom in a story that combines a concern with song (literary technique connected to voice) and moral landscape.

7

Slang, Theme, and Structure: Loyle Hairston's "The Winds of Change"

Many readers cannot recognize contemporary uses of dialect because the transcription techniques of most of the writers have changed from those early stories of Paul Laurence Dunbar, Charles Waddell Chesnutt, and Zora Neale Hurston. While Jean Toomer's complex celebration of African American folk traditions centered on orality of narrative voice, rhythm and intonation, and dramatic procedures and character revelation, he, like these earlier writers, wrote dialect with orthographic changes. Although he used less "eye dialect" and ellipsis than they did, his dialect transcription technique resolved itself into such language as the following: "But words is like the spots on dice: no matter how y fumbles em, there's times when they jes wont come. I dunno why."[1]

Most of my African American literature students don't recognize dialect or what Sterling Brown prefers to call "folkspeech" (because of those early stops of humor and pathos). The reason is that contemporary transcription techniques don't reinforce the sense of linguistic parody or caricature and regard the language as autonomous rather than as a simple distortion of Standard English, in the same way that the Americanness of Standard American English is transcribed as an independent, autonomous language without reference to the "King's English." (Only from the point of view of an Englishman might American English be written as "dialect.") Contemporary writers seem to want to mold African American English in the same way that Ernest Hemingway and Gertrude Stein molded *American* language, without taking the linguistic attitude that it was somehow a lesser language for literary uses than the continental variety. Likewise the Canadian writers (such as Margaret Laurence) exercise their linguistic autonomy of hearing the speech and recreating it in ways that distinguish the individual writer and at the same time assure its distinction from the American and British varieties. The new transcription techniques depend less on orthographical changes and ellipses and more on syntactical systems and to some extent vocabulary, attempting to explore the whole context of literary uses. Thus when I once raised the question of whether Ernest Gaines wrote in dialect (we had already read Dunbar and Hurston), most of my students said no, he wrote in English. Just with this shift in ways of transcribing the language (in Gaines's case the Southern regional Louisiana vernacular, only one of many varieties), the language gains a new authority. Hemingway or Stein, for instance, would not elide or misspell words because their characters pronounced them differently from the way a Britisher would, and as Harold Courlander points out, in many of the early writings only black speech suffered such peculiarities of orthographic change, while a similar vernacular of whites was transcribed with full linguistic value. This literary double standard persisted until certain contemporary writers decided to take the same kind of control over how their language was represented in literature as their European American peers had done.

Loyle Hairston's short story "The Winds of Change" (1963) reflects these changes in transcription technique and the sense of autonomy of the character telling his own story in his own voice without the early problems of recording dialect in literature. His story also clears up another misconception in its distinctive use of slang. "Slang" and "dialect" are not interchangeable, contrary to media stereotypes and misconceptions; from inside the language these forms are certainly not the same. In his short story Loyle Hairston uses this "slanguage" to bridge a connection between the telling of the story and his message of change. With Hairston we return to a discussion of the speech and vocabulary aspects of oral tradition and the relations among speech, vocabulary, and thematic concerns. In his article "The Language of Hip," Clyde Taylor calls slang expressions "verbal equivalents to the affective communication in jazz." Slang is one of the linguistic "tributaries" of jazz, and so it is apropos that Hairston use this "slanguage" to tell his musician's story, which is also a "critique of Western social order"[3] and aesthetic values.

In nearly every creative writing textbook writers are warned against the use of slang in serious writing. While sometimes permissible in dialogue, it should as a rule be avoided as stringently as the cliché, except again in dialogue or stream-of-consciousness thought. Slang is not good usage, though in colloquial expression it may be vivid and fresh. In literature, however, it is a "rogue's language."[4]

"The Winds of Change" uses slang, however, and not just in "spots and places" (Hurston) but in the overall narrative voice and thematic structure of the work, its characterization and social history. Other writers have made use of slang to redefine an aesthetic identity distinct from European American and to energize vocabulary. Its entrance into the Black Aesthetic poetry of the decade was especially notable. The poets of the "decade of change," even more than the fiction writers, brought slang into poetic vocabulary for its magic to "raise up, return, destroy, and create."[5] They used "sounds that previously were not considered part of the poetic language, and . . . therefore frequently looked for inspiration to the language of the 'street.' [They] . . . felt that 'elevated' language took some of the energy out of the immediate human expression, and . . . hoped to revitalize poetic language through the reflection of the word from the streets."[6] It is this sort of "destruction of the text" (Larry Neal) that has always held the new possibilities of poetic language.

Far back in literature Chaucer energized his poetry by introducing what was for his day "the language of the streets" into *The Canterbury Tales*. And it was this language which helped to make the characters "interesting, alive and thoroughly human"[7]—diverse personalities that had never before inhabited English poetry. Edmund Wilson in *Axel's Castle* speaks of more recent examples in his discussions of the French poets Tristan Corbière and Jules Laforgue. Wilson speaks of Corbière's poetry as "a poetry of the outcast: often colloquial and homely, yet with a rhetoric of fantastic slang."[8] Laforgue he calls "grandiose-slangy"[9]: "He and Corbière had introduced a new variety of vocabulary and a new flexibility of feeling."[10] It is especially the poetry of Laforgue, claims Wilson, that influenced the "irregular metrical schemes"[11] of T. S. Eliot and provided one basis for his own new poetic idiom, although being the greater artist Eliot transcends his "Symbolist predecessors"[12] and their shortcomings with his more precise images and maturer workmanship. But Laforgue and Corbière, like the early writers discussed in these pages, "discovered the possibilities."[13] These possibilities then came to fruition with richer artistic voices.

The African American poets of the sixties utilized the potential of the oral traditions of slang and street vocabulary although they recognized its shortcomings. The African American poet Haki Madhubuti (Don L. Lee) uses slang in "But He Was Cool," for instance, but at the same time recognizes the shortcomings of slang when it is a superficial interpreter (or influencer) of behavior and meaning. That is, some people allow slang to limit their sense of meaning, self, and possibility. But though poems in slang can have apt and insightful themes, we tend to see slang as lightweight. In "But He Was Cool" it is difficult to distinguish between the protagonist's shortcomings and those of the author. For though the author recognizes that indiscriminate slang limits his character, he uses third person slang to mirror the character's style, vocabulary, and world view. It is easier to make the distinction when we have a multilinguistic poem such as West Indian John Figueroa's "Portrait of a Woman," where wider linguistic resources are used, or Melvin Tolson's poems in which language ranges from abstruse lyricism to simple statement, where slang is more clearly delineated as portraiture. This can also sometimes be achieved in the mixing of slangs and dialects, where the meaningful range of slang itself is extended.

In the short story "Just Like a Tree" Ernest Gaines distinguished Southern rural speech from Northern urban dialect with his urban outsiders' use of a slangy, rapid-paced and racy idiom:

> Let me go on back here and show these country niggers how to have a good time. All they know is talk, talk, talk. Talk so much they make me buggy round here. Damn this weather—wind, rain. Must be a million cracks in this old house.
>
> I go to that old beat-up safe in the corner and get that fifth of Mr. Harper (in the South now; got to say Mister), give the seal one swipe, the stopper one jerk, and head back to that old wood stove. (Man, like, these cats are primitive—goodness. You know what I mean? I mean like wood stoves. Don't mention TV, man, these cats here never heard of that.) I start to dump Mr. Harper in the pot and Baby catches my hand again and say not all of them like it. You ever heard of anything like that? I mean a stud's going to drink eggnog, and he's not going to put whiskey in it. I mean he's going to drink it straight. I mean, you ever heard anything like that? Well, I wasn't pressing none of them on Mr. Harper. I mean, me and Mr. Harper get along too well together for me to go around there pressing.[14]

Rudolph Fisher has also made a similar dialect distinction in his short story "The City of Refuge." This conversation between two Northerners (one a transplanted Southerner who's been in the city longer) has the density and speed of slang and urban metaphor:

> "Chief, I got him: a baby jess in from the land o' cotton and so dumb he thinks ante bellum's an old woman."
>
> "Where you find him?"
>
> "Where you find all the jaybirds when they first hit Harlem—at the subway entrance. This one come up the stairs, batted his eyes once or twice, an' froze to the spot—with his mouth open. Sure sign he's from 'way down behind the sun and ripe f' the pluckin'."[15]

Hairston too uses the dynamics of slang—its "rhythm, intonation, timing, modulations in volume" [16]—to define his urban musician's voice. If frozen this could become a stereotype of urban speech, so it must be supported and modified with variety, imaginative use, and character dimension. Fisher, in his story, keeps it from freezing by offering a range of distinct colloquial voices, expanding further the possibilities of dialect in a rich tapestry of urban dialects, including West Indian, Italian, and a racy colloquial brogue of two white policemen. Hairston gives slang dynamic use in the voice of a whole story and developing personality.

From the beginning of the story the listener/reader is placed in the perspective of this language as it recreates the voice of the storyteller, Waddell, the young musician. It is an oral tradition that combines seriousness, humor, exaggeration, and verbal speed. (Taylor uses the word "kinesis" to describe this expressive energy, improvisation, and spontaneity.)

> It was my big day and I was so hopped up I woke up before the alarm went off. Geez. The house was quiet except for Sis hummin' out in the kitchen. I set my watch by the clock and gauged my time; then laid out my vine, a clean shirt and things on the bed. After I brushed my kicks, I looked my wig over in the mirror. My stocking cap slipped off my head when I was sleepin' and the waves in my hair done unstrung and was all tangled up. [17]

We know the changeability of the vocabulary; it "animates the text" [18] but it is also set by the text in that we get the meaning of "hopped up," "vine," "kicks," "wig," from the context, as well as their metaphorical implications. This procedure also enables us to enter the character from the beginning of the story. He is more visible than Jube Benson because he makes himself visible, inside and out. In addition, the reader, like the storyteller, is hopped up, waiting to see what the big day will bring. There is the hint that the paraphernalia will somehow fit into the meaning and resolution of the story, in redefining values—since the character's sense of who he is seems strongly connected with them: "I had to have a marcel!"

From the point of view of its literary use, it is the slang that seems to provide the most visible distinction between the urban, hip voice of Hairston's world and the slower, fuller Southern rural voices of both Gaines's and Fisher's Southern characters, though it should be emphasized that the urban and rural voices share some syntactical similarities, as in "and the waves in my hair done unstrung and was all tangled up." We see the Southern rural speech as source and predecessor of much of the Northern "urban hipness."[19]

The banter between Waddell and his sister while their father is trying to "cop a snooze" intensifies the pace, the mobility, and timing of the beginning, spurring the story on with its exchange:

"You takin' a bath?" . . .
"I'm gon wash my head."
"Aw, naw! Don't tell me that wavy-wigged-Waddell's gonna wash out his beauty tresses!"

Waddell's thoughts participate in the dialogue, play off the sister's comments to contribute to the forward movement, the function of any good "spiel" in literature: "I mean what's she know. She think I'm gon make a audition lookin' like a creep. You think they're lookin' for talent in the raw; appearance is half the game. A black-head knows that. If you ain't pressed and got the right spiel, you ain't sayin' nothin' to the silks; it's the only language they can dig." Waddell, we learn, is going to audition for a gig. Information comes into the story through dialogue, thought, and narrative, but the story stays active. The writer doesn't interrupt the progression of events, but we gather information in progress, kinetically, as things are happening. In addition, here in foreshadowing the author introduces key thematic phrases whose full (and ironic) implications won't be revealed until later: "appearance is only half the game" is another recognition of the double-consciousness defined by W. E. B. Du Bois in *The Souls of Black Folk*. Waddell is acutely conscious of how whites ("silks") see him and validate his sense of identity, both through *appearance and language,* key arenas of sensibility: "If you ain't pressed and got the right spiel, you ain't sayin' *nothin'* to the silks; it's the only language they can dig."

Like the double-conscious storytellers of previous decades, Waddell is highly aware of his audience: "Silks think you can't talk nothing but slang," he says later. And this story, though written (told) in slang, projects a sense of it as a deliberate thematic and structural choice. The reader (black and white) also gets the impression that this is only one of many possibilities of American idiom; that the author can master (or has mastered) them all, but has simply chosen this one.

The element of choice is important, and it implies other things as well. In his article on "The Language of Hip," Clyde Taylor speaks of the double standard toward inventiveness and choice in African American uses of divergent speech: "Notice, though, the neologisms of Black folks were satirized as malapropisms in minstrel shows and in the works of 'literary comedians' like Artemus Ward and Petroleum V. Nooby as evidence of the Negro's illiterate backwardness, while cognate neologisms from frontier speech are celebrated in the works of nationalistic American scholars as evidence of the inventiveness of endemic American speech. The local colorists who recorded frontier humor were as likely to observe the contributions of Black folks to this speech as they were to make Blacks the central heroes in their stories."[20] This unacknowledged participation might be equally seen to carry over into the American-ness of literature in general. Taylor's remarks suggest another problem in regard to linguistic and literary experimentation in the works of African American writers. In order to prove that they could handle the other language—indeed *write*—many such writers often remained conservative while their European American counterparts felt free to be inventive. For an African American writer to depart from the European American mainstream is to assure the "mal" rather than the "neo" response. The African American writers' deviations are seen as evidence that they can't follow the models or that the models are outside the range of their vocabulary, rather than as evidence of inventiveness, new and not silly compositions. For the African American writer a thing must have been done before by a European American before it is valid; yet when he does it the way it has been done and shows his mastery of the approved technical strategies, he is accused of being "imitative" or "artificial."

When such writers' works do compete with the literary innovators of their time (often inspired by models from oral tradition, though not always), the innovation is not acknowledged as such (by European American critics) until someone within the European American literary tradition has "discovered" (and therefore validated) it. In John O'Brien's *Interviews with Black Writers,* Ishmael Reed, who has been called "the most original poet-novelist working in the American language," noted in answer to the question, "Is innovative writing by black writers particularly ignored by critics?": "In fact, our worst enemies are radical liberals because they have so much influence on how we look in the media and in American culture. They have a vested interest in making us look bad. They are only interested in the social realist, the 'experience' of black people . . . When I came out with my books I was ignored by the eastern cultural establishment. I was completely ignored on *Pallbearers* because the book didn't fit their mold of what a black writer ought to be doing. When a black writer experiments he gets mugged for it. Then white imitators can come out and claim his innovation. This double standard can be seen, among other places, in the treatment of a book by John Seelye, *The Kid*. This book has been touted by its publishers and reviewers as being unlike any other Western novel, that it's a departure in the Western novel . . . In *The Kid* there's a character, a black cowboy, who has ESP and supernatural abilities. I was the first in this country to write a Western about a black cowboy with supernatural abilities and ESP, and here is this guy getting all the credit for it, as though it's some kind of innovation."[21]

Another case in point. Ntozake Shange's poetic drama *for colored girls who have considered suicide/when the rainbow is enuf*, though highly praised play, is not entirely recognized as the innovative poetic drama it really is. In fact Shange's drama ironically seems to make good an earlier, failed attempt by T. S. Eliot. As Edmund Wilson says, "the two episodes from 'Wanna Go Home, Baby' which [Eliot] has published in *The Criterion* seem rather promising. They are written in a sort of jazz dramatic metre . . . and there can be no question that the future of drama in verse, if it has any future, lies in some such direction."[22]

Creating "jazz dramatic metre" (minus "sort of"), Shange takes it in "some such direction" resolving in poetic drama of the "dark phrases of womanhood"[23] the tension between literary and oral motives and pointing toward a "future of drama in verse." For Shange, too, oral tradition is a laboratory for making experiments with Western literary traditions. Yet the works of other African American writers, often on the surface conservative or in the canon of social realism, less obviously innovative in language, structure, and content than Ishmael Reed's or Ntozake Shange's, are still heavily influenced by that tradition. Because of the tensions between written and oral literature, any effort to bridge the two while attempting to maintain a sense of the integrity of the oral forms turns necessarily in an experimental direction and a consistently changing and innovative one. This is clearly evident in the poetry of Langston Hughes, who is not as easily acknowledged along with the other literary innovators of his time as he should be. (Indeed, Robert A. Bone depicted Toomer as the only literary innovator of his generation in African American literature!)

Waddell, too, makes choices full of verbal discovery and "subverting the language"[24]—what Houston Baker, Jr., called "anti-mainstream aesthetic."[25] But at the same time double-consciousness continues as Waddell enters the place of audition. However, a new aesthetic is born when Waddell first sees the African woman, Oleta. Appearance becomes the initial metaphor for the "Wind of Change":

Then three more, one of 'em a member, bolted out of the dressin' room and sailed over to where we was . . . But this member—daddy, she was a real fox! Her big nut-shaped eyes was so bright it made you squint when you looked straight at 'em; and she musta been playin' the part of a African in the play because she wore her hair short and natural, like Miriam Makeba. But the way her big gold-looped earrings gleamed against her long satin-smooth neck, she looked like a African Princess! Without comin' outa my freeze, I dug her the most.

. . . . .

When I got inside and seen five cats in the middle of the floor stripped down to tights, squattin' behind them long-bellied African drums, I got a feelin' in my gut that I didn't like. In nothin' flat, the cat in charge let me know what the feelin' was. They done changed the "locale" to a African settin' and when I told him that I never done no primitive dancin', he told me, with a lotta friggin' double-talk—to blow!

There is a difference between the aesthetic reality offered by Oleta, the African woman, and the aesthetic "vogue" suggested by the above commercial exploitation, though this too offers its own parallels in social and psychic reality. But the ironic juxtaposition is skillful. When Waddell first sees Oleta he thinks she is merely "playing the part of an African," but the implications soon travel beyond the "play."

Waddell learns that Oleta's brother is a member of the United Nations delegation and he goes with the two women—Oleta and the "silk"—to the UN. "But when I got upstairs and seen all them African cats settin' round the tables on the main floor, I damn near flipped! Some of 'em wore reg'lar blue-serge; some showed off their native styles . . . Oleta pointed her brother out to me, settin' with a lotta young cats with smooth black round faces and woolly hair cropped even all over. They all was beamin' like they had Charley's number; and Charley was settin' there fussin' with his notes like he knowed it. I mean it was all I could do to keep from jumpin' up on my seat and bust out clappin'. No wonder the NEWS say the joint's run by Reds!" The function of the news media in image-making and interpretation should be acknowledged here in the juxtaposed remark; nevertheless, a new conception of beauty has been offered with the appearance of Oleta, and here, along with the new aesthetic, is a new possibility of identity and character, self-defined and autonomous. We move from the superficial, the vogue identity offered in the performance, to the substantial, the cultural, personal, and political change seen at the UN: at any rate, the potential for something substantial, a positive new moral order of values and human relationships. The

Africans—their own new character reinforced by the newly emerging independent African states—provide the counter aesthetic.

Waddell's story, written at a time of world-wide Black Liberation movements and Malcolm X's transformations of value and conceptions of black manhood, includes a new vision of a different world, but while he recognizes the new aesthetic and ethical guide, he doesn't internalize it. He continues to think about his *process:* "It was only Monday and by Friday my process'd need retouchin'; so I went by Ray's and made an appointment with Sonny for Friday." Ironic juxtaposition is again used when Marilyn Monroe, the European American standard bearer of beauty, but at the same time an exploited and commercialized image, is mentioned near the end of the story: "Marilyn Monroe was playing at the Loew's." Monroe, a natural brunette, also had to manipulate the mystique of blondeness in the unreal image-and-appearance game in order to achieve her precarious position. Un-blonde white girls and women, like black ones, are often confounded and victimized by "the bluest eye" (Morrison) and "fairest of them all" mythology/metaphor/aesthetic. It is an intraracial tyranny as well as interracial one; most whites themselves don't question the aesthetic and when they don't fit the image, alter themselves to conform to it. It is significant, though, that this sentence and evocation of Monroe precedes Waddell's dream of Oleta. It is a form of "signifying" as well as demystification which reinforces the major theme of the story: "Marilyn Monroe was playin' at the Loew's; only soon's I got comfortable I went to sleep and dreamt I was with Oleta by the lake in Central Park, playin' my bongos, and she was dancin' for me; and I was watchin' her Fine Brown reflectin' in the water shinin' with golden moonlight. Then she'd come over and stroke my hair; and in the gleamin' pools of her eyes I seen myself holdin' her close; only I was stripped down like an African warrior and my hair was woolly like them cats at the UN."

Finally, "The Winds of Change" is resolved as Waddell comes into his own assertion of the new aesthetic and identity, only beginning with appearance: "After gettin' my kicks shined and my fingernails honed and polished, I set down in the barber chair, rubbin' the fuzz on my chin and thinkin' about Oleta and how fine she was in a way I ain't never seen in a girl, member or silk. Sonny stopped gassin' with some guys in the back and put the cloth round my neck. I told him to give me a shave. And he started crankin' the chair back. 'Not my face, daddy—my head!'"

Slang, then, is a function of characterization and plot strategy. And because slang is the language that constantly changes—affected by time, place, and history—it suggests a relationship between the language of change and the theme of change. The transformation of the appearance of the language through modified transcription techniques recreates the authentic and autonomous voice of Waddell. Aesthetic autonomy here too precedes other autonomies. And there is of course a double meaning when Waddell shouts, "Not my face . . . my head!" Appearance is only half the game. Real and substantial—internal—change must come after the story.

8

Jazz/Blues Structure in Ann Petry's "Solo on the Drums"

In "The Winds of Change" we considered a writer who gained fictional autonomy through an effective union of "slanguage," theme, and character. Another African American writer who has employed techniques from oral tradition to control and liberate the structure of a story, its organization of events, and presentation of character is Ann Petry. "Solo on the Drums" lacks chronological and sequential dramatic scenes, but the storyline achieves flexibility and intricacy from the musical African American oral traditions of jazz and blues.

Many African American fiction writers and poets acknowledge the superiority of the black musician as artist, and from their early efforts to reshape literature to their own cultural dynamics these writers have made thematic and stylistic references to African American music as guide, with the recognition that the music possesses a greater capacity for complexity and scope. Of course much of the music's refinement is due to its remaining, as an art form and ritual, an unbroken though modified continuum of oral tradition, whereas the "writers" (*griots*) had to readjust to written literature in an environment that discouraged or banned such efforts as criminal, from the black codes of slavery to the Jim Crow laws and attitudes of the South (including Louis Simpson's infamous criticism of Gwendolyn Brooks: essentially, that her work would never be important as long as her characters were Negroes). The exchange between Richard Wright and the white woman employer in *Black Boy* crystallizes it all. When she asks him why he's still going to school (he's in the seventh grade), he replies that he wants to be a writer. "For what?" she asks, astonished.

> "To write stories," I mumbled defensively.
> "You'll never be a writer," she said. "Who on earth put such ideas into your nigger head?"

"Nobody," I said.
"I didn't think anybody ever would," she declared indignantly.[1]

This attitude did not apply to music. During the slave period, though the "talking" drums were banned because of their potential for insurrrection, music seen as entertainment was encouraged; as James Baldwin observed, the white listeners often "enjoy it without ever hearing its harsher notes."[2] The meaning underneath the surface sound is seldom heard: "You think it's a happy beat / listen to it closely / ain't you heard something underneath?" (Langston Hughes) Two things seemed to be working in support of the musician as artist: internally, there was the cultural connection with the oral traditions of Africa; externally, music did not hold the same threat to whites as literacy (relegated to folk utterance or performance, it also did not hold the same status), and certainly much of its combative intent went unheard. There were and still are tensions and misjudgments between the Western (European) conceptions of musical art and African American music in regard to harmony, chord structures, rhythms, kinds or uses of instruments, cadences, voice and phrasing, modes of construction, ranges of tones and intonations, presentation and purpose. Likewise some people continue to see differences of orientation as wrong or celebrate the music for the wrong reasons—for instance, Europeans' liking for jazz because of its "raw and savage gaiety" expressive of "an underworld of instinct" which "breathes a simple honest sensuality" and expresses "the mood of childlike happiness."[3] Yet the music continued to flourish because—in spite of the suppressions of the talking drums—there was never the same break in artistic tradition, and the divergences from the Western mainstream that in literature would have triggered rantings of "aberration" could be more readily admitted as innovative and deliberate, even avant-garde. However, again it was easier for Western critics to appreciate the innovations when they were taken up by the European American artists themselves, as in the syntactical aberrations of postmodernist literature and the literary-artistic claims of improvisational technique of certain contemporary Western writers. Yet even here, what African American tradition means by improvisational, that is, something informed by tradition and mastery of its techniques which allows the improvisational riffs, and what European Americans generally mean by it, that is, something "thrown together" or "tossed off," are quite different matters. In fact, much of the structural and thematic integrity of African American art vis-à-vis the West revolves around a problem of meaning.

91
▼

But to get to the height and depth of structural and psychological complexity of the music, black writers, when they began to experiment with their own artistic traditions, began to look to the music as a significant—indeed the most significant—extraliterary model. In an interview with Beverly Guy-Sheftall in *Sturdy Black Bridges,* Toni Cade Bambara, speaking of a "fearless and courageous and thoroughgoing" way of "dealing with the complexity of the black experience, the black spirit," says that "music is probably the only mode we have used to speak of that complexity."[4] Such writers recognize the potential for literature to be so used, and we will examine, beginning with Petry, ways in which African American fiction writers have attempted to mine that grand territory. At the same time, African American writers continue to acknowledge and look to the musician as the artistic vanguard and range finder, the most modern and often futuristic artist. Ernest Gaines in an interview with Charles H. Rowell in *Callaloo* made this acknowledgment: "Well, I feel we have expressed ourselves better in our music traditionally than we have done in our writing. The music (blues, jazz and spirituals, for example) is much better than our prose or poetry. I think that we have excelled in music because it is more oral. We are traditionally orally oriented. What I'd like to see in our writing is the presence of our music."[5] And Alice Walker has said: "I am trying to arrive at that place where black music already is; to arrive at that unselfconscious sense of collective oneness, that naturalness, that (even when anguished) grace."[6]

Ann Petry's "Solo on the Drums," then, is also an effort to bring that black musical presence into the writing. No African American writer has yet fully accomplished what the musician has, but it is significant that many black writers see music's potential for modifying the European American fictional forms—in the handling of theme, time, character, dramatic event, and moral-ethical import—differently from even the Europeans who celebrate it, because the black writers hear different things in the music. The European (and European American) is open to only one level of possibility; for the African American the range is pluralistic; jazz frees the imagination; *is* free imagination that is also disciplined, the latter almost always going unheard by the European ear. Michael S. Harper tells it this way in a poem for Miles Davis:

> A friend told me
> He'd risen above jazz.
> I leave him there.[7]

Petry's jazz effort certainly does not mean that she cannot write the traditional short story. She has had, like many American writers, to prove that she can. But like Hairston she makes a deliberate choice here. And unlike the early African American writers, who were double-consciously and continuously working to avoid being considered outrageous or "embarrassing" while proving themselves to white audiences—even to their own people who, like their early European American colonial counterparts, could not imagine a literature written for themselves, and sometimes even about themselves—Petry and other writers of new stories assumed an autonomy over their structures, languages, and characters.

The protagonist of "Solo on the Drums" is a jazz drummer named Kid Jones. Petry not only takes her subject and milieu from the musical oral disciplines of jazz and blues, but combines these in a musical-literary form in the mobility of her narrative, the selection and organization of events, the conflict and resolution.

Petry opens the story in the same way that a jazz musician would introduce major themes: "The orchestra had a week's engagement at the Randlert Theater at Broadway and Forty-second Street. His name was picked out in lights on the marquee. The name of the orchestra and then his name underneath by itself. There would have been a time when he would have been excited by it. And stopped to let his mind and his eyes linger over it lovingly. Kid Jones. The name—his name—up there in lights that danced and winked in the brassy sunlight . . . He used to eat it up. But not today. Not after what happened this morning."[8] The author gives an inkling of the problem, tells us there has been a transformation. She introduces the theme, welds the musical procedure to the narrative, and as the story progresses the initial situation is repeated, its contexts amplified, its meaning solved or explored through jazz solos and blues-speech interpolations. The motif of blues repetition and the self-assertive motives of blues are expressed in "the name—his name . . . his name . . . his name." Themes of identity and recognition are archetypal in all blues dramas. Blues pulls together and asserts identity (self and other) through clarification and playing back of experiences and meanings. While he "gets his music together" Kid Jones will be "getting himself together." But we still want to know what happened this morning and what has changed.

Next, Petry's "music" sounds staccato rhythms and a percussive syntax of the sentences which suggest a reverberating drumbeat solo: "He hit the drums lightly. Regularly. A soft, barely discernible rhythm. A back-

93
▼

ground. A repeated emphasis for the horns and the piano and the violin. The man with the trumpet stood up, and the first notes came out sweet and clear and high. Kid Jones kept up the drum accompaniment. Slow. Careful. Soft." More of the content of the story is revealed: "He wanted to cover his ears with his hands because he kept hearing a voice that whispered the same thing over and over again. The voice was trapped somewhere under the roof caught and held there by the trumpet. 'I'm leaving I'm leaving I'm leaving.'" The indirect monologue combined with drums and repeated blues lyric suggested by rhythm and syntax continues the musical process and fictional suspense.

As the story unfolds, the past is reiterated and clarified. The equivalents of improvisation on the initial situation become more intricate as more of the story is revealed. Finally, we learn that the piano player has taken Kid's wife. (A revelation that had been foreshadowed through blues double-entendre in the homonyms "marquee-marquis": "the Marquis of Brund" is what they call the piano player.) The conflict is expressed as a musical one, and we discover that the musical-literary structure holds throughout. The jazz-blues lapidary cuts and polishes complication and resolution of the action.

> And now—well, he felt as though he were floating up and up and up on that long blue note of the trumpet. He half closed his eyes and rode up on it. It had stopped being music. It was the whispering voice, making him shiver. Hating it and not being able to do anything about it. "I'm leaving it's the guy who plays the piano I'm in love with him and I'm leaving now today." Rain in the street. Heat gone. Food gone. Everything gone because a woman's gone. It's everything you ever wanted, he thought. It's everything you never got. Everything you ever had, everything you ever lost. It's all there in the trumpet—pain and hate and trouble and peace and quiet and love.

His wife's words and Kid Jones's memory of her speech become yet another lyric. The intensity and kinetic pace of that memory is duplicated by the prose. Together with the indirect monologue his thoughts are always expressed in the form of a lyric where the narrative functions as colloquial blues genre. Blues subject matter, meaning, improvised repetitions, slurs and worrying the line, double-edged paradoxes, patterns of light and shadow are clearly evident. In her essay "The Blues Roots of Contemporary Afro-American Poetry," Sherley A. Williams defines "worrying the line": "Repetition in blues is seldom word for word and the definition of worrying the line includes changes in stress and pitch, the addition of exclamatory phrases, changes in word order, repetitions of phrases within the line itself, and the wordless blues cries which often punctuate the performance of the songs."[9] The substance of the story, like the rhythm of the drums, has "to be listened for . . . insidious, repeated." The flashbacks are never repeated word for word, but with changes in texture, event order, punctuation, and motive.

As we move toward the climax of the story Kid Jones "becomes one" with the drums: "He began to feel as though he were the drums, and the drums were he." In the same way music and literature are joined, and the story itself is a jazz solo on drums. Even so, it does not reach the intricate blending we will find in Amiri Baraka's "The Screamers," where text itself becomes music, where the whole word-sound choreography seems to be the musical composition. This occurs, too, in Leon Forrest's *There is a Tree More Ancient Than Eden* where music and verbal text are one in the paradoxically controlled "free improvisation" of a jazz collage:

> Hawk-haunting down the ravaged sleeve of the enveloping raven forest and deep down the whispering flares of light in the distance and spellbound in the powdered dust of the magnolias, swinging scale-like in the breeze and the maypoles of chiaroscuro and fleeing the crowd lord to get back to the old fouled and dawning deed yoking the word into a waxy horror, yes and switching back into the neon cross etched against the moon shaving, oscillating upon the pavement gutters and breaking across a scarecrow plantation, jimmying the locked up bloodhounds leaping over the fencing and deep down the winding woods and the hounds ripping through the high grass and spear-like trees after the shackle-liberated heels; lord yes and clothing patched with ripped-away newspapers and dripping with dreaming long past the whites of their eyes, past the woods and rivers towards the north star swinging sweet and low, where he rode upon a milk-white horse drawing a chariot, in which a rectangular wooden box did rest yes and lord up through dreams of dates and promises and canceled checks, and numbers, and melancholia sliced across the faces, deep to the quick of the aching, weary, troubled bones, as delicate as wings, as prodigious as a ringing hammer, yes and river-wire and lord river-deep . . ."[10]

Actually, there are blues, jazz, spiritual, and sermonic rhythms and imagery all welded here; but it is jazz, I think, that first opened the possibilities of such "sound running" prose and gave directives for a whole verbal form that becomes music. Petry's story provides instead multiple structures within the traditional short-story form; it incorporates jazz and blues solos within a traditionally readable text; and the interface between the musical and literary remains clear. Her story stays a hyphenated mixture where fictional territories (or boundaries) are distinct and recognizable. In the Forrest excerpt there are no such visible junctures; there is a truer welding and a sense of the imaginative heat and power of that achievement.

But Kid Jones is an articulate musician, and the narrative describes and renders the effect of drumming: "The theater throbbed with the excitement of the drums. A man sitting near the front shivered, and his head jerked to the rhythm. A sailor put his arm around the girl sitting beside him, took his hand and held her face still and pressed his mouth close over hers. Close. Close. Close. Until their faces seemed to melt together. Her hat fell off and neither of them moved." The choice of vocabulary provides good musical equivalents: throbbed, shivered, jerked, pressed, melt, moved. The staccato recital suggests the drumbeat, and the vocabulary also fits the passion and ritual movement of the lovers. Their unity is juxtaposed to and reinforces the kinetic energy and unity of Kid Jones and his drums.

The theme of oneness continues with variations, from the drum motif to the patron lovers to Kid Jones's personal reminiscences and the initial predicament of the story recapitulated yet again: "The drummer forgot he was in the theater. There was only he and the drums and they were far way. Long gone. He was holding Lulu, Helen, Susie, Mamie close in his arms. And all of them—all those girls blended into that one girl who was his wife. The one who said, 'I'm leaving.' She had said it over and over again, this morning, while rain dripped down the window panes." But there is more than repetition. The scenic context—what we see and know of that morning—broadens. As we listen we gain more background and information, for the story's mode of organization is dynamic, fluent, and improvisational. Again, the scenes are not traditionally isolated and dramatic, with extended dialogues and chronological sequences of character revelations and emotional pivotings. Instead, the jazz-fictional scenes are descriptive and lyrical; the drums recreate the emotions, atmosphere, and metaphors of transformation.

The drum solo becomes more fierce in its warring with the piano player: "When he hit the drums again it was with the thought that he was fighting with the piano player. He was choking the Marquis of Brund. He was putting a knife in clean between his ribs. He was slitting his throat with a long straight blade. Take my woman. Take your life. The drums leaped with the fury that was in him." This unity of man and drums in the warring effort is the turning point of the story. From it the past and present, the personal and collective, form adjacent regions and then interpenetrate. The traditional African function of drums as message bearers becomes rhythm and music translated into word and meaning: "The drums took him away from them, took him back, and back, and back, in time and space. He built up an illusion. He was sending out the news. Grandma died. The foreigner in the litter has an old disease and will not recover. The man from across the big water is sleeping with the chief's daughter. Kill. Kill. Kill." The broader social-historical context, significant to the intent of the story, reclaims an aesthetic which reinforces the narrative and dramatic vision of the New World story.

In *Oral Literature in Africa,* Ruth Finnegan discusses drum literature and the drum's historical and ritual uses, noting that "The instruments themselves are regarded as speaking and their messages consist of words."[11] Kid Jones's performance reclaims this kind of communication, but he cannot forget the words he wants to: his wife's "I'm leaving." He is led back from the past, the protean metamorphosis of time/space, to his personal dilemma and his own need for emotional recovery. This collective memory develops Petry's structure and links it to other contexts of oral tradition. Again the drums start talking about his own life; other women are brought in, more details are given. This stuff of the blues and the blues relationships compound the central one of the story—the relationship between Kid Jones and his wife. Finally, Kid Jones forgets everything but the drums: "He was welded to the drums, sucked inside them. All of him. His pulse beat. His heart beat. He had become part of the drums." We are carried further than the incipient unity described earlier. This is the true blues/jazz unity. It is no longer *as if* he were one with the drums; he *is* one with them. Blues paradox arrives in the assertion of what this story—what all the storytelling—has been about: "The sound seemed to come not from the drums but from deep inside himself; it was a sound that was being wrenched out of him—a violent, raging, roaring sound. As it issued from him he thought, this is the story of my love, this is the story of my hate, this is all there is left of me."

When Kid Jones finally stops playing, the story itself winds down. But the blues experience has contributed to making this the best jazz drum solo he has given. The drumming has functioned as a kind of catharsis, a purgation ritual. Through his music, Kid Jones has done something, said something. He has "killed" the Marquis effectively in a musical ritual, so he won't have to do it in the world; the central confrontations have been transfigured. But the last note of the story, like the last note of a previous trumpet solo, seems to stay up in the air. "Yeah, he thought, you were hot all right. The jitterbugs ate you up and you haven't any place to go.

9

Folktale, Character, and Resolution: Ralph Ellison's "Flying Home"

The folktale became one of the earliest literary texts of the oral tradition. Ralph Ellison's short story "Flying Home" is an example of how a folktale can function dramatically in a text and participate in reinforcing theme, character, composition, and dramatic movement. During the turn-of-the-century the folktale not only was framed as in Dunbar's "The Lynching of Jube Benson," but existed as a bit of local color and indication of the quaintness of the storyteller, as in "The Wife of His Youth" and "The Goophered Grapevine" by Charles W. Chesnutt.

"The Goophered Grapevine," which appeared in 1887 in the *Atlantic Monthly* and was later collected in *The Conjure Woman and Other Stories* (1899), is a useful example of the framed folktale—the same pattern one sees in the Joel Chandler Harris renditions of the Uncle Remus stories. Chesnutt both incorporates and bends this manner of presentation. The story within the frame is in dialect and told by the black folkteller Julius McAdoo.

The narration is in highly formal—almost artificial—standard English. The first-person narrative perspective of the exterior story is that of the white character from the North who has come to look at a vineyard he wishes to buy. The two levels of storytelling are clearly separate in the territory they hold and in the transcription techniques used to render them. The primary audience, like the primary audience of most turn-of-the-century fiction (Dunbar's too, we recall), is presumed to be white. Chesnutt is true to his white narrator's perspective as he carries that character's description of Julius and analysis of Julius's character into the narrative: "He was a tall man, and though slightly bowed by the weight of years, apparently quite vigorous. He was not entirely black, and this fact, together with the quality of his hair, which was about six inches long and very bushy, except on the top of his head, where he was quite bald, suggested a slight strain of other than Negro blood. There was a shrewdness in his eyes, too, which was not altogether African, and which, as we afterwards learned from experience, was indicative of a corresponding shrewdness in his character."[1] The black man's shrewdness, due to the admixture of white blood, is an aspect of Julius's character that we are to look for. But the observation is made from within the frame of the Northerner's perceptions; and again, this tells us more about the psychology of the white man and the psychology of his time than it does about the character he describes.

From here we move to Julius's trickster tale as he tells the Northerner that the vineyard is goophered—conjured, bewitched, put under a magic spell. Julius controls this story as he tells the Northerner how the grapes came to be goophered. Dugal, the original owner, set spring guns and traps to stop the slaves on the plantation from stealing the grapes; when this didn't work, he went to a conjure woman. She put on the goopher, and a black stranger, not knowing about it, ate the grapes. Each spring after that the man (Henry) would grow young, then in the fall his hair would fall out and he would get old again. Dugal, also a trickster within the multiple trickster tale, would make money out of Henry by selling him in the spring when he was young and supple for $1,500, then buying him back in the fall for $500. Another trickster, a Yankee stranger, said he had a new "scientific method" for making the vines bear twice as many grapes. The grapes did indeed grow larger and faster, but then they shriveled up. When the vines withered, Henry died. It took three or four years before the vines started to bear again; the master was killed in the war, his daughter moved, and the vineyard has not been cultivated since. Julius advises the white man not to buy it.

From there we move back into the exterior frame. The white man assures us that he has bought the property. From his position of authority he tells us that the whole point of Julius's story was to trick him into not buying the vineyard. Nevertheless, the question of authority is open; we're not sure really who controls the story; Chesnutt keeps us wondering which of the stories is true and who has gained from the transaction. The white man feels that he saw through Julius's trick. Yet there is still the possibility that Julius wanted him to buy the vineyard so that he could work there and tricked him into believing the reverse—knowing how to manipulate the white man's psychology.

The Chesnutt story is an example of the early uses of the folktale, essential to the story, but the landscape and imagination of the folktale is separate from the story proper, and usually introduced by an outsider who frames and interprets it. The deeper texture and controlling values of oral tradition are often excluded from the interpretation. In Ellison's short story "Flying Home" the folktale interpenetrates the story's territory and shares the same space with it. The fundamental values of the tradition are pushed to the forefront of the story. We do not have the sense of the folktale violating the traditional story, or the traditional story freezing the folktale. In "Flying Home" the folk character not only shows astuteness and wit, but also assumes a legitimate and authentic dramatic place in the whole story. His tale belongs there, not framed but integrated. Literature is his province as well.

As in *Invisible Man*, Ellison chooses an "articulate hero" and writes from his viewpoint, from within his consciousness. "When Todd came to" is the first phrase of the story of a black pilot who crashed in a field. Like many of Ellison's beginnings the meaning is dual—"the end is in the beginning" *(Invisible Man);* the story itself is a story of Todd's coming to an awareness, or to continue the metaphor of *Invisible Man,* an illumination.

When Todd sees two faces suspended above him, he can't tell if they are black or white. It is the voice that clues him: "It was a Negro sound." "Say, son, you hurt bad?"[2] He doesn't know if he is. He watches them—an old Negro and a boy—warily, remembering jagged scenes of his tailspinning plane.

The painful distance Todd feels is also the distance between the elite and the folk, the latter represented by the two characters. With a sensation of remoteness Todd thinks, "I'd never make him understand." This distance, carefully delineated in the works of certain earlier African American writers, is given classic depiction in James Weldon Johnson's *The Autobiography of Ex-Coloured Man.* In Johnson's novel dialect was the only thing that sparked a feeling of interest or human recognition from the narrator regarding the lower class that otherwise repelled him. Here too the voice, the dialect, cause an initial spark of recognition. But another leap of recognition will be necessary.

Todd's double-consciousness is clearly expressed when the old man offers to ride him into town on old Ned, an ox. Todd thinks of streets full of whites watching this spectacle, a thought which brings "swift images of humiliation." He thinks of a letter he got from his girlfriend. She was growing suspicious that, though a trained pilot, he was not being assigned for flights. "I sometimes think they're playing a trick on us. It's very humiliating," she had written. He wondered what she knew of humiliation. For Todd, humiliation is in the whites' rejection of him as an individual. His mistakes are held against the whole race; the characteristics of others of his race apply to him as well. And though he acknowledges that the old man is "all right. Nice and kind and helpful," he doesn't want to identify with an "old black ignorant man." "But he's not you," he says to assert his identity—to authenticate himself as separate from the old man, whom he can only see as one-dimensional.

The black character's viewpoint, voice, and vision introduce a central dilemma of consciousness and identity. It is essentially the dilemma of Kabnis in Jean Toomer's *Cane;* it was originally named double-consciousness by W. E. B. Du Bois in *The Souls of Black Folk:* "It is a peculiar sensation, this double-consciousness, this sense of always looking at one's self through the eyes of others, of measuring one's soul by the tape of a world that looks on in amused contempt and pity. One ever feels his twoness,—an American, a Negro; two souls, two thoughts, two unreconciled strivings; two warring ideals in one dark body, whose dogged strength alone keeps it from being torn asunder."[3] Todd voices the double self when he anticipates that his personal mistakes will be taken as collective; this applies as well to the need to dissociate himself, his ego, and his condition from the "mistake" of the old man. However, Todd's girlfriend's letter does not only document a problem of character. Like the Trueblood episode in *Invisible Man,* it documents an old problem of African American literary endeavor: the efforts of certain writers to prove themselves by artistic dissociation from such characters as the old man. Such "colored people" may "live on the street," to paraphrase James Weldon Johnson's narrator, but they don't have to shamble into literature.

I should stress here that double-consciousness is a recurring theme in twentieth-century African American literature, particularly in character depiction, motivation, and revelation. It is also a mechanism for elucidating the relationship between personal experience, history, and society. The recurrence of this theme parallels the continuous appearance and reappearance of *identity* as a theme in world literature, and certainly in American literature. And as Ellison has stated time and again, the problem of identity is an American problem of value and image. W. E. B. Du Bois's specific application of this universal literary theme of identity helped to clarify a central problem of Africa-America (indeed this can be extended to any contradictory conceptions of self) and to make double-consciousness *visible.*

After Du Bois, the problem of identification was no longer one of authorial conflict of value and image as it had been a century earlier in the slave narratives and the abolitionist novels. It began to be a deliberate, central, and self-conscious theme, from the works of the Harlem

Renaissance to "true self-consciousness" in Toomer's *Cane,* Hughes's *The Dream Keeper and Other Poems,* and Sterling Brown's *Southern Road.* Ellison's *Invisible Man* (1950s) moves to such true self-consciousness ("I was looking for myself and asking everyone except myself questions which I and only I could answer"); Amiri Baraka's "The Screamers" (1960s) moves to "clear images of ourselves"; Alice Walker, Toni Cade Bambara, Ntozake Shange move to contemporary themes of womanhood and images of wholeness and self-creation.

The concept of double-consciousness, a continuing dilemma in African American character and literary history, also applies to other minority groups in the American experience. Moreover, it is useful to remember that European Americans themselves were double-conscious in reference to the Old World and their need to develop "self trust": "Even ardent nationalists uncritically continued to evaluate their own literature in European terms; to them, a native author was successful if he could do what a foreigner did."[4] Japanese American author Joanne Harumi Sechi discusses this double-conscious dilemma as it applies to the Japanese American perspective of America.

> I'll never forget the "ching, chong Chinaman" phrases we heard or the etchings of slant-eyed Oriental faces on the walk in front of a Chinese home. If they had to call me names, I thought they could at least call me by the right name. I was made to feel different, if not weird; I learned to despise that element in me which would induce those taunting words. To resolve my discomfort over "sticking out like a sore thumb," I was determined to be the "best." I had to prove to myself that I was just as good as, if not better than, the white kids . . . Playing the duality role didn't really satisfy my questions about who I was when I tried to believe in it and to live it. I felt that I had to be expert on things Japanese. I had to know the proper Japanese names for objects, the correct origins of ceremonies. I always tried to present "my" culture to others on a silver platter before they could attack it . . . I over-achieved in efforts to prove my capabilities to myself. I had to wash myself of feelings of deviancy.[5]

Sechi traces her movement from double-consciousness—what she calls "the duality role"—and its manifestations and its complex interactions: interracial, intragroup, and sexual—to self-trust and true self-consciousness, which is almost always (like the Invisible Man's) a recognition of one's own human contradictions and multiple possibilities.

To return to "Flying Home." The letter from the flyer's girlfriend, then, touches all the bases of double-consciousness: the media images;

the need for counter-stereotypes and burden of proof; collective versus individual identity; public versus private; and the ironic counterpoint of Blacks' stereotypes of one another. For instance, Todd refers to the old man as a "peasant." But the reader wonders whether the old man will be all, and only, what Todd perceives him to be. "With all I've learned I'm dependent upon this 'peasant's' sense of time and space." There will be further irony here, for the peasant's sense of time and space (certainly revealed through his folklore) will perhaps be more complex than Todd can imagine, deepening and complicating both the organization and meaning of his own story. One is reminded here of the equally complex organization and time/space sense of Louis Armstrong's music in the prologue of *Invisible Man,* a music where one can "slip into the breaks and look around . . . I found myself hearing not only in time but in space as well." The folktale suggests a prelude to the intricate time/space of *Invisible Man.*

Todd himself feels naked without the flying machine, as if the plane were a suit of clothes or his only dignity. It is the machine that confers dignity, though with embarrassment and wonder. The question asked in Ellison's *Invisible Man* was: What does an old black peasant have to do with humanity? Or with dignity? The story may try to answer these questions.

The theme of invisibility begins in stereotypical metaphors: Todd talks of the old man's "childish eyes." This intraracial stereotyping complements the interracial stereotyping of black characters by white narrators in previous chapters (Dr. Melville's Jube Benson, for instance). Todd cannot communicate with the old man; he cannot make him understand what he feels. He recalls other old black men who came to the airfield to watch the pilots. In the beginning, he'd felt pride and meaning in their presence. "But soon he realized they did not understand his accomplishments and they came to shame and embarrass him, like the distasteful praise of an idiot. A part of the meaning of flying had gone then, and he had not been able to regain it." Caught in the double-conscious terrain between "ignorant black men" and "condescending white," Todd wants his true worth recognized. But neither with these men of his own race nor with the white men does he feel he can measure his identity. The old man asks why he wants to "fly way up there in the air?" He thinks but doesn't say, "because it's the most meaningful act in the world . . . because it makes me less like you." Instead, he says simply because he likes it.

Craft and wit of the old man begin to emerge in dialogue, reflecting the oral tradition from which they came:

". . . so I went and found me some colored angels—somehow I didn't be-lieve I was an angel till I seen a real black one, ha, yes!"

The insightful humor of the old man's dialogue culminates in a folktale, which he imbues with the authority, sense and sensibility, and *substan-tiality* of his own voice. "Well, I went to heaven and right away started to sproutin' me some wings. Six good ones, they was. Just like them the white angels had." Manifesting the whole context of oral storytelling, the old man makes gestures of flying to a crowd of imaginary listeners, as he tries out his wings. He discovers that "colored angels" had to wear a special kind of harness when they flew. A black angel "had to be extra strong."

The image of a real black angel affirms the old man's identity, certainly contrary to Dr. Melville's demoniacal imagery for Jube Benson, or Creel-man's belief that Booker T. Washington must have "bewitched" the white women. The storyteller redefines an aesthetic with the same energy and imagination as his "flight." In this way he also restores our perspective, as Brother Tarp does for Invisible Man. And the folktale, though it is surreal in its transmuting of the tangible world, is not fantasy but a means of gaining control over social reality. The old man, Jefferson, might be an example of what the folklorist Alan Dundes calls "an active bearer of tradition."[6] The fantasy is clearly related to social background and social reality, and it functions in the context of that reality. The social reality is a precedent, a catalyst for the folktale, but the folktale provides an imag-inative freeing from the constraints of that reality. The tale is an "outlet for expression,"[7] a metaphor and "means of exploring the problem."[8] It is a free and freeing form.

In storytelling the oral tradition reinforces, complements, and acts on the reality. The old man tells Todd he too is a "flyer"; and in flying he also asserts his manhood, skill, and personality; it is through folklore that he can reveal himself and identify himself; folk tradition reestablishes and affirms humanity, restores perspective, and the truer and better self. As the hero of his own story, he refuses to wear a harness. "Cause if God let you sprout wings you oughta have sense enough not to let nobody make you wear something that gits in the way of flyin'."

Restored through his own storytelling, the old man turns articulate. He himself becomes the counterstereotype to Todd's first images and preconceptions of him, and the structures of both stories open into each other. The old man is the pilot of his story. His humanization and self-perception are not—at least in the context of the oral tradition—defined or redefined by outsiders. In *Native Son* the essential problem of Bigger

Thomas is that there is no tradition in which he can become articulate. So he cannot liberate his personality from the restrictive terms of men such as Britten; and, ironically, even from the abstract, sociological-Marxist restrictions of Max, who defends him in theory but is terrified to see his *real human being*. But within his own authoritative tradition, the old man is able to show his intelligence, his wit, his candor, his perceptive humor. He is also satirical; in an ironical reversal of symbolism, "I started flying up to the stars and divin' down and zooming roun' the moon. Man, I like to scare the devil outa some ole white angels. I was raisin' hell. Not that I meant any harm, son. But I was just feeling good. It was so good to know I was free at last." In his folktale the old man presents the archetype for Todd's own story of "modern flyer."

In the folktale the oral tradition reflects the reality, but the resourceful, hyperbolic wit of the oral tradition prevails: "I accidentally knocked the tips offa some stars and they tell me I caused a storm and a coupla lynchings down here in Macon County . . ." However, Todd misinterprets the old man's motives, feels he's mocking him. The tale means something different to Todd (as audience) than it means to the folkteller. There is no manifest communication. Then the story develops into a "joke" that is double-edged and serious. The black angel proves to be too good a flyer and is twice called before Saint Peter for speeding. Saint Peter finally says "Jeff, you got to go!" "Son, I argued and pleaded with that old white man, but it didn't do a bit of good. They rushed me straight to them pearly gates and gimme a parachute and a map of the state of Alabama." "So I told him, 'Well, you done took my wings. And you puttin' me out. You got charge of things so's I can't do nothin' about it. But you got to admit just this: While I was up here I was the flyinest sonofabitch what ever hit heaven!'"

"At the burst of laughter Todd felt such an intense humiliation that only great violence would wash it away." The laughter is double-edged, like blues humor. An excellent example of this double-edged humor is again from Ellison's own *Invisible Man,* when Invisible Man first enters Harlem and meets up with Peter Wheatstraw (a name given to old blues singers, according to critic Robert O'Mealley). Sings Wheatstraw:

> "She's got feet like a monkey
> Legs like a frog—Lawd, Lawd!
> But when she starts to loving me
> I holler Whoooo, God-dog!
> Cause I loves my baabay,
> Better than I do myself."[9]

This kind of humor is a persistent dimension of African American folklore and Ellison uses it again and again in *Invisible Man*'s multilevel jokes. The young pilot's response is one that some audiences also give to this comedic tradition, and it illustrates the difficulty that black comedians sometimes have in transferring comic situations to art. Because some of the procedures of comedy are related to the process of stereotyping, it is often hard for African American comedians (particularly those within the folk tradition) not to appear to be supporting stereotypes (Flip Wilson's "Geraldine" and "Reverend LeRoy" would be examples). The audience may find itself struggling between feelings of disapproval and the recognition of cleverness and timing in the blues joke. This problem applies to writers as well. Both comedy and stereotyping depend on forms of exaggeration and parody, ignoring the complete personality in favor of comical displacements (for example, a particular dimension raised to absurd proportions). When this happens the result is often the same failure of recognition that we have in this story: the pilot is quick to feel that the old man is making a joke of him. In such cases it is difficult to separate the comedic from the stereotypical, which also depends on caricature, parody, exaggeration. Both of these elements of the joke enter in Ellison's work—the relationship between comedy and serious social criticism—the blues laugh—and also the process of carrying us beyond the apparent stereotypic to the deeper levels of personality and meaning—the double-vision of the blues' hyperbole. (Again this progression is evident in many of the characterizations of Ellison's later novel.) But here Todd feels that the old man is laughing at him and it is another occasion for humiliation, double-consciousness, and stereotypic vision. He can only see the old man as a grinning clown telling the sorts of tales that whites like to hear. The story and the reality that the old man is inventing holds no meaning for the reality Todd faces. He searches the old man's face for mockery, but sees it "somber and tired and old." Again it is difficult for him to distinguish between self (and therefore group) parody and self (and therefore group) scrutiny.

At this juncture the story makes a transition from the third to first person, a curious though easy transition that brings us Todd's thoughts of childhood and the first time he ever saw a plane, a model airplane, an exhibit at a State Fair. It is a fascinating toy and he vows someday to have such a toy. He makes a makeshift plane of wood and asks his mother over and over when she is going to buy him one. She considers his entreaty crazy and foolish. Besides, model airplanes cost too much. Then one day he sees a real plane, made small by distance. Reaching out and trying to grab the plane, he grabs nothing but air: "It was like sticking my finger through a soap bubble." The plane flies on. This is the initiation of the hero. "Boy, is you a fool?" his mother asks. "Don't you see that there's a real airplane 'stead of one of them toy ones?"

The shift to first person provides a complement to the old man's story; it is social reality from another viewpoint, as well as the hero's thought functioning as interior story. Personal memory provides an initial link between Todd and the old man and foreshadows the recognition that will come in the story's present. Following this there is a conversation that begins the shattering of the distance between Todd and the old man. After the boy leaves to "hustle down to Mr. Graves to get him to come," old Jefferson explains: "Everybody knows 'bout Dabney Graves, especially the colored. He done killed enough of us." When Todd asks what they did, Jefferson replies, "Thought they was men."

Contradictions, ambivalence, and paradox, prevalent in *Invisible Man,* are themes here too, as the old man goes on with the story of Dabney's jokes. This is another version of the American blues joke (boomerang joke?) and the terror at the center of it. "Dabney Graves is a funny fellow," Jefferson says. "He's all the time making jokes. He can be mean as hell, then he's liable to turn right around and back the colored against the white folks. I seen him do it. But me, I hates him for that more'n anything else. 'Cause just as soon as he gits tired helping a man he don't care what happens to him. He just leaves him stone cold. And then the other white folks is double hard on anybody he done helped. For him it's just a joke." Finally, Dabney Graves arrives. He doesn't care what the Army has told Todd to do. "Nigguh, Army or no, you gittin' off my land! That airplane can stay 'cause it was paid for by the taxpayers' money. But you gittin' off. An' dead or alive, it don't make no difference to me." To "Jeff" and Teddy, he says, "I want you to take this here black eagle over to that nigguh airfield and leave him." At this point it is a recognition of connectedness that will release Todd from his sense of isolation. In perceiving Jefferson and Teddy's manhood he recognizes his own. "And it was as though he had been lifted out of his isolation, back into the world of men."

Since Charles W. Chesnutt's "The Wife of His Youth" (1899) a number of stories have focused on bridging the gap between the "talented tenth" (Du Bois's term) and the folk. In some stories, such as Robert Boles's "The Engagement Party," the incipient rapport has been aborted and the painful distance persists between an aeronautical engineer and a caterer and his daughter; other stories, such as James Baldwin's "Previous Condition," describe the uneasy (and unresolved) tension of recognition between the racially self-exiled actor and those he encounters when he goes "home to Harlem." Martin Delany's *Blake,* a nineteenth-century exception to the rule in many respects, not only bridges the intra-racial social gap—Blake moves in all levels of society, black slave and free, educated and uneducated—but goes beyond this to action—that is, Blake has a plan for mutual liberation.

This initial recognition of full humanity of others (within the race) rather than the easy denial (Peter Wheatstraw to Invisible Man—"You trying to deny me?") was an important first step. An exchange between Michael S. Harper and James Randall in *Ploughshares* comments on this idea of human recognition, its high frequency levels of awareness. Randall remarks on the impressive ability of black intellectuals to "deal with people from all levels of society and change their personalities and speech to do this." Harper replies: "'Change the joke and slip the yoke,' is what Ellison called it; many white people didn't realize they had their bags carried by Ph.D.s. That was my own experience working in the post office. I learned much about literature, politics, and the aesthetics of living from the studied eyes of friends; their survival depended on it—they had to improvise. They also knew they were human; that was never in doubt."[11] This is essentially the difference between Todd, who thinks about being more human, and the old man, who knows he is human without any doubt.

Since the difficult reconciliations of such 1950s exiles' return stories as Ellison's "Flying Home" and Baldwin's "Previous Condition," it is often the folk character who contains the key to true self-conscious humanity. We find such characters again in the "incorrect" women of Alice Walker's contemporary stories.

In "Flying Home," then, the folktale introduced in the story becomes a mirror for the dilemmas of character and circumstances which have to be resolved in the story. This is an important stylistic and thematic development of the use of folklore in fiction. To compare, the turn-of-the-century story by Chesnutt merely incorporated the text of the folktale, whereas Ellison opens up the entire story to its form and humanity. The folktale not only functions dramatically in the texture of the story, but the tale and the pilot's story provide *contexts* for each other and together form the linguistic community of the story. Instead of erecting a boundary, the folktale and the story share territory and reinforce meaning, as

10

The Freeing of Traditional Forms: Jazz and Amiri Baraka's "The Screamers"

If Ralph Ellison brought folktale, folkspeech, and character into freer territory, breaking through the earlier traditional fictional borders, Amiri Baraka (LeRoi Jones) opens up even more space. In "The Screamers" he makes use of the musical dimension of oral tradition—jazz—in a way similar to Ann Petry's "Solo on the Drums." Although Petry did not achieve the fullest potential of this usage, she pointed the direction to further modifications in dramatic structure, organization of space, event, time, and texture. Baraka's 1963 story does more than that—it frees us from the traditional form in a modern and modernizing text and also carries us beyond the merely technical implications of that freedom by making broader claims in the relationship between aesthetics and social morality.

Since Baraka mentions the word "dada" in the text, it may be useful to discuss his narrative in the light of this European phenomenon. This anticonformist art movement, launched in Zurich in 1916, flaunted satire and mockery, even contempt for traditional conventions—artistic as well as social. Chance and spontaneity were prized, as were the capricious, arbitrary, the unexpected, the antilogical. It was a free form which affected art, films, poetry, and drama. Its elements of fantasy and "irrationality" paved the way for such surrealists as Salvador Dali and Max Ernst, who later moved from dadaist discoveries to work which by comparison was more ordered in its whimsy, and poets Tristan Tzara, André Breton, Paul Eluard, Louis Aragon. The abstract painter and sculptor Jean Arp was one of the founders of dadaism, and the French poet Guillaume Apollinaire was influenced by it in his curious juxtapositions and simultaneities of image, metaphor, and meaning. The dadaist movement also had adherents in Germany, England, Russia, Holland, Italy, but it was art (sometimes called antiart) consciously in opposition to previous European artistic standards and conventions.[1] There is comparison, then, with the procedures of "The Screamers" and its improvised variations, which stand in opposition to European American literary tradition and in the context of what critic Houston Baker, Jr., has called a literature of repudiation.

But though African American innovative writers sometimes share or seem to mirror some of the forms of these European-American non-traditionalists, it is important to make distinctions and to look for distinctive purposes. For instance, when we compare Jean Toomer's use of stream-of-consciousness literary technique in *Cane* with that of James Joyce in *Ulysses,* we discover that the exploration of interior landscape and consciousness of African American character and personality *adds value* because African American character had not been explored from *the inside as complex and serious.* European American writers did not do it because they did not believe it to be either; African American literature neglected it because the drama of personality was often secondary or background to the drama of oppressive interracial confrontation (compounded, as in "The Lynching of Jube Benson," by problems of audience and perspective). In these cases the technical device became a morally (ethically, politically, socially) responsible act. But when we learn of the interior workings and imaginations of Joyce's Leopold Bloom, Stephen Daedalus, and Molly Bloom, we are not necessarily carried beyond the technical and thematic arenas. In the relations between Ireland and England, and in Englishmen's stock characterizations of Irishmen (similar to African American stock characterizations) the reader might see implications of social revolt, except for Joyce's own nonpolitical stand. In fact, Joyce's portrait and conception of the (self-exiled) artist would celebrate the divorce of the social and the aesthetic, as Stephen does in *A Portrait of the Artist.*

Within the context of the literature of repudiation it is also necessary to acknowledge Baraka's connection with the Beat Generation—writers such as Jack Kerouac (who named the movement), Lawrence Ferlinghetti, John Clellon Holmes, Gregory Corso, and Allen Ginsberg, all of whom reached artistic maturity after World War II. These writers also rejected conventional forms and Western cultural tradition and sought formal liberation through spontaneity and the openness of oral improvisation.[2] (This formal rejection affected dress and behavior as well as art forms and values.) However, in the critical perspective of *Cane, The Invisible Man,* and certainly in Baraka's own story, our concern is with what Ellison refers to as the relationship(s) between "art, society, and morality." Therefore, even though Baraka shares some of the techniques of the

Beats—the juxtapositions, "loose" structure, nonstandard or slang diction, he never shares with them "valuelessness" but only nonconformity.

The nonconformity of most innovative African American writers with the traditions they have rejected or repudiated is to propose new values. We acknowledge that some of these new values have been problematic, especially when they are simple reactions and blanket rejections of European American values as expressions of revolt. In the words of Albert Camus, "in order to combat evil, the rebel renounces good, because he considers himself innocent, and once again gives birth to evil."[3] This is the boomerang of Ellison's *Invisible Man*. It is what Edmund Wilson means in *Axel's Castle* when he talks of Rimbaud's combating "merciless domination" and in so doing being driven "to take the part of Satan."[4] To be sure, there are other genuine ambivalences, paradoxes, and confoundings of vice and virtue (and the double-standards of virtue) that one notes in works from Douglass to Wright. Nevertheless technical nonconformity attempts to lead toward value rather than away from it. The Beat Generation's rejection of old values could imply new values—a new morality—for many of them were also interested in transforming the world, like the French surrealist poets of an earlier rebel generation. But there was not always a sense of a necessary connection between form and value, so that the flouting of conventions could more easily be both the means and the end (as with dada). Although the Beats had lost faith in their own cultural traditions, ironically these still remained as anchors for them and their alternative moralities (as well as measures of their humanity and value, denied to Blacks within these traditions). In short, their departures into the irrational could be seen, paradoxically, as a component of intellectual history. For the African American writer, however, these divergences seemed mere justification for attitudes and oppressions already held by the arbiters of those anchoring traditions. That is, the writers themselves were illogical and irrational, rather than being conscious, mindful, and moral literary or social rebels. As the writers of one literary history of the United States say of the early Americans' relationship to Europeans, they were "nourished by differences" and "they could not but question what the European took as a matter of course."[5] This can be said surely of the African Americans' relationship to the European Americans. The implications of this can be seen also in the new attitude toward sexuality in the writings of black writers of the sixties and those who came of age during that time. Donald Gibson's comments in *Introduction to Modern Black Poets* are also relevant to Baraka's short story: "Highly irreverent toward conventional notions of sex and sexual morality, black poetry tends to be very free in its dealing with the sexual act and in its use of sex-oriented Anglo-Saxonisms. Language scatological in nature is allowable as another means of expressing the poet's desire to escape the restraints of the system of institutions and conventions which oppress him. Yet, despite a surface lack of concern with morality, black poetry is highly moralistic, attempting to convince its audience of the meaningfulness and significance of moral order superior to that reflected in American institutions."[6] What for the Beats could be a challenging of the superficial in Western moral order and a concern with the meaningful and the significant in human relationships, can for the African American be seen as mere justification for a sexual mythology and stereotyping already held by whites. This is why most African American writers before this generation scrupulously avoided any reference to sexuality. Certainly the uplift writers did so, though there were occasional outbreaks of freedom in the poetry of Langston Hughes, who wasn't afraid of any aspect of personality, or in the fiction of Claude McKay, who was readily condemned as "low-down" by Du Bois and others. Certainly Jean Toomer's explorations of sexual landscape and "sins against the soul" (as being the greater sins) and Ralph Ellison's comic-blues depictions of American sexual mythology are also exceptions. Nor was Zora Neale Hurston afraid of sexuality, though she sometimes used indirection and metaphor. The problematic relation of black women, social class, and sexuality was also one of Nella Larsen's themes. Nevertheless, sex becomes more easily controversial and *noticed* in works by African American writers, although Ishmael Reed gives the opposite impression in characterizing Clarence Major's first novel, *All-Night Visitors,* as "a departure from the Afro-American literary tradition, *marked by a reserve in sexual matters*"[7] (my italics). Yet if Henry Miller's or even D. H. Lawrence's works were modern African American texts, a whole array of meanings and values would become askew in moral projections of "unregenerative humanity."

To understand Baraka's endeavor it is necessary to delve deeper into the connection between technique and social morality and rebellion, especially in his relationship to jazz. The comments of Kimberly W. Benston, in an article on "Late Coltrane," are relevant:

> The revolt of the Afro-American artist against specific literary or social conventions is, at bottom, a rebellion against authority and the memory of imposed systems. As trumpeter Clifford Thornton . . . declared, true revolution of consciousness begins by a radical "un-learning" of existent modes . . . Thus, while the new "black aesthetic" turns inside-out all the pieties of life and art, speaking outlandishly in no language we ordinarily

hear, it still speaks for the life and increase presumably afforded by a new syntax of desire . . . The "new wave" jazz—having extended and mastered the contribution of bebop—opened the floodgates of passion, anger, pain, and love, and aroused that fury for liberty which is the essence of the new black art. It joined itself to earlier, major epochs of black music by reaffirming the creative union between the improvising soloist and the total musical collective. *But it also forged a new role for the music in the hierarchy of black expressions—that of guide rather than mere analogue to other communicative modes* . . . [my italics].

The thought of giving to words and prosody values equivalent to music is an ancient one, in African and Afro-American as well as Western culture. But with modern black literature, it assumes the force of a specific idea: the notion that black language leads *toward* music, that it passes into music when it attains the maximal pitch of its being.

Benston is careful to assess differences in the apparent affinities with European American avant-garde music:

The music of the white avant-garde, in its revolt from the "purposeful," teleological art of Western culture, is anti-tonal in order to be directionless, unkinetic, goalless. Its systematic use of chance as a technique of composition is designed to create sounds without syntactical-grammatical relationships, sounds as individual, discrete, objective sensations . . . Trane and his followers' music is, as Frank Kofsky has observed, *not* atonal. They find themselves exhilarated, not exhausted, in the face of formal possibility. But the distinction between them and their Euro-American contemporaries runs deeper than the mechanics or even philosophy of form. For, to the Afro-American artist in search of his nation's potential, what would be more horrid than the denial of human will?[8]

The reader might also see some parallel here in the work of the French modernist novelist Alain Robbe-Grillet regarding the position of human will and consciousness in the new art (despite his "scientific" argument for the change in the position of object versus subject reality). And the Beat Generation's connection with jazz is undeniable, as is the fact that jazz seemed to attain a special visibility in European American culture during the times of principal literary innovations and upheavals. But certainly the desire of the Beats to capture "both the openness and the outrageousness of American experience" and to "enhance the participation of literary audiences"[9] would lead them to this music and its sources.

"The Screamers" is like a free-form jazz solo. Many readers find it difficult because of its adroit blurring and blending of visual and temporal details, its shifts in time, setting, and emotional sequences; its fragments of biography, history, and sociopolitical commentary. Reading the story, then, is like solving a puzzle of space, time, character, chronology, event, and description. There are jazz-dada-surrealist shifts in accents; scenes and themes are introduced, reiterated, and amplified in solos within solos, where jazz is both meat and meteor, providing the substance and movement of the story.

The setting that gives the story a certain textual coherence, however, is the jazz club, Graham's, where Lynn Hope plays. The musician is introduced even before the narrator introduces himself. Thus, although the narrator witnesses, tells, and interprets the narrative, Lynn Hope is the hero and central figure, the one who resolves the dilemma or provides the possible source for the resolution of the contradictions of society, character, and circumstance. In the many hierarchies depicted in the story, he is supreme, the guide who (paradoxically) unifies.

The first paragraph introduces Lynn Hope and then the major theme in an oblique, impressionistic way, using syncopated rhythms and riffs. A "yellow girl" won't dance with him, nor will "Teddy's people" or "Haroldeen, the most beautiful, in her pitiful dead sweater. Make it yellow, wish it whole. Lights . . ."[10] The wish is to be made whole. The problem is fragmentation: personal, historical, cultural. It is essentially the double-consciousness dilemma again. The basic tune, the motif of intraracial double-consciousness is introduced in this first paragraph and will be repeated and broadened with improvised variations and scenic compressions. Though interracial conflict isn't the subject of the early part of the story, we are aware of the interracial background of many of the pre-sixties hierarchies of value, and the need for redefining moral aesthetic as well as form.

The narrator recognizes the isolation of others as well as his own, and conveys this in satirical and cynical tones as he investigates the meanings of the dilemma and makes labyrinths of place and time. Like the Invisible Man, he is nameless. As we listen to Lynn Hope, we also experience the voice and rendering of another musician—his verbal horn, his staccato rhythms, shifts in accent and invention. He is the witness to Lynn Hope's and his own essential music, as they both "shuffle lightly for any audience"—at least in the beginning. Lynn Hope is the catalyst of the experiences in the story; the narrator is the one who gives them meaning. There are paradoxes of identification: "Laundromat workers, beauticians, pregnant short haired jail bait separated all ways from 'us,' but in this vat we sweated gladly for each other. And rubbed." The problem is intraracial division, separation by class and external conceptions of value. The musician is the common hero, who offers the possibility, the stimulus, and potential for wholeness, for self and group realization. The narrator acknowledges this function as he recreates Lynn's methods through alliterative and onomatopoeic riffs.

Though the narrator tells the story, Lynn is the central and visible dramatic figure, the vehicle of the wish. Along with the others the narrator himself is in need of wholeness. He admits his own isolation, his flaws of character, his intellectual arrogance: "Who would I get? (Not anyone who would understand this.)" The interracial psychosexual ambivalence applies also to other dilemmas of consciousness, offering perverted hope or paltry substitute for a more essential hope of wholeness. Before we move to the regenerative possibilities of the music, we learn about its misuses. This psychosexual theme is brought up in *Invisible Man* in the vet's dialogue: "Why, of course, but remember, Crenshaw, he's only going to be there a few months. Most of the time he'll be working and so much of his freedom will have to be symbolic. And what will be his or any man's most easily accessible symbol of freedom? Why, a woman, of course. In twenty minutes he can inflate that symbol with all the freedom which he'll be too busy working to enjoy the rest of the time. He'll see."[11]

Other contemporary writers have explored the social and psychological contradiction of sexuality. One finds this especially in the works of James Baldwin—from the European American Southerner's perspective of sexual myth, metaphor, and racism in "Going to Meet the Man"; from the African American perspective in "Previous Condition"; and in his most notable novel, *Another Country,* about sexual ambivalence, interracial duplicity, and forms of cruelty. Alice Walker's stories and novels also deal with sexuality from the African American feminine and masculine perspectives in all of these ways. And John A. Williams's "Son in the Afternoon" is an excellent example of psychosexual terror leading, ironically, to both revenge and visibility. In addition, this theme certainly has its historical basis in the slave narrative period and its combinations of sexual myth and interracial cruelty.

Although "The Screamers" challenges Western tradition in its obscuring and fragmenting of detail, it nevertheless maintains the complications of a traditional beginning: conflict and establishing the circumstances of character, society, and historical situation that must be resolved. As Baraka continues his jazz improvisations on divisiveness and solitude through the "slow or jerked staccato," the narrator makes initial efforts at communion, but it is only a communion of perception and intellect, not of feeling; he like the others remains a "valuable shadow, barely visible . . . Chanting at that dark crowd." Throughout the story, notes run together in a musical collage of identities and images: "Big hats bent tight skirts" in a "mingled foliage of sweat and shadows." The narrator is aware of the poorer Blacks' misperceptions of him as "that same oppressor" and acknowledges his own arrogant and disordered misinterpretations of their mystery.

In flashbacks and fragments of biography the narrator sings a solo of his double-conscious days, when he wanted girls like Erselle but his hair "wasn't straight enough." (Now, though, he has "good hair.") Yet Baraka is speaking of more than the double-consciousness of social and personal relationships and intraracial prejudice. In African American literary history such middle-class heroines as Erselle were sometimes summoned as window-display or used merely as the objects of satire. The narrator's reference to such girls and their purposes has a satirical tone, but rises above satire to become a struggle of artistic conscience as he defines his situation in relationship to them, and their situation in relationship to their own thwarted potential for wholeness and regeneration. "Important Negroes . . . plotted in their projects for mediocrity . . . only the wild or the very poor thrived in Graham's or could be roused by Lynn's histories and rhythms. America had choked the rest . . ."

African American literature was thus mediocre because of its lack of risk-taking and its unchallenging imitation of American aesthetic value— ultimately because of its own "haughty" relationship to its subject. Long before Baraka's 1966 essay "The Myth of a Negro Literature," however, Richard Wright in his 1937 article "Blueprint for Negro Writing" repudiated this literature, seeing his own as a departure from it.

> Generally speaking, Negro writing in the past has been confined to humble novels, poems, and plays, prim and decorous ambassadors who went a-begging to white America. They entered the Court of American Public Opinion dressed in the knee-pants of servility, curtsying to show that the Negro was not inferior, that he was human, and that he had life comparable to that of other people. For the most part these artistic ambassadors were received as though they were French poodles who do clever tricks . . . The mere fact that a Negro could write was astonishing . . . Either it (Negro writing) crept in through the kitchen in the form of jokes; or it was the fruits of that foul soil which was the result of a liaison between inferiority-complexed Negro "geniuses" and burnt-out white Bohemians with money.[12]

In seeking an alternative identity and aesthetic and in moving away from the mediocrity of the bourgeois realists, the narrator takes the plunge that so many writers took later in the 1960s. They tried to redefine themselves and their allegiances in terms other than those of the "oppressed minorities" whom Lenin observed as "often reflect(ing) the techniques of the bourgeoisie more brilliantly than some sections of the bourgeoisie themselves"[13]—they tried summoning new subjects and new "peers": ". . . old pinch faced whores . . . celebrity fags with radio programs, mute bass players who loved me, and built the myth of my intelligence. You see, I left America on the first fast boat."

To leave America on the first fast boat is symbolic of the new literature of repudiation (Baker's term). The narrator finds kinship with these outsiders, all contrary to the respectable girls summoned in the beginning of the story. This is an alternative to the mediocrity of the aesthetic of mimicry, but it also suggests how the heroes of some sixties literature became problematic. Baraka's "black magic" poem "Black People!" also highlights this theme. The poet Haki Madhubuti (Don L. Lee), in his poem "We Walk the Way of the New World," likewise writes about the necessity of going beyond the initial break with the white man and his America to produce new images and new values.

Both poems address the problem of values. Baraka's poem, but not Madhubuti's, embodies the paradox: in the attempt "to leave America" by mocking and flouting bourgeois standards, the poetic message reinforces the negative stereotypes of that America, a liability of rebellion not held by the Beat Generation and Wright's monied Bohemians. Frederick Douglass in his *Narrative* expresses another aspect of the essential paradox: "What he most dreaded, that I most desired. What he most loved, that I most hated. That which to him was a great evil, to be carefully shunned, was to me a great good, to be diligently sought; and the argument which he so warmly urged against my learning to read, only served to inspire me with a desire and determination to learn."[14] Although fear of the "evil consequences" of his learning to read is justified in this instance, and in many such instances where the master and slave must necessarily see the world differently and where in the master's world the slave "isn't even human,"[15] it nevertheless suggests the paradoxical nature of this stance. In "The Screamers" the narrator pursues his own path of paradox: "Willing for any experience, any image, any further separation from where my good grades were sure to lead. Frightened of post offices, lawyer's offices, doctor's cars . . . Lynn's screams erased them all." We are reminded again of Camus's statement in *The Rebel* and of the confounding of values when questions of race and color and interracial confrontation are involved.[16]

Lynn's music seems to provide the only ethical and holistic alternative. His music offers a new mode, a new entity, a different context and a positive value. In the words of Lloyd W. Brown, author of *Amiri Baraka,* "he legitimizes his literary art by associating it, in a variety of ways, with the oral traditions of black American culture and with the musical tradition which he recognizes as the only true art form to evolve from the black American experience."[17] The jazz art, then, offers a new source of identity as well as artistic form.

A study of jazz and the whole of American literature would be welcome—one which compares and contrasts the uses of the music in the works of both African American and European American artists. This is not the place for it; a few observations must suffice. Thus Michael S. Harper has noted how the "essentially . . . black form"[18] of jazz has worked in F. S. Fitzgerald's fiction as "a commentary on character and plot."[19] Critic Edmund Wilson has mentioned T. S. Eliot's play "Wanna Go Home, Baby," "written in a sort of jazz dramatic metre."[20] And of course the seminal poem of the twentieth century, "The Waste Land," incorporates jazz and jazz rhythm in the language ("O O O O that Shakespeherian Rag—") and in the sense of free improvisation, shored fragments, and perpetual possibility of form. We have mentioned the Beats, the Jazz Age, the possibilities of jazz in Gertrude Stein; even Carl Sandburg has a "Jazz Fantasia"; it would be interesting to see where all these lead. In the discussions of Ann Petry's "Solo on the Drums" and Michael S. Harper's poetry we noted the European tendency to hear only the eroticism. In his poem of cultural decadence, degeneration, and spiritual sterility Eliot seems to think of jazz as the "disgraced white girl" with "halting speech" and "paltry humanity" (to use Baraka's images), yet when jazz enters the poem, the negations are overpowered by it in the rhythmical life and intensity of the poem itself. Another negative note sounds in Carl Sandburg's "Jazz Fantasia," where the author essentially stays outside the jazz character (in most black poetry the character is the center—the inner space of the poem—as in Harper's Coltrane and "Bird" poems, and Sherley Williams's Bessie poem). The focus of Sandburg's poem is on the music as sound and on the mechanics of instruments and instrumentation. When the jazzmen are recognized, named, and made visible, however, the recognition leads to destructive results: "You jazzmen . . . make two people fight on the top of a stairway and scratch each others eyes in a clinch tumbling down the stairs."[21] This is the antithesis of the Baraka story, which represents spiritual joining and transcending. Baraka's jazzman is hardly the one to make the people fight. Though the music itself was born out of cultural and racial dislocations and fragmentation (the scene at the beginning of Baraka's story) it leads the black hearer/reader to spiritual regeneration—that "clear image." At the end of Baraka's story, as we will see, the music is mis-heard, the act of communion misinterpreted (deliberately?). The end thus seems to (again) suggest how the music functions in the "other literature." For even though these European American writers may be genuine in terms of their own literary history, sensibility, and needs, their jazz is generally antithetical to African American uses of a music, which in their stories, poems, and dramas rescues people from chaos and fragmentation and restores to wholeness. And it is more than an "avante garde routine" as Lloyd W. Brown's statement would verify; it offers an unambiguous integration of art, society, and personality, a reclaiming of perspective and value. To say that "the length of the music was the only form" is to assert a new definition of self and possibility, together with a new artistic form of open, self-inventing structures, as the narrator continues his literary jam session.

As in *Invisible Man,* the artist-hero of "The Screamers" is attempting to rebuild a self (individual and collective). Jazz offers a metaphor for freedom of movement—spatial, temporal, and imaginative. The improvisational nature of an art without boundaries and its multiple levels of fluidity are manifest in the narrative consciousness, the juxtaposition of themes, episodes, and judgments; the musician is the artist-hero's alter ego. As the author describes the musician's performance, he is describing and clarifying his own, the responsible literary artist and the musician sharing motivation. Here the narrator speaks of a new form called the honk that pushes "its insistence past music"; a product of a "dipthong culture," it embodies hatred, frustration, secrecy, despair: "There was no compromise, no dreary sophistication, only the elegance of something that is too ugly to be described, and is diluted only at the agent's peril." But these "uglier modes" are paradoxically beautiful, provide connections and redefine an aesthetic not "forever at the music's edge" but at its center. Jay, another musician, makes the initial breakthrough in "the only other space that form allowed" as his "horn spit enraged sociologies . . . We hunched together drowning any sound, relying on Jay's contorted face for evidence that there was still music, though none of us needed it now."

The word gets back to Lynn what Big Jay had done, and "to save face" he must outdo him. So Lynn blasts all night, until he gets his riff:

III

The Novel

Dialect and Narrative:
Zora Neale Hurston's
Their Eyes Were Watching God

Their Eyes Were Watching God (1937) is a transitional novel in the dialect tradition. Though a small work, it is not about a little world of dialect; it is a hypercharged little book which coordinates and resolves certain early dialect problems while initiating and anticipating many of the concerns and conceptions of contemporary writers. Like a shining hummingbird, it flies backwards (as only the hummingbird can) and forwards, pointing to the past and anticipating the future dialect novel.

A glimpse of dialect's function in the nineteenth century African American novel reveals the same presuppositions of the minstrel mode we found in Dunbar's "The Lynching of Jube Benson," with similar effects on the interplay of dialect and personality. William Wells Brown's *Clotel* (1853)[1] is a well of such presuppositions. Chapter XII, "A Night in the Parson's Kitchen," illustrates the author's and the age's attitude toward dialect. In this important chapter, for the first time in African American literature the reader is introduced to slaves in a social and communicative context. Here dialect follows one of James Weldon Johnson's tenets: it enters only as comic relief. Therefore, the chapters which dramatize the relationships between blacks exist chiefly as amusing interludes. This stylistic attitude and its consequence—like the aesthetics of the central character Clotel, "indistinguishable from a white woman" and the leading victim of slaveholders' duplicity and sexual abuse—appear to contradict the purpose of the book: that is, to show (prove?) the humanity of blacks as well as expose the cruel conditions of slavery as an abolitionist argument. None of the Blacks in the book is given full portrayal, either in character, scene, or language. This treatment resembles the European literary tradition (and hence Brown's literary model) of treating servants and the lower classes comically, or as background figures (even when they were pulled to the foreground as in *Don Quijote,* they remained essentially comedians, when not villains, though Cervantes modifies tradition somewhat by Sancho's Quixotic metamorphosis). In *Clotel* both the black slaves and the Southern poor whites are treated to a similar pattern of comic relief or minstrel humor. Likewise, in nineteenth-century European-American literature the routine opinion was that "'low' scenes and characters could appropriately be dealt with only as comic," as seen in the mining stories of Bret Harte. Walt Whitman, the only pre-Twain writer who thought otherwise, felt that "vernacular [was] adequate to meet any demand a serious writer might make on it."[2]

Chapter XIII of *Clotel*, "A Slave Hunting Parson," scenically parallels Chapter XII; here, treated like the Blacks in the previous chapter, the poor whites assume the role of Mr. Bones to the white parson's Interlocutor. Moreover, the dialect of the poor whites is virtually indistinguishable from the slaves' diction. Rather than liberating the dialect, Brown's intention is perhaps to allow it to become a part of the antislavery argument too: the refusal to educate the poor white and the general low condition of these people, linguistically and otherwise, are yet another consequence of slavery. To show the "despicable language" of slavery being used by whites as well as Blacks was precisely one of the antislavery techniques, and the fact that the chapters are annexed verifies this tactic. The novel's purpose aside, the scene in the kitchen registers the adverse influence of the minstrel tradition on the use of dialect in the novel, and discloses its human and experiential limitations. Without quoting the scene, the bit of verse that precedes the chapter serves to crystallize its function:

> "And see the servants met,
>   Their daily labour's o'er;
> And with the jest and song they set
>   The kitchen in a roar."[3]

The only nineteenth-century black novel which admits intelligent and complex speakers of dialect and "elevated uses" is Martin Delany's *Blake*, but Delany notably departs from many other obdurate conventions. According to Black Aesthetic critic Addison Gayle, the writer's paradigmatic hero is "handsome, black, intelligent." But even though Delany admits and displays a variety of characters using dialect, his central character—an educated man—speaks standard; indeed, a very rarified, formal, stylized, impeccable English. This is another variation in the dialect-standard ambivalence. Many African American writers hesitate between dialect and standard. For some the standard language becomes precious, that is, too respectful, observant, and attentive to the rules, too meticulous, too punctilious and seemingly "derivative" without the versatility and easy informality of writers who take their tradition and language for granted. This can also happen to European writers from different social groups: those who take their cultural modes for granted often more freely innovate and originate, are less modest and moderate in what they will do with the standard and its forms. There are exceptions, of course, such as D. H. Lawrence and James Joyce, but Joyce after all had an elitist, Jesuit education. Still Joyce could do nothing to please certain of his "social betters" such as Virginia Woolf, who called *Ulysses* "illiterate" and "underbred."[4] Even D. H. Lawrence had at least moral if not social objections to the "deliberate, journalistic dirty-mindedness" of the book. *Ulysses,* as we know, is neither illiterate nor journalistic, and if dirty-minded, it is rarified, exalted, stellar dirty-mindedness. Yet perhaps his social placement did make for Joyce's *push,* to prove that he could do anything and everything in the language.

But to get back to that other punctiliousness: it often carries into characterization itself, where even virtue is formalized—what Sterling Brown called "plaster of Paris saints." Yet this formality, more noticeable perhaps in black writers because of both the dialect stereotyping and the linguistic reality of many speakers, is really no different from that of other writers who come from dialect regions. Standard language often acquires a rare elegance, and actors and writers from St. Louis are often mistaken for (upperclass) Englishmen (even Virginia Woolf would approve). One is more attentive to the standard. One listens deeper. One becomes at times, too literate. (It is interesting that in French a sign of the educated speaker is the *liaison*—the running-on of letters, whereas in many Southern American communities—black and white—the educated speaker pronounces *all his letters*—occasionally those not meant to be pronounced.)

Delany's *Blake* speaks standard. Even in scenes with other slaves the minstrel pattern is absent. He does not assume the role of Mr. Interlocutor with his "ignorant fellows." Blake's interchanges with speakers of dialect are not for comic relief; indeed very complex situations are often recognized and recreated. Here a dialect-speaking woman is introduced in a way that contrasts significantly with the traditional pattern: "'How de do, sir!' saluted she, a modest and intelligent, very pretty young black girl, of good address."[5] In *Blake,* intelligent personalities are still visible through dialect, are allowed to speak it, and may still be moral, serious, and complex human beings.

In nineteenth-century pre-Hurston fiction, it was generally simply taken for granted that the central character, along with his moral and intellectual superiority, would also be a speaker of standard English (and his language proof of these other qualities); this was unquestioned and unquestionable. This is not the case in Hurston's work. Janie does not speak standard, yet she is the central character. She does not speak standard, yet she is intelligent and complex, and her dialect is part of what Whitman would call the "taste of identity."[6] I might add here, however, that one of my students who was reading Hurston's *Their Eyes Were Watching God* laughed when he got to the dialect—Janie's speaking dialect was unexpected. We talked about his reaction and possible reasons for it. I suggested two: that he was used to the leading black character's speaking standard in the participant-observer novels of earlier black writers; and that his was a conditioned response to *any* dialect, and marked the persistence of the minstrel attitude. For instance, we continue to see the usage of not only ethnic but regional dialect in the media, even though many of the literary writers have long since abandoned that comic or satirical intention. In films especially, unless they are comedians or villains, even white Southerners do not speak like Southerners, perhaps because this would trigger too much laughter when the intent is dramatic. Usually the leading characters whom the audience must identify with speak standard. White Southern writers, on the other hand, have liberated their own voices, so that they at least bring authentic American voices into their fiction, often to the forefront of American letters. Nor are these voices restricted to dialogue, but enter every mode of expression. Occasional movies and television shows, taking their cue from the literature, also allow these voices (for their "flavor"), but I believe most audiences still *hear* them as quaint, picturesque, or minor; and speakers of regional dialects are often described, no matter how loquacious, as "inarticulate," (this is how a New York critic referred to the garrulous characters in the stories of Bobbie Ann Mason). And as I mentioned in the chapter on Hurston's short story, it could have been the attitude of the reader, not the writer, that cued Wright to dismiss Hurston's intent out of hand as minstrel.

Hurston's dialect, however, is linked both to her concern with the authentic possibilities of the black voice in literature and to variegated dimensions of character. *Their Eyes Were Watching God* is a transitional dialect novel because it extends the innovations in the dialect tradition the author began in her short story "The Gilded Six-Bits," and because it more fully actualizes the potential of literary dialect than did the fictions of Dunbar or Chesnutt, or the antecedent novels of William Wells Brown and even Martin Delany, though *Blake* provides a sturdier bridge to Hurston's work and its aims than do any of the others.

As with Hurston's short story, the dramatic focus of Hurston's novel is *within* an African American community. The theme is a woman's search for love that leads to a new conception of freedom and identity. Hurston stresses the psychology of character and complexity of relationships, all providing a background of fictional value to complement the linguistic innovation—an innovation which perhaps again seems slight to contemporary readers, but is noteworthy for the emotional and experiential range and sense of human possibilities released by both Hurston's redefining perspective and literary dialect. Though she is not talking specifically of Zora Neale Hurston here, novelist and poet Alice Walker defines this necessary, important shift in perspective:

> even black critics have assumed that a book that deals with the relationships between members of a black family—or between a man and a woman—is less important than one that has white people as a primary antagonist. The consequence of this is that many of our books by "major" writers (always male) tell us little about the culture, history, or future, imagination, fantasies, etc. of black people, and a lot about isolated (often improbable) or limited encounters with a nonspecific white world. Where is the book, by an American black person (aside from *Cane*) . . . that exposes the subconscious of a people, because the people's dreams, imaginings, rituals, legends, etc. are known to be important, are known to contain the accumulated collective reality of the people themselves.[7]

To receive the full weight of this observation, one must compare Walker's statement with two other critical perspectives: first, the black protest tradition, concentrating on interracial conflict at the expense of intricate character relationships, and second, the white critical perspective, assuring black writers that the "broader perspective" was never their own, militated against this "accumulated collective reality" in black fictional imaginings.

Below, Rebecca Chalmers Barton's praise throws light on her view of a black writer's perspective: "Nor does the boundary of color bar the promising new writer, Ann Petry, from the broader perspective. Her latest book, *Country Place,* exposes plenty of seaminess in New England small town life without recourse to racial questions. In fact, there is only one Negro character, and she is cast in a minor role."[8] In an otherwise well-written and astute book, Barton here manifests the critical atmosphere of her time (and ours?). To deal with whites in a small town is "broad," even laudatory, but to deal with Blacks in a small town (à la *Winesburg, Ohio* or *Dubliners;* even *Madame Bovary* is provincial, but "French provincial") is "narrow" and a "recourse to racial questions."

Unfortunately, not a few black readers themselves share this sensibility, and works where only Blacks are visible or have the major visibility in the text are dismissed by themselves as racial material. A simple test would be to repaint some of the faces without changing the work technically and see how instantly "racial material" becomes universalized (meaning improved) or vice versa.

Ideally, the black writer, like any writer, should be able to write about *anyone anywhere anytime*—Greek farmers, Swedish businessmen, Bolivian mathematicians, Chinese professors of Italian literature, African astronauts—including his own, to show that sort of human as well as technical diversity and dexterity; but to confuse the issue, as it is still being confused, is to suggest that an Irish writer *must* write about Spaniards to be universal. Indeed, if black writers are castigated for writing about Blacks, mainstream white American writers should be castigated for writing about mainstream, middle-class white Americans (in their major roles). The only time I've seen this was when reading a book on science fiction writing; aspiring writers were informed that most of the world was *not* middle-class, white American and were advised to consider putting some Indians, Africans—or—let's not be too difficult—at least some Italians in outer space! (That is, as space *heroes*.) It is refreshing to hear middle-class white American writers being called to such a high standard, since they have so often accused others of not being universal if they do not include *them*, preferably in *their* leading roles. But enough of this—racial material and political motive and social psychology will probably continue to be confused with objective literary criticism. As black sculptor Mildred Thompson once said, "gallery personnel could not look at the work for looking at me!"[9]

The black writer needs, in spite of others' confusion, to control and restore his own perspective as the norm. Michael S. Harper has expressed this well: "for me, Blacks are the norm, the individual context from which all can extrapolate. The particular is always the key to the universal, so I've never thought I had to get away from anything."[10] In *Their Eyes Were Watching God*, dialect voicings break the boundaries of convention to restore perspective and tell us about "culture, history, future, imagination, fantasies," the internal and external reality of the characters in Hurston's world. For Hurston, too, "Blacks are the norm."

Dialect in Hurston's world has "the beauty and power of heard speech and lived experience." It is not restricted to the comic in any of its forms: grotesque, parody, burlesque, satire, or the pathos. Hurston's dialect demonstrates its capacity for a broad communicative range, through a variety of emotional transformations in many scenes, in shifts of mood and atmosphere, and in the quality and depth of assorted relationships. Here, as in Hurston's short story, dialect is still capable of humor, but it is the imaginative humor of the oral tradition—such as the storytelling on the store porch; it is the humor that one laughs *with,* the humor of boast and tall tale and comic balladry. Or it is a dialect capable of wit and biting satire, but never denying the intelligence or full humanity of its users. It is also a language that can go beyond pathos to the tragedy of Tea Cake's death and the incidents surrounding it; to express the heroism of Tea Cake's saving Janie during the hurricane, and the magic of their whole relationship.[11] There are no fixed conventions. Like condensed energy suddenly made articulate, it can express any wonder, voice any meaning.

For Hurston, Janie is an articulate woman who "happens to" use dialect. The folk heroine, no longer quaint like Charles W. Chesnutt's "The Wife of His Youth," has become the complicated center of the work. However, Hurston maintains certain dialect conventions. For example, though Janie tells her story to her friend Phoeby, Hurston does not let her narrate the whole story in her own voice. She sets up the storytelling, then returns to the standard authorial voice. Let's refer again to John Wideman's comment that the framed story legitimizes and gives authority to black speech.[12] Wideman goes on to discuss different frames and how they dramatize the assumptions of dial :t, locking it into formulaic molds, determining the kinds of experien :s, subject matter, and emotions it is allowed to express. And though the technique of the framestory is old in Western literature (Chaucer and Boccaccio used it; Joseph Conrad later employed it widely) we can see how a seemingly innocuous stylistic technique in African American literature transcends itself to say something (or not say something) about human value and possibility.

In *From behind the Veil,* Robert Steptoe speaks further of this aspect of *Their Eyes Were Watching God* and the wider thematic implications regarding the articulate heroine: "Hurston's curious insistence on having Janie's tale—her personal history in and as a literary form—told by an omniscient third person, rather than by a first-person narrator, implies that Janie has not really won her voice and self after all—that her author (who is, quite likely, the omniscient narrating voice) cannot see her way clear to giving Janie her voice outright."[13] Steptoe's discussion rivets the connection between voice and character liberation. And it also suggests a contrary standard regarding Western and African American literature. In Western literature, as I believe Oliver Wendell Holmes noted in an essay on writing novels, most "great books" (he said *all*) have been third-person narratives; in African American literature from the slave narrative on, the importance of telling one's own story has been the thrust (*Invisible Man* is often distinguished in this tradition). I think this is an important instance where the higher technique in one tradition is not recognized as the higher technique in another. Its influence on how most African American literature is read and received outside the tradition is probably greater than suspected. (All well and good, but what can you do in third person? says one standard. Yes, but I'm winning my—or my character's—voice and self, says another.) What this could imply for contemporary work could be something like judging English drama by Racine's dramatic method: oh what loose, illogical, flighty, chaotic dramatists the English are!

Janie's grandmother's slave narrative—"Ah was born back due in slavery and it wasn't for me to fulfill my dreams of what a woman oughta be and to do"—prefaces and foreshadows Janie's own story and provides the dramatic and revelatory pattern for it. Thus the slave narrative is also framed within a novel that dramatizes a modernized version of it, although freedom here involves not only physical escape, but spiritual renewal and escaping constricting ideas of self. Therefore, Janie searches for a new freedom, a new idea of what a woman should be and do, and she creates her own values, through patterns of illusion and disillusion, until, after her fulfilling, emancipating relationship with Tea Cake, she grows into whole womanhood. Though their relationship is important, as Robert Hemenway notes, Tea Cake is not the *cause* of Janie's growth but a complement for it: "While Jody would not let her take part in storytelling sessions, with Tea Cake it is perfectly natural for her to be a participant . . . It is important to note that Janie's participation comes after she has learned to recognize sexism, a necessary preliminary to her self-discovery."[14] Because there are no models for Janie of what she must be, she must more or less create herself. With Tea Cake that self-creation can develop wholly, after she has redefined her own horizon as distinct from that of her grandmother, her first two husbands, and perhaps her whole community: "She had been getting ready for her great journey to the horizons in search of *people;* it was important to all the world that she should find them and they find her. But she had been whipped like a cur dog, and run off down a back road after *things* . . . Nanny had taken the biggest thing God ever made, the horizon—for no matter how far a person can go the horizon is still way beyond you—and pinched it in to such a little bit of a thing that she could tie it about her granddaughter's neck tight enough to choke her."

Often, as here, fiction in the African American tradition contains models not of what one might be or become but the reverse: examples of what one must escape, nets to avoid in order to achieve wholeness. While some works contain examples of autonomous, self-realized characters who provide moral revelations or possibilities for the unrealized ones, central characters are often like Janie, emerging to recreate or create themselves without guideposts or blueprints except their own, or signs telling them where not to go. Of course this latter method can be tricky. A writer generally has three options for moral revelation: (1) representing characters as they should be (romanticism, idealism); (2) representing them as they are, or as he believes them to be (realism); or (3) representing them as they should *not* be (sometimes but not always in the context of naturalism, satire, irony, and so on). The black writer who chooses the third option is often misread and accused not of exposing the human condition but of stereotyping it (there is always a fine line, for example, between stereotyping and satire or satirical irony, which often distort or exaggerate in order to characterize; moreover, most readers end up understanding the character as negative if Black and stereotype are synonymous). Black writers who write linguistically and stylistically composite novels are also moved to some composite form of character portrayal in which the romantic ideal and its opposite or variants coexist. (Isn't this *Don Quijote* again or those marvelous nineteenth-century Russian novels?) Yet often one writer's romantic idea, even here, can be another's stereotype; certainly the masculine ideal as conceived by a woman writer, for example, might seem unlikely to a masculine reader. For example, Janie's (and Hurston's) "heroic, handsome, sensitive, generous-spirited" Tea Cake appeared to some (male) critics as merely another variant of the "guitar-strumming, irresponsible" (not free-spirited) black man stereotype. It is often the case that characterization is especially ambiguous among groups that have been the victims of unrelenting and even vicious stereotyping by others (like the Irishman in English literature). For such writers the dominant literary traditions and the creative act are often at variance. Again, my students provide an accessible example. Like most "revolutionary reformers," the students who had been the most vocal in denouncing the apparent stereotypes in the works of black writers (including Hurston) and specifying how those characters (and writers) erred, would quite often produce fictional works that others found equally questionable in their portrayals. Possibly lack of craft (necessary in creating any whole character), lack of fictional models (in or outside tradition), or inexorable "subliminal conditioning" (media) produced this result. But the reasons for the gulf between creative theory and creative act are not easy to explain in any tradition and it is always easier to talk the work to be done than to produce it.

Perhaps the only workable ideal black masculine character to have appeared in the literature is again Delany's Blake, a man capable of holding what are often seen as opposing or contradictory virtues: "He was bold, determined and courageous, but always mild, gentle, and courteous, though impulsive when occasion demanded his opposition."[15] Unlike many one-dimensional ideals, Blake can be multidimensional without being contradictory: he adds up to a whole. Still, this remains on the level of description, which is easy, and though Blake achieves much of this characterization in fine and diverse scenes, they are not as skillfully dramatized as one would like, not as skillful as Hurston's or later writers (Wright, Ellison) with even more controversial characters. To be sure, Wright's Bigger Thomas is not meant to represent anyone's ideal, but rather the unrealized personality comparable to Joyce's *Dubliners* (and their implications vis à vis the Englishman's "Paddy"), who are unrealized versions of what Joyce, to his lights, might have been if he had stayed in Ireland. (Joyce later moved to the composite portrayal, the impressive intellect of Stephen Daedalus and the warmth and humanity of Leopold Bloom, in the midst of a multitude of Dubliners as they should not be.)

After Janie succeeded in realizing herself, her story as told to Phoeby assumes the patterns of revelation, the episodic scenic structures, and the geographical movements of the slave narrative, although, unlike the traditional narrative in the genre, Hurston, as we have seen, does not maintain Janie's voice throughout. But although Hurston does not go as far as later writers in breaking the frame and freeing Janie's whole voice as self, we should notice a narrative tension between the two linquistic traditions, a sense of new foundations being laid against an old wall. *Their Eyes Were Watching God* extends the instances that we first noticed in "The Gilded Six-Bits," where the vocabulary, syntax, metaphors, and thought processes of the characters invade the language and authorial voice of the narrative. Hurston's first attempt at breaking the frame occurs when she reports Joe Starks's initial conversation with Janie. The narrative breaks into the rhythms, vocabulary, and world view of Starks:

> Joe Starks was the name, yeah Joe Starks from in an through Georgy. Been working for white folks all his life. Saved up some money—round three hundred dollars, yes indeed, right here in his pocket. Kept hearin' 'bout them buildin' a new state down heah in Floridy and sort of wanted to come. But he was makin' money where he was. But when he heard all about 'em makin' a town all outa colored folks, he knowed dat was de place

he wanted to be. He had always wanted to be a big voice, but de white folks had all do sayso where he come from and every where else, exceptin' dis place dat colored folks was buildin' theirselves. Dat was right too. De man dat built things oughta boss it. Let colored folks build things too if dey wants to crow over somethin'. He was glad he had his money all saved up. He meant to git dere whilst de town wuz yet a baby. He meant to buy in big. It had always been his wish and desire to be a big voice and he had to live nearly thirty years to find a chance. Where was Janie's papa and mama?

Here Hurston uses indirect dialogue to break into the integuments of narrative. She modifies the narrative by paraphrasing Joe's speech to Janie. He also in a manner of speaking—though intended ironically here—becomes a "big voice" in the narrative. (And Joe could be someone's romantic idea; Janie—illusively in this text—initially sees him as one.)

Hurston modifies and revivifies the text on other occasions by using the language that Janie might have used—imagery, vocabulary, rhythms, sentence structure, and so on. Though maintaining the third person, she approximates the transcription techniques of contemporary writers who have broken out of the frame. Unlike Joe's monologue, the language isn't distorted with "eye dialect" but is transposed by rhythm, word choice, and syntax much like a contemporary text. In the following excerpt, Hurston breaks into the narrative suggesting Janie's voice and imaginings, her thought processes:

She rather found herself angry at imaginary people who might try to criticize. Let the old hypocrites learn to mind their own business, and leave other folks alone. Tea Cake wasn't doing a bit more harm trying to win hisself a little money than they was always doing with their lying tongues. Tea Cake had more good nature under his toe-nails than they had in their so-called Christian hearts. She better not hear none of them old backbiters talking about her husband! Please, Jesus, don't let them nasty niggers hurt her boy. If they do, Master Jesus, grant her a good gun and a chance to shoot 'em. Tea Cake had a knife it was true, but that was only to protect hisself. God knows, Tea Cake wouldn't harm a fly.

And here is an instance of Janie's syntax and vocabulary organizing and embellishing the narrative:

She looked hard at the sky for a long time. Somewhere up there beyond blue ether's bosom sat He. Was He noticing what was going on around here? He must be because He knew everything. Did He mean to do this thing to Tea Cake and her? It wasn't anything she could fight. She could only ache and wait. Maybe it was some big tease and when He saw it had gone far enough He'd give her a sign. She looked hard for something up there to move for a sign. A star in the daytime, maybe, or the sun to shout, or even a mutter of thunder. Her arms went up in a desperate supplication for a minute. It wasn't exactly pleading, it was asking questions. The sky stayed hard looking and quiet so she went inside the house. God would do no less than He had in His heart.

Of course this is one of the narrative writing techniques in which oral tradition and literary again coincide (co-mingle?). In the works of James Joyce and Gustave Flaubert readers frequently assume the narrative territory to be exclusively the territory of authorial voice in diction, vocabulary, and articulation. Hence Joyce and Flaubert are often accused of possessing the romantic sentimentality that they were satirizing. (Joyce's attitude toward Stephen Daedalus might more precisely be called ironic.) Other writers, such as Elizabeth Bowen, make sure that the reader "gets it" by parenthetically stressing that the narrative renderings are the way the character would see, think, or express a thing. She announces what she is doing as part of the ironic structure of the narrative. Irony and satire, not solely dramatic characterization, are often motivations in Western literature for this technique. J. F. Power's "Dawn" does it through Father Udovic's thought processes, vocabulary, and mawkish logic restructuring narrative; another example is Henry James's "central intelligence" method in which much of the verbosity and circumlocutions that we take simply for James's style are third-person narratives that center in the minds of characters and indirectly reproduce their personalities, their rhythms, prolix thoughts, and parlance. The depiction of Gerty in *Ulysses* makes this technique clearer. Because Gerty is a woman, so there are no autobiographical parallels, and because the architecture of *Ulysses* is more multifaceted than that of *A Portrait of the Artist as a Young Man,* it is easier for the reader to know that the intent is satirical, the attitude ironic. On the other hand, if a woman had written a book entitled *Gerty* using this method of indirect dialogue and monologue, many readers would suspect the author and narrator were one; the ironic attitude would have been more difficult to convey and sustain; the author might have had to announce what she is doing. However, Hurston's intent here is not satirical or ironic. She is not satirizing Janie's way of expressing things or organizing thoughts. Nor is she Janie. She is simply allowing us to enter Janie's world.

The author also brings oratory from the African American folk sermon into Janie's and the narrative's vocabulary, amplifying and ornamenting the folk voice and interior revelation. The same thrust and narrative dynamics permeate nearly all of James Baldwin's fictions. James R. Bennett in *Prose Style* found it odd that Baldwin might share this vernacular expression with Southern white writers: "Although Southern writing can be as laconic as other American colloquial prose, it also indulges in that public oratory we habitually associate with the Southern politician, and which we often hear in the prose of Thomas Wolfe and William Faulkner, of Robert Penn Warren and William Styron, and even, ironically, of James Baldwin . . . the oratorical mode shares the characteristics of the colloquial. Its exclamations, repetitions, uncertain backings and fillings, accumulation of synonyms, and rhetorical emphases all originate in the extemporaneousness of speech, the spontaneous jetting of language that maintains its equilibrium by constant movement forward."[16] Knowing that oratorical flourishes are migratory, this does not seem odd to this reader/listener, especially because of the invisible linkings in Southern black and white races and textual relationships (Baldwin's ancestors were transplanted Southerners; nor do we always know in this Southern tradition who is influencing whom in rhetorical strategy). It is what Ellison would call the "true interrelatedness of blackness and whiteness."[17]

Hurston admits Janie's language, imagination, and perspective in many places. However, these are probably places where, says Robert Hemenway, "the narrative shifts awkwardly from first to third person." This narrative awkwardness or tension may be read as Hurston's attempt to give a certain validity and articulate authority to Janie's expression, thought, and experiences; her attempt to make Janie's language do even in small ways, the things that other languages, taken for granted as literary languages, can do.

Not until James Baldwin, Ernest Gaines, Ellease Southerland, Toni Cade Bambara, Ntozake Shange, to name but a few contemporary writers, did the folk language become flexible enough to enter the fabric of the narrative to tell the whole story. Southerland, for instance, breaks into the third-person narrative with the syntax, vocabulary, and metaphors of Abeba's speech community without feeling it necessary to first make the shift to the first-person storyteller, and she resolves the narrative tension in a more shimmering, malleable prose:

Jackson didn't have good sense. He had all the sense he was born with, but that wasn't enough. He was a great big boy, sixteen years old and what'd he do all day? Go on up the road to the midwife's place and play just as content with the little girl there. Playing tea party. That ain't no way for a grown boy to be. Just two years ago, the little girl fix mud cakes and all. Took weeds and fixed it sos it looked like greens and laid a twig beside the dinner for a fork then called Jackson to the table to eat and that great big boy picked up the little mud cakes and bit right into them. And Abeba Williams that's the little girl, put her hand on her hip just as she see the midwife do and said, "Jackson, you to play eat, not to eat mud sure enough." And Jackson got it straight after that.

Like Ernest Gaines's *The Autobiography of Miss Jane Pittman,* Ellease Southerland's *Let the Lion Eat Straw* extends the work Hurston began in breaking down some of the barriers between dialect and narrative in fiction. Nevertheless in her territory there is still the problem of the look of ease and apparent lack of complexity and implication. (Also, what is innovative in one tradition often appears conventional from the point of view of another where freeing one's voice is not the issue. In American popular music, for instance, the so-called innovations and breakings-out of early rock 'n' roll were not distinguishable from conventional black music, for jazz had already been there and gone. Conventional literature in one culture may likewise surprise another culture while "innovative" literature might hold nothing new. From the point of view of the frame then, we speak of innovation.)

This "look of ease" is something that must be addressed in the African American tradition as in all other literary traditions. How to render the colloquial voice authentically, break out of the frame, and yet be impressive literarily? For instance, the colloquial voices in *The Waste Land* or the interior monologue of Molly Bloom still impress us; is it because these colloquial, natural voices play against the more elaborate unnatural voicings? But if first-person voice is seen as the higher standard, how could a convincing contrast be devised? Perhaps more of the expansiveness and opulence of the sermonic mode could be used to play against the colloquial. But first one seizes authority over one's own voice (and voices), then develops, cultivates, enhances, heightens, intensifies, sets a style.

In Western literature there are essentially two stylistic streams, often interfaced as in *The Waste Land;* one of clarity and one of complexity. Some writers and readers see style as superior the easier it is to understand (decode?). Others deem superior styles that one must work to penetrate, that reveal significant unity or coherence. The more difficult the writing the more the allure. This is the distinction between Frost and

Eliot, Hemingway and James (or Joyce). One either tries, like Frost, to "make little orders," or to make profound secret puzzles—evoke a fictional reality that is as incoherent as the real one. The world itself is not a simple notion. Contemporary African American writers with oral motives in the latter stream are Leon Forrest, Ishmael Reed, Steve Cannon (interestingly, they are all men). They produce the difficult texts, something the reader must decode, as if the text were an arena not simply of creation, to use Kimberly Benston's term, or simply of communication, but of intellectual combat. This is not the place to explore the implications of this differing perspective. At its best the masculine text has an impressive adventuresomeness. Even among student writers, the men more often tend to use satire or irony, the more difficult tones and styles which demand more visible displays of cleverness or wit. The women's texts tend to be more low-keyed and to have more of a surface conventionality, with subtler textual subversions, often unnoticed, and which must be pointed out. However, before any adventure, the territory was first seized; the voice first freed.

Seizing some of her territory, then, Hurston, even in the final paragraph of *Their Eyes Were Watching God,* makes the reader feel the oral tradition breaking through—colloquial and heightened—here, as in Toomer's *Cane,* in narrative made to be heard and felt as well as read. Janie's voice welds sermonic rhetoric and oratory with the musical traditions of blues and spiritual:

> The day of the gun, and the bloody body, and the courthouse came and commenced to sing a sobbing sigh out of every corner in the room; out of each and every chair and thing. Commenced to sing, commenced to sob and sigh, singing and sobbing. Then Tea Cake came prancing around her where she was an the song of the sign flew out of the window and lit the top of the pine trees. Tea Cake, with the sun for a shawl. Of course he wasn't dead. He could never be dead until she herself had finished feeling and thinking. The kiss of his memory made pictures of love and light against the wall. Here was peace. She pulled in her horizon like a great fish-net. Pulled it from around the waist of the world and draped it over her shoulder. So much of life in its meshes! She called in her soul to come and see.

12

Riddle: Ralph Ellison's Invisible Man, *or* "*Change the Joke and Slip the Yoke*"

Ralph Ellison's novel *Invisible Man* is such a luxuriant novel that it might be used as a model to discuss a multitude of traditional oral forms and motives in speech, metaphor, and architectonic structure. Jazz, for one, informs and complicates the structure and personalities of the novel and enhances Ellison's vision of the "fluid American reality" as well as his creative resolution of a world of possibility. In 1936 Ellison came to New York to study sculpture and musical composition, and among his numerous jobs he had been first trumpeter in a jazz band. He had also written brilliant articles on music and musicians. It is therefore no wonder that the deep structural influence of music on his fictional composition accounts for much of the complexity of his style, and along with elements of expressionism and surrealism accounts also for his breaking away from the "narrow limits of naturalism." He discusses some of these developments in the speech he gave after receiving the National Book Award for *Invisible Man* in 1952: "As for the rather rigid concepts of reality which informed a number of the works which impressed me and to which I owe a great deal, I was forced to conclude that reality was far more mysterious and uncertain, and more exciting, and still, despite its raw violence and capriciousness, more promising . . . I was to dream of a prose which was flexible, and swift as American change is swift, confronting the inequalities and brutalities of our society forthrightly, but yet thrusting forth its images of hope, human fraternity and individual self-realization. I would use the richness of our speech, the idiomatic expression and the rhetorical flourishes from past periods which are still alive among us."[1] Jazz itself "struggled with form," "challenges the apparent forms of reality," reveals its "mad, vari-complicated chaos, its false faces," "until it surrenders its insight, its truth."[2] Jazz musicians recompose American reality, "making music out of invisibility," "slipping into the breaks," and "looking around."[3] Such music is in tune with the fluidity of American experience and language. Its "diversity and swiftness of change"[4] creatively resolves by using whatever is contradictory, ambiguous, or ambivalent, far beyond "sociological interpretations" *(Shadow and Act),* often in surreal vision.[5]

In describing black artist Romare Bearden's work Ellison might well be talking of his own literary strategies: "he delights us with the magic of design and teaches us the ambiguity of vision . . . insists that we *see* and that we see in depth and by the fresh light of the creative vision . . . his ability to make the unseen manifest . . . visual possibilities of jazz." Ellison too is an explorer "of the frontiers of human possibility."[6]

The prologue of *Invisible Man,* like a boomeranging jazz prologue, initiates the major themes, scenes, symbols, literary techniques and technical combinations which we see reiterated and redefined in structured improvisation. The book deals with themes of irony and ambivalence, questions of identity, and the protean nature of reality, history, and freedom. The prologue, the initial solo, introduces, anticipates, and foreshadows every essential dramatic method and motif in the book, its strategies of making the "unseen manifest." The novel describes not a static but a mobile reality of perpetual discovery: "unity in diversity . . . the widest possible spectrum . . . a vibrant living continuum."[7]

In the prologue Ellison acknowledges the African American musician as the great artist, for it is the "black and blue" music of Louis Armstrong that enables the storyteller to first "slip the yoke" and "slip into the breaks [spaces] and have a look around." And he is thus able to hear "unheard sounds," to hear himself "not only in time but in space as well." Through music, he enters a new world, descends into its depths, and makes his first "acquaintance with ambivalence." Now he is able to ask crucial questions: "Could this compulsion to put invisibility down in black and white be thus an urge to make music out of invisibility?" He must learn what freedom is; he must see with inner eyes as he moves through the "waking nightmare" in his quest for visibility: self-definition and the recognition of his own (and others') humanity.

Music and jazz as metaphor in *Invisible Man* have been often highlighted by critics. Moreover, several discussions in this book have already been devoted to the influence of jazz on prose and poetic structures. Therefore, I would rather explore another oral traditional motif, one that might itself be a seen/unseen oral form: Ellison's use of the riddle and the riddle-as-joke or joke-as-riddle. The riddle is motif itself broadly connected with jazz, since Ellison makes jazz-like use of his riddles; that is, riddles are introduced, they recur, and metamorphose improvisationally throughout. However, this does not mean that *Invisible Man* is improvisational in the sense of being unplanned—Ellison's numerous interviews and essays on its design assure that it was not; this is merely to suggest that its intricate structure has the vibrancy of improvisation—a sense of perpetual discovery.

Like jazz, then, the riddle establishes and complicates the pattern of *Invisible Man*. In some ways *Invisible Man* might be called a dilemma tale, with its complex integration of realistic, expressionistic, surrealistic stories ending up in a dilemma. Its riddle, however, seems to combine the question-and-answer form of the American riddle and the description of the African riddle as oral literary form, as statement. Ruth Finnegan's definitions are useful here: "The popular European or American picture of a riddle is of an explicit *question* to which a respondent must try to puzzle out the correct answer. African riddles are not altogether like this. The 'question' is usually not an interrogative at all in form but, outwardly at least, is a statement. An answer is expected but very often the listeners are not directly asked to guess but merely faced with an allusive sentence referring analogously to something else which they must then try to identify. The point, furthermore, is normally in some play of images, visual, acoustic, or situational, rather than, as in many English riddles, in puns or plays on words."[8]

The prologue and initial chapters of *Invisible Man* define the novel's riddles through generalizations, images, statements, puns, paradoxes, questions, so that their context—chapters, situations, characters, modes of behavior, ambiguities, and so on—become a series of possible answers, and therefore possible meanings.

The focal and principal puzzle is the grandfather, who introduces the first boomerang riddle of the book:

> On his deathbed he called my father to him and said, "Son, after I'm gone I want you to keep up the good fight. I never told you, but our life is a war and I have been a traitor all my born days, a spy in the enemy's country ever since I give up my gun back in the Reconstruction. Live with your head in the lion's mouth. I want you to overcome 'em with yeses, undermine 'em with grins, agree 'em to death and destruction, let 'em swoller you till they vomit or bust wide open . . ."

The protagonist had always known his grandfather to be a quiet, meek man. That he could also be dangerous—a spy and a traitor—became a constant and unanswered puzzle. The adventure and the dangers of the hero's travels aim at discovering the meaning of this riddle, this paradox.

In his search the hero will not only find many possible and probable meanings for it, but will weld together other statements and circumstances that appear contradictory, incongruous, impossible, as he attempts to discover how "yes" can be both affirmation and denial. But Invisible Man is not the only character to face his riddle. In the second chapter we meet Trueblood, who likewise embodies ambiguities of character beyond any sociological or psychological interpretation.

Sometimes riddles come in the form of dreams, prophetic or not, which Ellison uses to clarify experiences or to anticipate new experiences. Invisible Man, a student at a pastoral college in the South, is asked to chauffeur Mr. Norton, a white philanthropist and trustee who speaks of the school as "a great dream become reality." The young man drives his passenger into "forbidden territory" which the school officials, especially President Bledsoe, would not want Mr. Norton to see. "I've never seen this section before. It's new territory for me," says Mr. Norton, in preparation for a scene that becomes a "nightmare become reality." Before Mr. Norton is introduced to Mr. Trueblood—the dreamer/riddler—we learn that his philanthropy is a sort of monument to his daughter, and that his feelings for his daughter seem to transcend fatherly affection.[10] This discovery foreshadows the Trueblood scene and serves to connect the two, for Mr. Norton also *contains* unknown territory (terror-story) that he has not seen before, has refused to see, or has not been able to see. Trueblood's story forces him to see the unseen, as the novel itself forces the readers to see, taking them too into unseen territory.

In a dream, or a dream-like state, or more precisely a "dream sin," Trueblood has committed incest with his daughter. He awakes intending to tell his wife about his "crazy dream," only to find himself "lookin' straight in Matty Lou's face . . . I'm too surprised to move . . . And I figgers too, that if I don't move it maybe ain't no sin, 'cause it happened when I was asleep . . ." Is one morally responsible for a dream sin? Freud asks this question in his "Moral Responsibility in Dreaming" and answers yes. And in Ellison's riddle, is "true blood" guilty or not guilty? As in other dilemma tales, he seems to be both at once. Nevertheless he accepts the moral responsibility for the dream sin, unlike the white trustee Norton, who is in a territory he has never seen before—his own interior landscape as well as Trueblood's. Selma Fraiberg in "Two Modern Incest Heroes" speaks of the connection between Norton and Trueblood: "Mr. Norton who listens to Mr. Trueblood's dream with dread and fascination is the witness to his own dream. Mr. Norton's dream-sin of incest is concealed from him and from the world. He atones by creating monuments to the sacred memory of his daughter, and his good works for the Negro are the symbols of his guilty partnership with the Negro: the Negro sins for Mr. Norton and Mr. Norton atones. Mr. Trueblood who sinned in a dream and wakened to find himself embracing his daughter is stripped of pretense and the protection of the myth. He is confronted with his naked self and the testimony of his dream and the act."[11] Trueblood, having solved his own riddle of conscience and consciousness, decides he is what he is: "I makes up my mind that I ain't nobody but myself."

The character Trueblood has offered his riddle and at the same time provided a key to the nature of Ellison's riddles: they contain both the question and the answer. They are paradoxical jokes. Alan Dundes in *Interpreting Folklore* calls this quality "the solution which maintains the contradictions."[12] This is also the nature of "the joke that always lies between appearance and reality."[13] Ellison has called America "a land of masking jokers." His riddlers are also jokers; and the jokers are double-edged—"the laughing teeth that kill."[14] Trueblood's dream-sin is such a tragicomic joke, a comic-serious riddle.

At the end of Trueblood's story, Invisible Man is torn between humiliation and fascination, while Mr. Norton is drained of color. The nightmare sin is a shared one and they are all caught in the same moral dilemma, the same ambivalence, the same riddle-joke. Trueblood, in the paradox, is both sinner and hero. He does not judge himself, cannot judge himself or his crime, but he confronts it, sees it, and behaves responsibly in the face of it. And with Trueblood, Ellison admits the kinds of character into the African American novel that the literary equivalents of Dr. Bledsoe would also consider inappropriate territory for the Mr. Norton readers. Therefore his inclusion of Trueblood and development of this character from the stereotype to full humanity is important in its implications, ranging from the "window display"[15] of the "uplift writers" to the concerns of Black Aesthetic critics. The question continues to be: what unseen territory might the black writers admit to the literature or exclude from it? And they continue to give variant answers, from Alice Walker's assertion that "The writer—like the musician or painter—must be free to explore, otherwise she or he will never discover what is needed [by everyone] to be known";[16] to Toni Cade Bambara's assertion: "Speaking one's mind, after all, does not necessarily mean one is in touch with the truth or even with the facts. Being honest and frank in terms of my own where—where I'm at at a given point in my political/spiritual/ etc. development—is not necessarily in my/our interest, not necessarily in the interest of health, wholesomeness . . . I try not to lend energy to building grotesqueries, depicting morbid relationships, dramatizing perversity."[17]

The next important riddler-joker who provides the question-answer is the Veteran, whom Invisible Man encounters in the Golden Day. More forbidden territory, the Golden Day is the place where local inmates of an insane asylum are allowed to have their day to visit the girls. Invisible Man can't believe that these men are lunatics. "Sometimes it appeared as though they played some vast and complicated game with me and the rest of the school folk, a game whose goal was laughter and whose rules and subtleties I could never grasp." Again riddles that contain the answer. The Veteran, a patient who had formerly been a doctor, says of the Invisible Man: "He's invisible, a walking personification of the Negative, the most perfect achievement of your dreams, sir! The mechanical man!" It is a riddle and prophecy of what the Invisible Man will discover in his boomerang journey. Later, after he is expelled from the school for taking Mr. Norton to the wrong territory, he again encounters the Veteran, who gives him some advice: "Play the game, but raise the ante, my boy. . . . You're hidden right out in the open—that is, you would be if you only realized it. They wouldn't see you because they don't expect you to know anything, since they believe they've taken care of that." This is the same advice his grandfather gave, reworded and viewed from another angle, by a man who is already altering his reality through improvisation, and has an ironic awareness of "the joke that lies between appearance and reality."[18]

Ralph Ellison too is subtly ironic about his use of folklore: "I use folklore in my work not because I am a Negro, but because writers like Eliot and Joyce made me conscious of the literary value of my folk inheritance. My cultural background, like that of most Americans, is dual (my middle name, sadly enough, is Waldo). I knew the trickster Ulysses just as early as I knew the wily rabbit of Negro American lore."[19] And certainly the riddle is one of the folkloric forms that lies at the back of literary tradition in thematic structures, plots and symbolism: riddles of character and circumstance, identity and illusion, nightmare and reality— the human ambiguities.[20] For example, James Joyce's major writings are tremendous riddle-books. Joyce too is fond of "the riddling questions" that "provoke riddling or ambiguous answers."[21] Ellison's methods of answering the riddles resemble Joyce's. Like Joyce, he will present abstractions first, then parables and concrete examples from Invisible Man's experience, episodes of symbolic history which parallel the unseen in American identity. Ellison has discussed this in *Shadow and Act:* "Obviously the experiences of Negroes—slavery, the grueling and continuing fight for full citizenship since Emancipation, the stigma of color, the enforced alienation which constantly knifes into our natural identification with our country—have not been that of white Americans . . . [Negroes'] sense of reality springs, in part, from an American experience which most white men not only have not had, but one with which they are reluctant to identify themselves even when presented in forms of the imagination."[22] Thus American reality too is a riddle of riddles, and again a "land of masking jokers."[23]

After Invisible Man violates the codes and is forced to leave the school, he loses what identity he thought he had and enters a world of reality, dream, and nightmare. He must rediscover who he is—his name, his history. A speech he makes to prevent an old black couple from being evicted brings him to the attention of the Brotherhood and Brother Jack, another riddler and masked joker. Jack says, "History has been born in your brain." Invisible Man, named by the Brotherhood (though the reader never discovers the name) and given an identity by them, becomes an orator. However, he breaks with the Brotherhood when he discovers that even to them he is invisible—an abstraction—as are the people in Harlem. They disapprove of his taking "personal responsibility" and we are reminded again of the processes of discovery in Richard Wright's break with the Communist party. "I had spent a third of my life traveling from the place of my birth to the North just to talk freely, to escape the pressure of fear. And now I was facing fear again . . . I was already afraid that the stories I had written would not fit into the new, official mood."[24]

The "race question" for the Brotherhood has been a matter of political expediency, easily supplanted by the "woman question." In attempting to use his grandfather's advice, Invisible Man tries to defeat the Brotherhood by yessing them. But the yessing boomerangs—another riddle-joke—and spurs a race riot in Harlem, which the Brotherhood, it seems, had wanted all along. Each solution to one riddle—each revelation—is followed by a contradiction, raised to a broader (and often more dangerous) context. Invisible Man realizes that the riot was part of the Committee's plans all along, and himself a tool. "A tool just at the very moment when I had thought myself free. By pretending to agree I *had* indeed agreed."

Like everything in this book, its riddles can be funny, dangerous, and sad at the same time. There is a connection here with African American comedic tradition in which the jokes contain such pluralistic levels of possibility. That riddler Ras the Exhorter becomes Ras the Destroyer is one of these multiple riddles. Ras, who sees liberation as separation, views Invisible Man as a traitor and during the Harlem Riot seeks to destroy him. In a strange transformation scene, Ras becomes an object of mirth to a group of men who re-tell his story while the hero overhears. "They were laughing outside the hedge and leaving and I lay in a cramp, wanting to laugh and yet knowing that Ras was not funny, or not only funny, but dangerous as well, wrong but justified, crazy and yet coldly sane . . . Why did they make it seem funny, *only* funny?" But this is the nature of the riddle-joke at the edge of danger, the comic and serious jammed into the same space, in the same way it does in the blues, which Ellison has called a "tragi-comic" form. But as a form of seeing it also enables us to penetrate the mysterious and familiar—"the imagery of the blues conceived as visual form, image, pattern and symbol."[25] This sort of jamming occurs in surrealism as well, and the Ras scenes are surrealistic in their unexpected juxtapositions.

Ras is a "fantastic image" and so is Tod Clifton, a member of the Brotherhood, who seems at first to be a heroic black figure like Delany's Blake. But after the fight with Ras, attempting to answer his own riddle, he "plunges outside of history" to be discovered in a contradictory scene selling Sambo dolls. The Brotherhood dismisses him as a traitor, but Invisible Man acknowledges that the question is not so simple: "He was a man and a Negro; a man and a brother; a man and a traitor, as you say; then he was a dead man, and alive or dead he was jam-full of contradictions. So full that he attracted half of Harlem to come out and stand in the sun in answer to our call. So what is a traitor?" One is reminded of jazz great Charlie Parker in *Shadow and Act,* whose character holds (and wholes) contradictions and paradoxes in one and the same space.[26] We must ask ourselves whether Tod can be a traitor and a hero at the same time. Is this not only one of the paradoxical jokes that can be answered only in a contradiction, in a solution that maintains the contradiction? Perhaps any whole personality is like any surrealistic painting, a road only to unexpected juxtapositions. Anna Balakian says that one characteristic of the surrealistic image is its contradictory nature: it creates a phenomenon that appears impossible. To illustrate this Balakian quotes from "Tiki" by André Breton: "Je t'aime à la face des mers / Rouge comme l'oeuf quand il est vert."[27]

The chameleonic Rinehart is another riddler the Invisible Man meets on his journey. The encounter teaches Invisible Man that there are two kinds of invisibility—one that is imposed and one that is chosen and used. To escape from Ras the Destroyer, Invisible Man dons a hat and dark glasses and inadvertently assumes the identity of Rinehart—a preacher, gambler, lover, numbers runner, a symbol of chaos and "dangerous freedom." "And sitting there trembling I caught a glimpse of the possibilities posed by Rinehart's multiple personalities and turned away. It was too vast and confusing to contemplate." Rinehart crystallizes the meaning of seen/unseen, inner/outer through his fluid character and multiple identities, and Invisible Man discovers through him that "The world in which we lived was without boundaries. A vast seething hot world of fluidity" and possibility. He also discovers another way of using his grandfather's advice, as Ellison tells us in *Shadow and Act:* "The final act of *Invisible Man* is not that of a concealment in darkness in the Anglo-Saxon connotation of the word, but that of a voice issuing its little wisdom out of the substance of its own inwardness—after having undergone a transformation from ranter to writer. If, by the way, the hero is pulling a 'darky art' in this, he is not a smart man playing dumb. For the novel, his memoir, is one long, loud rant, howl and laugh. Confession, not concealment, is his mode."[28]

After Invisible Man's escape and descent "inward" into the "hole," he has a dream that frees him of illusion. The dream also functions as a riddle-solution: "How DOES IT FEEL TO BE FREE OF ILLUSION." Invisible Man says that in spite of the dream he is whole.

Perhaps it would be good to stop here—to slip into this break and look around at the meaning of hibernation and going underground. How is it a descent inward, and how does it make the hero whole? A good parallel is the central and revealing scene in *Don Quijote*[29]—another great tragicomic novel. Miguel de Cervantes's hero also descends into a cave, which also represents an answer for the hero, for the very question of its existence is a central riddle in that book. The Cave of Montesinos chapter in *Don Quijote* about his going underground is a transitional episode in Don Quijote's search for himself. Sancho, who has himself been transformed in this wonderful story, upon their return to their village expresses the philosophical significance of Don Quijote's whole journey when he says, "viene vencedor de sí mismo" (he returns a self-conqueror). Don Quijote's victory is "el mayor vencimiento que desearse puede" (the greatest conquest one can wish for), and the Cave of Montesinos can then be seen as the hero's descent into himself in his aim to conquer himself.

Don Quijote has throughout the book played with his own possibility and the possibility of others. There have been times when he thought he "controlled his own story," only to discover that others controlled it. Don Quijote, like all the people he has encountered (and like Invisible Man), is made up of his "actualities and potentialities" (Jean Toomer, *Essentials*). By the introduction of the dream of the cave, which remains a question (which can only be answered by a contradiction?) and thereby permits the author to maintain a tension between the dream and the real, the actual and the potential, Cervantes amplifies the theme of potentiality. In a like manner Ellison amplifies *his* theme of possibility through Invisible Man's dream and going underground. In both books, reality itself often appears as dream—hasn't Ras also really "invented reality"? And others in their retellings have reinvented it. In escaping from his underground, Invisible Man will seek to invent his own reality. The Cave of Montesinos chapter in *Don Quijote* reveals the hero's imagination in action; dream, reality, biography, myth, folklore blend to form Don Quijote's (and likewise Invisible Man's) sense of possibility and destiny. Those in the dream *see* Don Quijote, recognize him as the knight he has made himself. He is not invisible to them, and it is this episode—this going underground—which allows him to continue to believe in himself when others do not. Those in the cave acknowledge his rights and responsibilities and the dream/reality therefore enables him to have some control over time and space/place. Similarly, going underground should also be read in *Invisible Man* as a transitional episode before the ascent, which will take place outside the framework of the book.

There are of course some negative aspects of the Cave of Montesinos chapter—or perhaps not negative but paradoxical. It is not necessary to discuss all of those here, except to say that Don Quijote must now see and test reality in a new way. Mainly, the Cave of Montesinos marks a crucial stage in the process of Don Quijote's self-recognition and self-creation into a truer and better self, by combining the good qualities of himself and Sancho and honoring the requirements for truth that both need, in each other's acts of will and imagination. In contrast, though underground, Invisible Man is whole, and we feel he will emerge whole.[30]

In the epilogue, Invisible Man attempts finally to come to terms with his grandfather's advice, his riddle. Again, the question-answer is supplied. In his ruminations, Invisible Man first asks whether his grandfather meant that we should say yes to the country's "principle"—the basic truths on which it was founded—rather than its men of violence. Then he asks: "Or did he mean that we had to take the responsibility for all of it, for the men as well as the principle, because we were the heirs who must use the principle because no other fitted our needs? Not for the power or the vindication, but because we, with the given circumstance of our origin, could only thus find transcendence?"

The book itself, Invisible Man's memoir, exists as a riddle and the riddle is carried to its conclusion/introduction and referred to the reader: "Who knows but that on the lower frequencies, I speak for you?" This is the book's final riddle which the reader himself must answer. Its inclusion makes the book both circular and open-ended.

Invisible Man is a multistructure of oral traditional forms—jazz and jazz solos, blues, oral storytelling, sermon, oratory, ballad. *Invisible Man* has also amplified the usually succinct form of the riddle as a way of complicating the form and pattern of the novel and the main character's attempts to deal with contradictory character and reality, ironic and ambivalent humanity, as he discovers the nature of his dilemma, the range of his own possibilities, and the possibilities of his world; as he attempts to take the risks of being human—as Ellison would say, being "stubbornly human."

13

Blues and Spirituals: Dramatic and Lyrical Patterns in Alice Walker's The Third Life of Grange Copeland

The narrative strategy of *The Third Life of Grange Copeland* (1970) is to alternate between blues and spirituals. The style and scenes swing from the actual blues conditions and thwarted potential of character and relationships to moments of transcendence—the future orientation, direction, and optimism of the spiritual motif. These oral forms provide dramatic and tonal patterns for the novel and its emotional and thematic content and progression from blues to spiritual, opening to hope and possibility.

Grange Copeland is the principal character whose "three lives" we experience as he travels the range from blues of the spirit to spiritual purpose. And when we first meet Brownfield, Grange's son, we meet his potential. We like the little boy, through whose eyes we see the novel's beginning; but the blues, hovering below the waterline of possibility, quickly overcomes the music of the spirit. After a visit from his cousins from the North, he feels how small is his knowledge, restricted to farming, compared to their "dazzling information" of automobiles, street lights, paved walks, and escalators. "They bewildered, excited and hurt him. Still, he missed them; they were from a world he had never seen."[1]

Brownfield's viewpoint controls the first chapter; his curiosity and openness is visible. But the realm of spiritual potential changes—into what Alice Walker will later call "the harmony of despair." The narrative prose reproduces the sad harmony through monotonous repetitions, vivid and tangible blues imagery, and "worrying lines" in Walker's description of Grange's tetter and tomato sores and the "languid slow order of jobs" he must do: ". . . he became fond of the calm, slow patience of the cow . . ." Brownfield's life is entangled in this particular time, place, and circumstances, in this specific socioeconomic cat's cradle which Walker vigorously describes with the judgment of event, detail, and ripe imagery. But from the beginning we come to understand Brownfield, to see things through his eyes, in a world that is jostled by Hurston's and Wright's worlds. The brutality and starkness of Wright elbows the round, vivid, metaphorical intensity one finds in the works of Zora Neale Hurston and Jean Toomer, two earlier writers whom Walker admires and celebrates. But this is not the insulated, protected world of Janie's childhood in *Their Eyes Were Watching God,* no carefree imaginings, no images of flowering pear trees or limitless horizons; even Brownfield's occasional daydreams are problematic, because the ideals of the American dream exclude him: the mansion, the chauffeured car, the model wife and children—"two children, a girl and a boy . . . showering him with kisses." But it is a strange and ambivalent daydream: "The face of Brownfield's wife and that of the cook constantly interchanged . . . his dreaming self could not make up its mind."

This depiction of "dreaming selves" in media metaphors is the standard movie image ideal which other black writers have employed to complicate character, from Richard Wright's *Native Son* to Toni Morrison's *The Bluest Eye* to the poetic themes of Amiri Baraka, Michael S. Harper, and others. In different ways these writers conclude that African American character must assert its wholeness against the reductive and dangerous imagery of the movies. Michael S. Harper's "Grandfather" poem is an explicit case in point:

> In 1915 my grandfather's
> neighbors surrounded his house
> near the dayline he ran
> on the Hudson
> in Catskill, NY
> and thought they'd burn
> his family out
> in a movie they'd just seen
> and be rid of its kind:
> the death of a lone black
> family is *the Birth*
> *of a Nation,*
> or so they thought . . .
>
> I see him as he buys galoshes
> for his railed yard near Mineo's
> metal shop, where roses jump
> as the el circles his house
> toward Brooklyn, where his rain fell;
> and I see cigar smoke in his eyes,

chocolate Madison Square Garden chews
he breaks on his set teeth,
stiched up after cancer,
the great white nation immovable
as his weight wilts
and he is on a porch
that won't hold my arms,
or the legs of the race run
forwards, or the film
played backwards on his grandson's eyes.[2]

The poet must "see" his grandfather and remake his own "image of kin" against the movie's version, juxtaposing African American character and American movie history. D. W. Griffith's film was praised for its technical innovations and discoveries, its camera positions, lighting and editing techniques, yet it set images and stereotypes that persisted in the European American imagination and movie depictions. Harper's poem portrays scenes that were enacted numerous times after the movie was shown, its images played backwards and forwards. It depicts, without wonder, the ambivalent interchanging of selves and the derangements of movie images. Note also the poem's own technical innovations in its use and absence of transitions; one has the sense of a film moved rapidly forward (or backward) blending and juxtaposing disparate images.

The beginning of *The Third Life of Grange Copeland* can be compared to Book I of Wright's *Native Son* entitled "Fear," in its predominant mood and feelings, the difficult, ambivalent, masked and shifting personalities. There is the problematic relationship between Brownfield's mother and father, a blues relationship in its contradictions: "Depression always gave way to fighting, as if fighting preserved some part of the feeling of being alive. It was confusing to realize but not hard to know that they loved each other."

The beginning of *The Third Life*, is intended to mirror the beginning of Richard Wright's *Native Son*. This assumption seems correct, because Walker later challenges (or modifies) Wright's theory of accountability in African American relationships as it is fleshed out in his own blues novel; we might therefore look for some parallels in scenes, literary allusions, key metaphors and phrases. As noted, both books begin with tension and confrontation within the family. Unlike Wright, Walker maintains her focus on the intraracial dilemma and complex personalities; but like Wright she does give us a sense of the social, political, historical, and economic forces and determinants. Yet she insists on paying attention to the African Americans as whole personalities (distinct from her phrase "survival whole"). She acknowledges the violence—physical and spiritual—that Wright described, and agrees with some of his assessments of the confusions and interferences in American reality. In an interview on National Public Radio Morning Edition Series (1981) she commented that several generations of poverty, racism, and the kind of social existence and struggle for survival we see in this novel "can corrupt human feelings." Energy and will can often turn against oneself and those close to one. In such circumstances, notes Walker, "the oppressed join the oppressors in oppressing themselves." It is necessary to grow beyond that, to liberate oneself from self-destructiveness. "I wanted to make black people more committed to themselves," says Walker. This acknowledged message to black people diverges from Wright's protest tradition, which addresses its essential messages to whites. The poet Etheridge Knight also spoke of the necessary transition from the protest tradition as it involved the writers of the Black Arts movement of the sixties: "Now any Black man who masters the techniques of his particular art form, who adheres to the white aesthetic, and who directs his work towards a white audience is, in one sense, protesting. And implicit in the art of protest is the belief that a change will be forthcoming once the masters are aware of the protestor's 'grievance' (the very word connotes begging, supplication to the gods). Only when that belief has faded and protesting ends, will Black art begin."[3]

In Walker's work the precedents of Wright and Hurston gain a sense of a formed whole. She maintains the intimate focus of Hurston, the perspective that Hurston restored within the African American community, and cultivates Hurston's interest in psychology, motivation, human complexity and possibility; but hers is a more violent and teratologic South than Hurston's, a South of social and economic terrors that still do not cause us to shift our attention from the black people themselves. Walker's book has got what James Baldwin in *Notes of a Native Son* (1955) said that Wright's book lacked: a "sense of Negro life as a continuing and complex reality." And Baldwin's own works, especially his novel *Just above My Head* (1979), crystallize this same complexity and same shift of our thoroughgoing attention. As one of his characters says: "When was the last time we sat down at this table and talked about white people? The only reason we talking now is because it looks like they've decided to desegregate this and desegregate that. I hope they do. It might make life a little easier for you and a little better for them . . . But just remember—it don't so much matter what they mean to do: it matters what we mean to do."[4] Baldwin too explores relations among blacks themselves. He doesn't ignore the social and historical realities, but they don't take precedence over individuals (nor do conversation about white people and their doings take over the dialogue). Black people form the significant center; they are not simply channels through which we discover "the ways of white folks." Baldwin keeps black people and their multiple complexities—including confusing loves—front and center. And as with Walker, forms from oral tradition are used to reinforce the spirit of this achievement.

In *The Third Life of Grange Copeland,* blues repetitions exist on the multilevels of narrative, dialogue, word choice and the overall rhythm and pace of the work, its plot structure, complications and resolutions of relationships. For instance, certain authoritative-submissive relationships echo each other: Brownfield's fear of his father, Margaret's fear and submission to Grange, Grange's fear and submission to the white man Shipley: "Their looks were a combination of small sly smiles and cowed, embarrassed desperation."

Grange, unable to bear the circumstances that he cannot change, leaves; Brownfield misinterprets his father's desertion and general behavior as a lack of love. Grange comes into Brownfield's bedroom, bends as if to touch or kiss him, but doesn't—another confusion, another difficult recognition of love. Octavio Paz in *Labyrinth of Solitude* has spoken of hermeticism in the Mexican character and the psychology of the mask, which seems to be also present in this episode: "Hermeticism is one of the several recourses of our suspicion and distrust. It shows that we instinctively regard the world around us to be dangerous. This reaction is justifiable if one considers what our history has been and the kind of society we have created . . . But this attitude, legitimate enough in its origins, has become a mechanism that functions automatically. Our response to sympathy and tenderness is reserve, since we cannot tell whether those feelings are genuine or simulated . . . Any opening in our defenses is a lessening of our manliness."[5] This dangerous hermeticism applies to Wright's description of Bigger Thomas: "He knew that the moment he allowed himself to feel to its fullness how they lived, the shame and misery of their lives, he would be swept out of himself with fear and despair. So he held toward them an attitude of iron reserve; he lived with them, but behind a wall, a curtain."[6]

Brownfield's life, after his father's desertion and his mother's suicide, becomes a repetition of his father's. For a brief "spiritual respite," Brownfield's and Mem's relationship opens up to some possibilities, the potential wholeness after a wearying journey: ". . . she was so good to him, so much what he needed, that her body became his shrine and he kissed it endlessly, shamelessly, lovingly, and celebrated its magic with flowers and dancing."

But again, forces, choices of will, *something* thwarts the transcendence and we descend again from the spiritual plateau to the blues valley. Brownfield's relationship with Mem repeats Grange's relationship with Margaret. The same questions are raised, questions of guilt and responsibility, of manhood and womanhood, pride and personality contending with conditions. Depressed by continuous and mounting debts, he thinks of suicide. He accuses Mem of betraying him with white men: "a charge she tearfully and truthfully denied. And when he took her in his drunkenness and in the midst of his own foul accusations she wilted and accepted him in total passivity and blankness."

In describing the conditions in which these characters must live, Walker asks the questions of responsibility which Wright answered in *Native Son,* preparing her own way for her own answer. We must account for the weight of economic and social factors in people's own acts of choice and will. The same problem comes up in Walker's short story "The Child Who Favored Daughter": how are "innocence and guilt . . . further complicated by questions of race and color"?[7] Here the questions center on Brownfield's ego, and how his attempts to shame Mem are tied up in the question (riddle) of manhood. Brownfield seems to justify his harsh treatment of Mem on the basis of his manhood or his idea of manhood. And many of the women in Walker's early works become what the men imagine them to be: it is a frequent theme in black women's fiction. It is Walker's "outcast" women who struggle against males' truncating images of who they are and might become, in the same way the males must contend with whites' truncating and obliterating metaphors for their humanity and possibility. Mem, once a school teacher, burns her books and begins to speak as Brownfield feels a "nigger" should speak. After he succeeds in humbling Mem—or she acquiesces in his abridgement of her—Brownfield returns to his affair with Josie, Mem's aunt and Grange's former lover, a blues character in her own right, her own spiritual potential betrayed. Later, when Grange returns to Baker County, Brownfield discovers that he is still afraid of his father. Grange and Josie marry.

The plot moves through harmonies of despair, incantatory blues experiences that sound like litanies, as the couple "move from one sharecropper's cabin to another." "Each time . . . Each time . . . Each time,"

Walker repeats, compounding Mem's despair in concrete, dispiriting images. "Her mildness became stupor; then her stupor became horror, desolation and, at last, hatred." Later we see Brownfield's own difficulties. We learn that he feels his life has no possibility of choice. At such moments we share his sense of a life that is destined and fated; that courage is in acceptance. Yet at other times there is the sense of spiritual possibility. But Walker gives only cursory attention to Brownfield's perspective, and mostly when it impinges on Mem's. Redemptive prose welcomes the birth of Ruth. Redemptive prose follows Mem when she tries to transform their conditions, to make things better by signing a lease for a house in town, deciding on her own to move—to overcome that oppressive reality through willful action. She threatens one of Brownfield's ideas of manhood with a gun, then moves to town. There is a sense of progress, but Brownfield is dissatisfied despite better conditions, because the move was not his decision but Mem's: "he complained about everything often and loudly, secretly savoring thoughts of how his wife would 'come down' when he placed her once more in a shack." There is the comedown, and Brownfield murders Mem.

Finally, when Grange returns from the North, reborn, with a sense of his own (and his granddaughter Ruth's) fulfillment, we enter the spiritual mode again. With these spiritual sequences there is a sense of freedom, of self-determined transcendent will, of full humanity and "survival whole." Survival whole is what Grange wants for Ruth: "Survival was not everything. *He* had survived. But to survive *whole* was what he wanted for Ruth." And it is what Walker wants: "You ask about 'preoccupation.' I am preoccupied with the spiritual survival, the survival *whole* of my people," says Walker in *Interviews with Black Writers.*[8]

After Brownfield murders Mem, Ruth goes to live with her grandfather and Josie. The relationship between Ruth and Grange is superb in its scenes and metaphors of wholeness; it is one of the full, rich, wholesome, spiritual sections. In their learning sessions, Grange tries to teach her about history and what he considers the proper attitude to have toward whites. There is blues humor in the tone of the narrative and in Ruth's pithy responses to Grange's eagerness for her to know. Grange, averse to whites, has even forbidden Ruth to play with white children. She asks why.

> "One," Grange said, "they stole you from Africa."
> "*Me?*" she asked.
> "Be quiet," he said. "Two. They brought you here in chains."

"Hummm?" she murmured. Looking at her slightly rusty but otherwise unmarked ankles.

"Three. They beat you every day in slavery and didn't feed you nothing but weeds . . ."

"Like we give Dilsey?" she interrupted.

Ruth's ideas about history and heroism are influenced by the imagination and mythology of TV Westerns where the good guys always win. She says, "But you're a good man Grange." Walker wants us to understand that heroism is often contradictory. Carlos Fuentes in *Where the Air Is Clear* also challenges the simplistic Manichean heroic ideal. "What wins is not always good [and] not always evil." The hero can be the one who has been defeated, if the defeat is regenerative, purgative, and leads to wisdom as it does in Fuentes's book. Says Manuel Zamacona, "Mexico's defeat . . . leads us to truth, to values, to knowledge."[9] Floyd Horowitz, speaking of Ellison, said "Yet defeat is a realization and a realization is a victory of perspective."[10] Walker, like Ellison (and Wright), is working here, I think, with the chameleonic American riddle-joke whose only solution might be a contradiction, or "maintain the contradiction."[11]

Grange has known defeat but he has also gained a kind of freedom, a self-sufficiency that he has chosen—apart from whites. There is duplicity though in his relationship with Josie, for in order to achieve that necessary freedom and "security," he has had to make use of her and her money. "Josie had thought it was love for her that made him such a seeker of privacy."

Ruth's claim that murder is the unthinkable crime prefaces a flashback sequence which continues to allude to Wright, at the same time that it marks Walker's divergence from Wright's assertion that racism is the determinant even in the most intimate relationships between blacks. Wright's theory is concentrated in the following excerpt from *Native Son*:

"You know where the white folks live?"

"Yeah," Gus said, pointing eastward. "Over across the 'line'; over there on Cottage Grove Avenue."

"Naw; they don't," Bigger said.

"What yo mean?" Gus asked, puzzled. "Then, where do they live?"

"Right down here in my stomach," he said.[12]

A flashback of Grange in New York tells of the murder (self-murder) of a white woman—like Bigger's, no premeditated intentional murder.

In fact, Grange had attempted to save the woman, but she refused his help (he was only a "nigger") even to save her life, and drowned in an icy lake. However, Grange, like Bigger, accepts the act as murder, and accepts the moral responsibility of it. For Grange (as for Bigger) this was a first glimpse of the white as a human being caught in her own blues relationship, with a soldier who got her pregnant, gave her money, rejected and deserted her. When the woman sees Grange, she dons her mask of fortitude, refuses his pity, refuses to see his corresponding humanity. After the "murder" he reacts with violence, fighting whites, calling for hate; finally "growing beyond that," he withdraws from them into his own sanctuary. Perhaps this is a parallel with what Wright has called a "defense of indifference": "For the time being, he would withdraw completely from [whites], find a sanctuary, make a life that need not acknowledge them, and be always prepared, with his life, to defend it, to protect it, to keep it from whites, inviolate." But Grange does not want to spoil Ruth's innocence or her love for him by telling her about his past. Ruth knows him as redeemed, as a reborn man. She does not know the cruelties that he has had to take or give.

Other passages also parallel and contrast with Wright's scenes. In the jail scene and the discussions of motive and choice, Brownfield feels an unseen force influencing his life, comparable to the unseen force behind Bigger's doings. But when Brownfield does discover a sense of "mobile, self-determined will," it is not directed toward self-creation or redemption but to plans of revenge against Grange. The greatest revenge would be to take Ruth from Grange, because he knows they love each other. Personally, Brownfield feels absolved from any guilt in his treatment of Mem because "something stood behind his cruelty to her" (in a point-blank reference to Wright, it is something like Bigger's white folks in his stomach).

Walker finally challenges (or modifies) openly, through Grange's speech to Brownfield, the idea of racism behind everything, and points to Blacks' own responsibility for their souls: "when they [whites] got you thinking that they're to blame for *every*thing they have you thinking they's some kind of gods!" Areas of choice and will exist in spite of circumstance. There are intimate places inside where whites cannot come. There is the possibility of wholeness and full humanity, of spiritual care, of taking care of one's own spiritual survival, the "survival whole."

The book's resolution brings a sense of unevenness. New characters are hastily introduced near the end—a young black couple, Helen and Quincy, involved in the Civil Rights movement. Because Brownfield has legal claim to her, in order to secure Ruth, Grange must kill Brownfield—and then wait himself to be killed by the white authorities. In this part of the book it seems as if the writer, coming to the end, were rushing to complete it. But this sense of rhythmic speed, of strong run-on, also directs the reader toward the future that lies outside of the text. The haste of this open-ended structure points us out again, away from the blues present; and what appears to be a flaw is not arbitrary but, like the spiritual, becomes a metaphor for the mobile, open resolution. Sharon Spencer speaks of this type of mobile construct, which in Walker's case is inspired by the open structures of oral forms: "the intention . . . is clearly to defy the convention of the 'rounded-off' ending and to insinuate an action that continues to develop outside, or beyond, the novel itself."[13] Ruth's quest for wholeness will take place beyond the novel. The young black couple introduced at the end of the book also represent a continuous possibility of spiritual redemption, and a redemption of the earlier blues relationships between black men and women. The open end points to this spiritual restoration, and is again oral in its root structure.

Walker thus moves us away from "Richard Wright's blues." *The Third Life of Grange Copeland* resolves as spiritual because it directs us to the future, from Grange to Ruth. The movement from the sense of the blues or harmonies of despair to the sense of amplified possibilities of her characters in the spiritual prose gives Walker's novel its dramatic and lyrical patterns. As in Toomer's "Karintha" or Michael S. Harper's "Uplift," here again oral tradition influences the "spirit and substance of action itself."[14] In *Shadow and Act,* Ellison said this about the blues, a blues in which the spiritual is also contained: "they at once express both the agony of life and the possibility of conquering it through sheer toughness of spirit." Grange's blues have been thus transformed: his going underground has been converted into Ruth's "will to confront the world" (Ellison's phrases), "a triumph of spirit."

14

Freeing the Voice: Ernest Gaines's
The Autobiography of Miss Jane Pittman

In *The Autobiography of Miss Jane Pittman* (1971)[1] Ernest Gaines realizes the potential of voice that was only suggested by Zora Neale Hurston in *Their Eyes Were Watching God*. As Robert B. Steptoe observed: "Hurston has created the illusion that Janie has achieved her voice . . . but . . . Hurston's insistence on having Janie's tale—her personal history in and as a literary form—told by an omniscient third person, rather than by a first-person narrator, implies that Janie has not really won her voice and self after all—that her author (who is, quite likely, the omniscient narrating voice) cannot see her way clear to giving Janie her voice outright."[2] It is Gaines, I think, who responds to the call (Steptoe's phrase) and has Miss Jane "win her voice and self" by telling her own whole story.

The novelist Barry Beckham has linked Gaines with the African writers' use of oral tradition as well as with the American writers' "fascination with folk speech": "Gaines's sure grasp of the elements of Louisiana bayou country dialect is not simply a natural extension of his familiarity with folk speech peculiar to that geographic area. The quality of voice which is the stylistic hallmark of Miss Jane Pittman's autobiography surely has a relationship to that vernacular propensity recurring throughout American literature since Mark Twain . . . I would like to suggest too that Gaines's cherishing of the oral tradition brings to mind the premium that his ethnic counterpart, the black African novelist, places on the primacy of the word. Reflecting a cultural tradition which sustains the transmission by voice of a voluminous body of legends, proverbs, songs, and stories as well as events demanding verbal facility, the African novelist—more naturally than the black American novelist—has long drawn from this oral tradition in ordering his fictional world . . . Gaines is not consciously working out of the African tradition, but his novel sustains an oral literary tradition whose roots may be more African than American, more Tutuola than Twain."[3]

Ernest Gaines may also be discussed as a writer whose black speech breaks out of the narrative frame, the story within a story. And because Miss Jane tells her whole story, Gaines extends the innovations of Hurston to *gain* the emotional, intellectual, and experiential range of the language in narrative and exposition as well as dialogue and thought processes. The language explores the dynamics of character, psychology, and social and personal relationships to reveal truths of personality and society. Miss Jane, like Hurston's Janie, is a complex, intelligent, articulate woman; unlike Janie, she tells her whole story, freeing self and voice in the way that Robert Steptoe has commended. She has a quality N. Scott Momaday ascribed to storytelling: "whole and consummate being."[4] In addition, Gaines strengthens the link between storyteller and audience by introducing the black historian as a character in the prologue. This validates the folk or oral historian, the relationship between auto-biography and history, and the autobiographical approach to history. (From the point of view of literary tradition, oral history is questionable.) In "Miss Jane and I" Gaines speaks of women like Miss Jane. Then he speaks of Miss Jane: "She knows much—she has lived long . . . Truth to Miss Jane is what she remembers. Truth to me is what people like Miss Jane remember. Of course, I go to the other sources, the newspapers, magazines, the books in the libraries—but I also go back and listen to what Miss Jane and folks like her have to say."[5] History is not background, but influencing force in character and event.

Similar freeings of voice occurred in other literary traditions, where it was necessary "to speak in a new way."[6] In Jamaican literature, for instance, there has been an exact parallel—in fact, the frame was shed earlier than in the African American fictional tradition. In his article "Discovery" Gerald Moore writes about the new speech of V. S. Reid's 1947 novel *New Day:* "The importance of *New Day* does not rest only on its central concern with Jamaica and its people. The same new confidence that dictated its theme extends into the style itself, for the whole book is couched in the form of a long monologue by the aged narrator as the crowds celebrating their new measure of freedom surge under his window. Hence it is written throughout in a style approximating to Jamaican country dialect of the mid-nineteenth century . . . To write an entire book in this despised dialect, albeit spoken habitually by nine-tenths of the population, and in off-moments by the rest, was radical indeed." The author of the novel uses transcription techniques which do not slow or distort the language of the people, but render it whole and visually intact. Says Moore, "Reid has in effect composed a *musical script* (my italics) with dialect features." In reproducing the dialect as any language given literary uses, Reid gives wings to it: "it was with *New Day* that a new generation of West Indian writers began the task of breaking free from the colonial cocoon and flying with wings of their own, in a distinctly tropical sky."[7]

American literature itself was involved in a similar freeing of voice from the dominant voice of Europe. John Neal, a novelist of the early nineteenth century, was among those who bemoaned an American literature with "hardly so much as one true Yankee phrase . . . It would not do for me to imitate anybody. Nor would it do for my country. Who would care for the American Addison where he could have the English?"[8] There are always those to call literary change "decadence"; one's sonorous music is often another's jagged noise. But before Neal, Thomas Jefferson had also expressed similar sentiments regarding American language that have applied here. Jefferson had been reproved by the *Edinburgh Review* for using the word "belittle" in *Notes on Virginia* (1784). He was unperturbed: "Had the preposterous idea of fixing the language been adopted by our Saxon ancestors, of Peirce Plowman, of Chaucer, of Spenser, the progress of ideas must have stopped with that of the language . . . what do we not owe to Shakespeare for the enrichment of the language, by his free and magical creation of words? [To be sure] uncouth words will sometimes be offered; but the public will judge them, and receive or reject, as sense or sound shall suggest."[9] He does not mean the English public.

There are clear and important parallels in European American and African American literatures, each moving toward its own literary independence through the use of oral modes. Like their European American counterparts, African American writers are concerned with the literary potentiality of their linguistic heritage. Their self-sanctioning explorations are not simply "imitative experiments,"[10] but produce veridical literature "having freed itself" and "saying only what it wanted to say and as it wanted to say it."[11]

Similarly, Gaines's freeing of African American voice through its colloquial base, "oratorical modes," and sense of "extemporaneous speech" and "artful sufficiency"[12] had to be achieved before more intricate structures could be developed in this literature. In another arena, Eudora Welty has worked at freeing the European American Southern vernacular, as seen in her popular "Why I Live at the P.O."; another example is Peter Taylor's "Spinster's Tale," a frequently anthologized story. Their characters assume a linguistic autonomy as they tell their own whole stories. However again, in these freeings of voices it should be observed that the African American Southern voice and character is framed within the freed European American Southern voice. Here is an example from Welty:

> There was a nigger girl going along on a little wagon right in front.
> "Nigger girl," I says, "come help me haul these things down the hill, I'm going to live in the post office."
> Took her nine trips in her express wagon. Uncle Rondo came out on the porch and threw her a nickel.[13]

Welty and Taylor are being true to the psychology of their Southern characters, their myths and histories, and world view; in the face of such writing, it becomes even more notable that while Gaines frees Miss Jane's voice, he doesn't diminish (or render anonymous) the possibilities of other voices. Even Albert Cluveau, the Cajun villain of the work, is able to control his own story, though it is a brutal and dangerous one. But because Gaines is concerned with "the truth of personality" (Sterling Brown's phrase) he notes the ambiguities and complexities in both the African American and European American voices. Cluveau does not set the ideological pattern for European American behavior, nor does heroic Jane set the ideological pattern for African American behavior. There is the sense of the range and dynamics of personalities in both communities, and theories (social or political) of how people should behave do not restrict the possibilities of relationships, character, or language. Gaines does not restrict the possibilities of the European American voice—which still ranges visibly from the Cluveau's to the Tee Bob's—because he is paying attention to the multiple ranges, varieties, and unpredictabilities of African American voice and character. (In contrast, the containment of the black voice seems the prerequisite of parallel freeings of voice in European American literary traditions.) Gaines is concerned not only with Jane's telling her own story; he is concerned with the full humanity of everyone. Likewise, children are freed in these stories from the restrictive autonomy of adults and we are able to distinguish their voices in vocabulary, selection of event, and character, something not always available in other writings in "Black folk English" (Alice Walker's phrase). John F. Callahan has said something of Ellison that applies well to Gaines and his works and motives here: "For [him] an individual is not wholly defined by history and ideology; always there is some act of will; always possibilities of an unforeseen, unpredictable nature intervene."[14] This is enhanced by the multiple freeings of voice.

It is the techniques of the oral story and the spirit of the "folk creators themselves" (Johnson) that made Gaines's achievement possible. Perhaps oral tradition and Gaines's connection with it accounts for his comfort with first-person narrative, as he points out in an interview with Charles Rowell: "when I start a book in the first-person point of view my characters take over very soon and then carry the story themselves . . . Usually I think of myself as a storyteller."[15]

Gaines has a sure attention to voice. The "I" of oral tradition also seems linked to a concern with a whole African American personality telling his or her own story and controlling the moral perspective of it, the images, the conceptions of value, the selection of events, the dramatic structure and significant conflicts. The oral aspect and the "I" are integral parts of Gaines's story and the storyteller's creative and regenerative energy.

Oral storytelling techniques abound in *The Autobiography of Miss Jane Pittman*. Miss Jane's speech patterns—syntax, vocabulary, pronunciation—are integral. Improvements in dialect transcription techniques add greater flexibility and readability. There is more sense of geographical accuracy and less dependence on orthographic changes and distortions through eye dialect. If Miss Jane pronounces a word a certain way and that pronunciation has a certain resonance or tells us something about the region (and the regional pronunciation), or the personality and sensibility, Gaines will use it, but not for comic effect, quaintness, or picturesqueness. Miss Jane is neither a folk comedian nor a pathetic figure. Her language contributes to rather than detracts from the force of her personality. Beckham lists some of these special words—*Luzana, restrick, Fedjal Goviment, invessagator, 'pending, lectwicity*—and says, "Gaines's purpose is not only to preserve authenticity of speech, but also to cherish the special quality, the fresh attractive novelty, of Southern black folk speech."

The lyricism in Miss Jane's storyteller's voice is achieved through repetition, reminding one again of blues structure, the first line being the "lead line," the rest of the paragraph "worrying the line":

> We didn't know a thing. We didn't know where we was go'n, we didn't know what we was go'n eat when the apples and potatoes ran out, we didn't know where we was go'n sleep that night. If we reached the North, we didn't know if we was go'n stay together or separate. We had never thought about nothing like that, because we had never thought we was go'n ever be free. Yes, we had heard about freedom, we had even talked about freedom, but we never thought we was go'n ever see that day. Even when we knowed the Yankees had come in the State, even when we saw

them marching by the gate we still didn't feel we was go'n ever be free. That's why we hadn't got ourself ready. When the word came down that we was free, we dropped everything and started out.

As in the form of content of the oral story, there are direct comments to the listener; the listener is as present as the storyteller. Sometimes Miss Jane gives advice to the listeners: "I reckoned I done ate much fish round here as anybody. It's good for you—fish. Fish and work. Hard work can kill you, but plain steady work never killed nobody. Steady work and eating plenty fish never killed nobody. Greens good, too. Fish and greens and good steady work. Plenty walking, that's good. People don't walk no more. When you don't walk you don't drink enough water. Good clean water and greens clear out your system."

There are the easy transitions in time that one finds in oral stories, easy shifts in tense—not only in transitions between past and present but in context of the historical past. These transitions help evoke the immediacy of the present moment, where the shift in tense occurs in the same scene, indeed, in the same sentence: "I never did go in the house, I just sat down in my chair on the gallery. I'm sitting there only a minute and here he come. Leaned his fishing pole against the end of the gallery and sat down on the steps."

In telling the story Miss Jane often jumps ahead of time. There are not strict chronological or linear sequences; she anticipates events, offers revelations of episodes before they occur. It is interesting to mention here that Billie Holiday, who would often "stay behind the beat" or jump ahead of it in innovative phrasing, also ordered her autobiography (*Lady Sings the Blues*) this way. In Jane's autobiography, for instance, we are told beforehand what will happen to Ned: "Ned used to write me, send me money all the time, but he never said anything about coming home. Not even he knowed he was coming back here till after he came from that war in Cuba. That war ended in 1898. He came here that next summer. And a year later, almost to the day, Albert Cluveau shot him down." And again: "Two weeks before Ned was killed he gathered us at the river." This anticipation increases the dramatic tension; and though we know what will happen we do not know how it will happen. This same method of dislocating and relocating time and place is used when we are told about Tee Bob's suicide: "Robert thought he didn't have to tell Tee Bob about these things. They were part of life, like the sun and the rain was part of life, and Tee Bob would learn them for himself when he got older. But Tee Bob never did. He killed himself before he learned how he was supposed to live in this world."

Gaines recreates the rhythmic spontaneity of dialogue in progress. One has a sense of the dynamics of real conversation. The ceremony of re-naming is one instance:

> Then somebody said: "My new name Abe Washington. Don't call me Buck no more." We must have been two dozens of us there, and now everybody started changing names like you change hats. Nobody was keeping the same name Old Master had given them. This one would say, "My new name Job." "Job what?" "Just Job." "Nigger, this ain't slavery no more. You got to have two names." "Job Lincoln, then." "Nigger, you ain't no kin to me. I'm Lincoln." "I don't care. I'm still Job Lincoln. Want fight?" Another one would say, "My name Neremiah King." Another one standing by a tree would say, "My new name Bill Moses. No more Rufus."

One could never say of Gaines's dialogue or indeed of the dialogue of most African American writers that they followed this advice from a book on writing techniques: "Some writers read their dialogue out loud to determine whether it sounds like the spoken word should sound. I never do this, although it may work for some. I believe it is sufficient for your dialogue to read—or scan—well, and never mind how it sounds. The reader is not going to read it out loud, and you are creating an illusion of speech."[16] I don't believe Gaines would ever say "Never mind how it sounds," no more than would most writers considerate of oral tradition. Gaines's dialogue throughout has the dynamics of spoken language: "I usually don't have any problems when writing dialogue—whether I'm writing it in the omniscient point of view or the first person."[17] I suspect it is because he *hears* it and because he thinks of himself as a storyteller who communicates with the written word. Even the long speeches, the dramatic monologues of characters, not only read but *speak* well. The whole of the book speaks well.

However, it should be added here that in certain works influenced by oral tradition, dialogue is not always direct but often reported. Since Beckham has mentioned Amos Tutuola in context of oral tradition, I want to quote such a passage from his *The Palm-Wine Drinkard:*

> . . . when the king saw the tiny creature, he called the whole of us to his palace.
> After that, the king asked him who was commanding the cleared-weeds of his field to rise up after the field had been cleared: The tiny creature replied that he was commanding all the weeds to rise up, because the king chose all the creatures of the "Wraith-Island" town but left him out, although he was the smallest among all, but he had the power to command weeds etc. which had been cleared to grow up as if it was not cleared at all.

But the king said that he had just forgotten to choose him with the rest and not because of his small appearance.

Then the king made excuses to him, after that he went away. This was a very wonderful tiny creature.[18]

This reporting is effective in Tutuola because of the wealth of detail, character, and magical event and imagery. Oral traditional influence doesn't always work when it becomes simple telling rather than showing; without the accompanying imaginative control of Tutuola, it could be merely an easy device to relieve the writer of dramatic responsibilities. But this is no worry in Gaines's work.

Descriptions of characters are also presented as if they were spoken. There is the sense of the moment, of the processes—continuity and discontinuity—of awareness. When Miss Jane sees Ned again after years: "I hadn't seen Ned in twenty years, but I knowed it was him the moment I saw him standing on the gallery. Not from the way he looked. He didn't look nothing like he did when he left here for Kansas. He was a great big man now. Powerfully built: broad shoulders, thick neck. I knowed it was him because I felt it was him." The description isn't concluded all at once. New observations are made upon reflection: "A boy had left here, a man had come back. Even his hair was turning gray. But when I looked at Tee Man I saw the resemblance. He was black just like Ned. Ned's teeth, Ned's grin, Ned's kinky hair. Looking at him was like looking at Ned when Ned was that size."

Other elements of the oral traditional storytelling techniques in the overall structure are the episodic patterns, the stories within stories and self-contained stories, and as mentioned, the sense of significant correspondence between storyteller and audience in the mingling of personal and private history and the personalizing of historical moments. Such is the story of Huey Long: "Huey Long came in the year after the high water. Nothing better could 'a happened to the poor black man or the poor white man no matter what they say. Oh, they got all kinds of stories about him now." Later, Miss Jane's voice validates and judges this historical moment. And then Miss Jane goes on with her own story. Truth is what Miss Jane remembers.

Because Gaines has Miss Jane tell her whole story, using many of the essential techniques from oral storytelling tradition, we have the sense of the whole oral traditional genre entering the literature. Instead of a hierarchy of linguistic modes there is an alliance. This is what Baraka achieved in "The Screamers"; in his story, however, jazz was the comprehensive oral genre. Here, the storytelling is the verbal mode, so Gaines avoids the confusion and puzzling meanings of the compressed improvisation jazz scenes. There is the clarity of crystal, the lucidity of obsidian; but both methods are contiguous with oral (and aural) tradition—from the racy precision of the blues to the arabesque jazz cadences. And both writers show directions in which other African American writers may go in modifying the whole text of a story, its form and values.

The text doesn't offer only bits and pieces of Miss Jane's story or mere paraphrases of her thoughts, but her complete voice—her metaphors, her thoughts, her manner—and the dynamics of her whole history and imagination. Gaines has carried us beyond Hurston's illusion of Janie's voice to the full value and reality of Miss Jane's tall-telling.

The freeing of voice seems obvious with the "I" narrator. The question then is how to keep the voice free and still maintain a third-person narrative. I have indicated some efforts at this in Ellease Southerland's *Let the Lion Eat Straw,* but even there the tensions are not resolved fully enough to permit revealing multiple elements of contemporary experience and expression. Southerland fails to achieve a "stable idiom from the vernacular" (Bridgman) and the freeing of "colloquial constituents from their naturalistic bondage" to "further possibilities." This, though it "legitimizes the presence of the colloquial mode," enables the prose to "effloresce into more intricate structures."[1]

In an interview with Mel Watkins in *The New York Times Book Review,* September 11, 1977, Morrison speaks of the texture of the oral tradition: "And sometimes when the language is right . . . I begin to react to the characters who say certain things . . . When the language fits and it's graceful and powerful and like I've always remembered black people's language to be, I'm ecstatic. It always seemed to me that black people's grace has been what they do with language. In Lorrain, Ohio, when I was a child, I went to school with and heard stories of Mexicans, Italians and Greeks, and I listened. I remember their language and a lot of it was marvelous. But when I think of things my mother or father or aunts used to say, it seems the most absolutely striking thing in the world. That's what I try to get into my fiction." Toni Morrison's *Song of Solomon* (1977) demonstrates this grace and power of the oral tradition and moves into more intricate structures.

One way of placing *Song of Solomon* is in the context of the folktale or "tall tale," with the oral storytelling beginning, and the vocabulary, rhythms, and motives of the folktale:

The North Carolina Mutual Life Insurance agent promised to fly from Mercy to the other side of Lake Superior at three o'clock. Two days before the event was to take place he tacked a note on the door of his little yellow house:

> At 3:00 p.m. on Wednesday the 18th of February, 1931, I will take off from Mercy and fly away on my own wings. Please forgive me. I loved you all.
>
> (signed) Robert Smith
> Ins. agent

Mr. Smith didn't draw as big a crowd as Lindbergh had four years earlier—not more than forty or fifty people showed up—because it was already eleven o'clock in the morning, on the very Wednesday he had chosen for his flight, before anybody read the note.[2]

This has the clarity, directness, assurance and double-edged realistic humor of the folktale. In addition, by welding together the vernacular and standard literary prose, Morrison has succeeded in overcoming and resolving our sense of the aesthetic tension that often exists in novels that merely incorporate folkloric elements, or that make use of them in the more obvious correspondences of the first-person narrative, though these too may be intricate, as in the works of Alexis Deveaux, Steve Cannon, Ishmael Reed, and James A. McPherson to name but a few. In *Song of Solomon* two traditions seem to coexist in the same time and space. The oral tradition is lifted out of the early confines of mere comedy and pathos, and given the complex tasks of any articulate, intelligent literary prose.

In addition to style, mood, tone, nature of character and event function in the context and texture of the folktale, deriving from a multitude of narrative and dramatic sources. For instance, throughout *Song of Solomon* there is the sense of the narrator talking to the reader, without, however, intruding into the territory of the novel. Like other story tellers, the speaker, with grace, makes an easy acknowledgment of the reader as hearer or listener; in this there is a kinship with both Gaines's and Tutuola's works. Likewise, the narrative about character backgrounds does not simply sum them up, but has the import of the spoken recollection of the past, a quality of discourse: "They each knew Mr. Smith . . . He never beat anybody up and he wasn't seen after dark, so they thought he was probably a nice man." The others, themselves a part of the audience, become witness to the character. Throughout the novel, various characters become audience-witnesses to other characters' sayings and doings, and often, as here, the narrative rendering possesses the understated blues-humor of the last line.

The technique of "multiple narrator and spectator" figures in the plays and fiction of the African (Ghanaian) writer Efua Sutherland and probably has longer traces in our tradition: "Within the structure of Sutherland's Anansegoro, the storyteller is both narrator and spectator, using the Moboguo to comment upon Ananse's schemes for the benefit of Sutherland's audience—while at the same time functioning as on-stage audience. This dual role underscores Sutherland's play-within-a-play structure. In turn, this structure contributes to the kind of audience involvement that is demanded by the Anansegoro format."[3]

Folktale combines with myth and legend in the figure of the flying man, which initiates the mythic and legendary structure and acts as a recurrent motif and metaphor. This metaphor links the beginning to the end/beginning, when Milkman, the central character, realizes that his aunt Pilate is the woman who "without leaving the ground . . . could fly," and Milkman himself becomes the flying man. In a 1977 television interview, Morrison discussed the imagery of flying and its African American folkloric background. Earlier, the significance of this imagery was glimpsed briefly in Ralph Ellison's story "Flying Home," with Todd the flyer and old man Jefferson the mythic flyer. The African myth was that black people could fly until they ate salt, introduced by the white man. (In a traditional African oral poem entitled "The European," the European is said to be "white as salt."[4]) Flying is wide-ranging topos in African American lore—in North America, in the Caribbean, and in Latin America—as a symbol of freedom, a legendary fact that may be drawn on by the African American with the same assurance that the European American artists draw on their various Daedalus mythologies. It is a central metaphor for *Song of Solomon,* through which Morrison plays with legend and possibility. In *A Treasury of Afro-American Folklore,* Harold Courlander has noted instances of the theme of the Flying Africans, especially stories of slaves flying back to Africa.[5] This myth—an instance of the surreal in folklore—also contributes to freeing "colloquial constituents from their naturalistic bondage."[6] This is another illustration of how the African American writer may turn to his own folkloric and oral traditions for surrealistic perceptions that one finds in the best of modern world literature. Gerald Moore has noted much surrealistic percipience in African folklore: "In Yoruba poetry we find often a cryptic juxtaposition of images; a refusal to explain and to build easy bridges for the reader from one part of the poem to another; coupled with an extreme power and conciseness in the images themselves."[7] One need only read Tutuola to get a sourcebook of surrealistic motivation from African folklore, in the possibilities of transforming reality and curious juxtapositions of fantastic images.

In *Song of Solomon* aunt Pilate is the fount of fantastic imagery and the character whom the author refuses to explain. Because Milkman is forbidden by his father (Pilate's brother) to see her, the forbidden quality of her reality seems to confirm her as legend. When Milkman first sees his aunt, he is spellbound; he knows that "nothing—not the wisdom of his father nor the caution of the world—could keep him from her." Milkman has heard "unbelievable but entirely possible stories" about his father's sister. This description reinforces Pilate's legendary, otherworldly, mythic quality and complex reality. Like one of Tutuola's characters in *The Palm-Wine Drinkard,* "She was not a human being and she was not a spirit, but what was she?"[8] But Pilate is both woman and spirit—some magical presence.

Milkman's own family life has been problematic and lacking something that Morrison champions even for Pilate, who stands apart in her adventurous freedom and independence: a holistic nurturing. Ruth, his mother, nursed him until he was well into boyhood because she was denied the emotional, spiritual, physical warmth of a whole relationship with her husband, Macon. Ruth herself harbors a pathological, obsessive love for her own father, details of which Milkman must hear and rehear in self-justifying versions of the story. Pilate is the first "whole" person Milkman has encountered. It is this wholeness and human warmth that he responds to. She is an intelligent, clever, adventuresome woman, unlike his mother or his "fragmented" (Melvin Dixon's phrase) restricted sisters First Corinthians and Magdalene, unlike even her own daughter and granddaughter, Reba and Hagar. Pilate has grown beyond the "dangerous" (Rinehart-like?) freedom of Morrison's previous character Sula. In the same 1977 television interview Morrison spoke of Sula as being "wholly free—no commitments"; but Pilate's freedom and self-sufficiency are committed and human-valuing. She is "fierce and nurturing" and a "genuine literary heroine."

In Pilate's story we transcend realism and enter the arena of the fantastic story or the tall tale, but the true tall tale, the entirely possible tall tale. Morrison has also captured some of the magic reality—the sense of fluid possibilities—we find in Gabriel García Márquez's *One Hundred Years of Solitude,* a novel she admires. And in the same way that we accept the transforming stories of Márquez as true, we accept hers as true. First there is the ritual of naming, which seems an indelible part of the legendary (and oral) beginnings. Her father picks out her name, randomly, from the Bible: "Pilate."

"Like a riverboat pilot?"
"No. Not like no riverboat pilot. Like a Christ-killing Pilate. You can't get much worse than that for a name. And a baby girl at that."

In a review of the book, Melvin Dixon has noted the pilot-Pilate inter-change, Pilate as "pilot"; like the mythic hero she serves as guide to others, as well as protector. She was the pilot for Milkman's birth. Once she decided that her brother Macon should have a son, Pilate gives Ruth an herb that induces Macon to make love to her. Puzzled, he does. When she becomes pregnant, Macon tries to force her to abort the baby (he suspects Pilate), but with Pilate's help, she withstands Macon and has the child. The description of Pilate's own arrival in the world provides a kind of mythology of birth: "After their mother died, she had come struggling out of the womb without help from the throbbing muscles or the pressure of swift womb water. As a result, for all the years he knew her, her stomach was as smooth and sturdy as her back, at no place interrupted by a navel." The true tall tale enters in other descriptive and metaphoric structures, such as the "woman who looked as though she might move the earth if she wanted to."

The truest tall tale, of course, is that of the ancestral Solomon the flying African; it is the connection between African American and African mythology and folklore. This is the pivotal legend of the book, the central revelation for Milkman in his quest for wholeness and the book's princi-pal metaphor. In legend, numerous African slaves, like Solomon (or Shalimar), flew back to Africa. This piece of African oral tradition and mythology is a talisman for Milkman's own possibility of flight and dis-covery of self and others. The legend also provides a new connection and an authentic link between oral and written literature. *Song of Solomon*, in its complex reordering and welding of oral and written literature, makes sophisticated use of the artistic conventions of the oral literature. The novel both reinforces tradition and maintains the African-African Amer-ican continuum of "artful sufficiency."[9] This welding continues to be important in Morrison's novel *Tar Baby*, in which the overarching sym-bol is also orally derived, and freed voice gives vibrancy to third-person narrative.

Many of the revelations in *Song of Solomon* come through story rather than the dramatic scene. Morrison uses the folklore technique—the "how come and why"—for character illumination, plot discoveries, and mean-ings. The revelation of Solomon's identity and supernatural exploit is but one among the various revelations of the identities of others and their natural and unnatural acts. Pilate is introduced to Milkman through stories told him by his mother and father. Macon justifies his actions toward Ruth by telling Milkman about the night Ruth's father died. In Macon's version of the story, he discovered Ruth "In the bed. That's where she was when I opened the door. Laying next to him. Naked as a yard dog, kissing him. Him dead and white and puffy and skinny, and she had his fingers in her mouth."

This is a galvanizing story which colors the readers' estimate of Ruth. But later Ruth tells her son her own version of the same story, answering Milkman's initial question and like any oral maneuver worth its salt or pepper, raising another one:

"Were you in the bed with your father when he was dead? Naked?"

"No. But I did kneel there in my slip at his bedside and kiss his beautiful fingers. They were the only part of him that wasn't . . ."

"You nursed me."

"Yes."

"Until I was . . . old. Too old."

". . . And I also prayed for you. Every single night and every single day. On my knees. Now you tell me. What harm did I do you on my knees?"

Further on, in her attempt to justify her life and motives, she explains herself and her self-value, derived from her father. She is not a strange woman, she says, but a small one. And although she refers to her father as an arrogant, often foolish and destructive man, "But he cared whether and he cared how I lived, and there was, and is, no one else in the world who ever did. And for that I would do anything."

Ruth contradicts Macon's story, but the two versions—interpretations of the same turgid reality—coexist in the tale and complicate the structures of identity, motives, and character revelation, in the end yielding the "whole story." Pilate also reveals her past to Milkman through story, and she seems the most convincing and truthworthy storyteller—so trustworthy that her re-telling is lifted out of dialogue and becomes part of the narrative declaration of the tale. Unlike Steptoe's sense of Hurston's wresting the story from Janie to assume control herself, preventing the liberation of her character's self and voice, Morrison grants this character the authority of the narrative itself, the part of the novel which presents and maintains the whole fictional world.

The use of stories to force dramatic and character revelations is also essential in the work of Carlos Fuentes. Like García Márquez, the Mexican novelist builds artistic bridges between oral tradition and literature. What Fuentes has said of language and the Latin American modifications of it parallels the African American (and African) perception: "Mexico is the only world radically cut off from Europe which has to accept the fatality of Europe's complete penetration and use the European words for both life and faith, although the being of her life and faith are of a different language."[10] A character in Fuentes's *Where the Air Is Clear*, like Milkman (except for his more enigmatic, "insubstantial" nature), acts as a kind of witness to the lives—to the stories—of others. We hardly ever learn more of Ixca Cienfuegos than we knew from the beginning—his name and where he comes from—but he represents the moral center of the work and listens to the intimate details of others' lives and imaginations (in this he seems both Pilate and Milkman). When the other characters don't tell him their stories freely he forces them, and through their stories we have a sense of the history of a nation forty years after the Mexican Revolution of 1910. By revealing their stories to Ixca, the characters are able to *see themselves* (and we see them), to come to some terms with their own dilemmas, their own nightmares. Like the characters in *Song of Solomon* (with the exception of Pilate) they attempt to justify their lives, rationalize the past, though they cannot destroy it. They make themselves visible through their stories. The context of story and storytelling and the relationship between story, revelation of personality, and identity seems similar in these two works. "In every man there is the possibility of his being—or, to be more exact, of his becoming once again—another man" (or woman?) says Octavio Paz,[11] and so say Fuentes and Morrison thematically and dramatically in their works. Both Milkman and Ixca—characters who "demand everything and offer nothing"[12]—must become "open, accessible," must be led to self-discovery, self-definition, self-knowledge, must affirm their personalities and identities as they affirm those of others discovering complete truths (the wholeness) from many (often contradictory) truths.

Pilate's story, told to Milkman and to the reader, is self-contained within a story, and her search and redefinition of her identity precedes, mirrors, and parallels Milkman's. In her own tale of "how come and why" she not only reveals her personality, but in a tremendous narrative passage shows the character re-creating herself. It reads in part: "when she realized what her situation in the world was and would probably always be she threw away every assumption she had learned and began at zero. First off, she cut her hair. That was one thing she didn't want to have to think about anymore. Then she tackled the problem of trying to decide how she wanted to live and what was valuable to her. When am I happy and when am I sad and what is the difference? What do I need to know to stay alive? What is true in the world?" The fact that she was born without a navel reinforces the sense of self-creation, becomes a metaphor for self-creation, or again, in Du Bois's movement from double-consciousness to wholeness, makes possible the merging of the double self into the truer and better self. The distinction between Pilate and all the others in the work is made.

Morrison draws many more elements of oral tradition in *Song of Solomon*. Like Ellison's *Invisible Man,* it is a multistructure of oral traditional forms—in language, characterization, treatment of episodes, dramatic dialogue, repetition and variation, the interplay of music and oratory in vocabulary, syntax, narrative vision, themes and motives, imagery and figurative forms—"texture, text, and context" as Alan Dundes would say. And like the best folktale or dilemma story, *Song of Solomon* is indirectly didactic. Pilate provides the model for Milkman and for the audience of the possibility of wholeness in the world. The integration of oral and written literary traditions adds the same sense of wholeness to the text.

Conclusion

"Freeing of voice" has been the essential metaphor for the direction of the literature discussed in these pages—the movement from the restrictive forms (inheritors of self-doubt, self-repudiation, and the minstrel tradition) to the liberation of voice and freer personalities in more intricate texts. This artistic liberation movement links the writers of African American literary tradition and is common to all literatures which have held (or assumed) a position of subordination to another literary tradition. Other critics have recognized and named this evolution. John Wideman put it in terms of "breaking out of the frame"; Robert B. Steptoe spoke of the black character's "controlling his own story." It is also a movement from literary double-consciousness to literary "true self-consciousness," to use W. E. B. Du Bois's terms. American literature once held a subordinate position to the literature of Europe. When writers such as Gertrude Stein, Ernest Hemingway, and J. D. Salinger "seized the word," it achieved its liberated voice and cultural independence. But within the wider category of American literature a variety of cultural traditions is struggling to do the same. Native American, African American, Chicano, Asian American, and voices of the American working class are grappling with visibility within the democracy. These writers, as James Weldon Johnson would say, seek the "wider compass" in literary creations that reveal their own "whole consummate being" (N. Scott Momaday) in naming themselves and their own possibilities. This is the quest of the liberated voice: to be self-authenticating (Steptoe's phrase), like Bessie in Sherley Anne Williams's "Someone Sweet Angel Chile" or like Angela Davis in "Poem of Angela Yvonne Davis" by Nikki Giovanni. The freed voice is the voice involved in the search for self and other, but that is self-defining. It is the voice of the grandmother in N. Scott Momaday's *House Made of Dawn,* who knows that "the simple act of listening is . . . crucial to human history."[1] It is Ixca Cienfuegos in Carlos

Fuentes's *Where the Air Is Clear,* who begins with "My name is Ixca" and concludes by naming and reaffirming all the others. It is the Invisible Man of Ralph Ellison, who becomes visible by telling his own story.

In most Third World writing there is a correlation between story-telling and the sense of whole being. "Grandchild, I am an old woman but I have nothing to tell about myself. I will tell a story," says Elizabeth Cook-Lynn's narrator in "History of Unchi," and in telling the story the old woman recreates herself. "Each evening I watch my mother fight / the meaning of words without pictures," begins Laureen Mar's "Chinatown 4." She fights to reassert her identity in a language wholly unlike Chinese. To do this, her words must "tilt upwards, cling to the air like leaves," but the poem reinstalls the pictures. Diana Chang does something similar in a poem in which "The landscape comes apart / in birds." The Filipino American writer Jessica Hagedorn acknowledges connection with African American oral tradition in the recreation of self in her poem "Sometimes you look like Lady Day." When the voice is restored to literature, the identity is restored. And it is often necessary to "speak in a new way"— certainly *in another way,* as illustrated by Marcela Lucero-Trujilla's Chicano American talk in her "Machismo Is Part of Our Culture." She completes the integration of two voices/languages by combining Spanish and American dialect in the poem's last two lines.[2]

In many of these works aesthetic, social, and moral identity is formed in counterpoint to Western forms and voices by modifying these forms with elements from other traditions. Thus N. Scott Momaday introduces ritual poetry in *House Made of Dawn* and Amiri Baraka, Leon Forrest, and Steve Cannon reassert in their poetry and fiction competing artistic traditions such as jazz. Whereas early African American writers were in-fluenced by Western models—the most destructive of which were the minstrel forms—many European writers are now being influenced (and modernized) by writers of the Third World.[3]

The break away from Western literary tradition was made possible by turning to the forms of oral traditions, at first with the "aesthetic vio-lence" of form in the prose and poetry of Amiri Baraka, Haki Madhubuti, Nikki Giovanni, Jayne Cortez and others. Their works have open-ended structures with voices that seem to travel outside of the landscape of the novel, short story, or poem in a literature of "no final solutions" and "unanswered questions,"[4] and in works containing "multiple narrators and spectators"[5]; these are modern, reinvented texts reminiscent of Afri-can dilemma tales in their resistance to Western novelistic resolutions.

Oral tradition offers continuity of voice as well as its liberation. It brings together the writers discussed in these pages. It is also a light for what each writer wishes to illuminate. Each writer in his or her own way resolves the tensions between orality and literature in the quest for the restoration of self as whole personality.

Because the influence of oral tradition has been so vital in modern African American writing, it is sure to continue in works to come, especially in the movement toward more complex uses and toward the freeing of literature from "naturalistic bondage."[6] As individual imaginations move beyond mere duplications of oral traditional form, they will possibly continue to move beyond mere representation of naturalistic reality, or will explore oral tradition for various nonnaturalistic modes. Oral tradition will continue to function as the broad foundation—a "complete and complex tradition in its own right."[7] With this foundation, the writers are free to reach, extend, and recreate new horizons of literary achievement and speech. As I have argued in these pages, writers from Chaucer to Cervantes to Lorca and on to modernist and postmodernist writers of the twentieth century have gained textual and contextual inspiration from their various oral modes. Oral tradition, then, exists in time—it is transmitted from generation to generation—but in literature it assumes a timelessness as it shares space with literary heritage.

To restate, most literatures that begin in a subordinate position to another literature or literary heritage—as European American literature once did vis-à-vis the literatures of Europe—experience a similar development. Colonial American writers, for instance, often wrote for European audiences, as early African American writers wrote to white audiences, in language and forms that were *approved*. When a writer did allow Americanisms to creep in he was often rebuked, as witness the conflict between Thomas Jefferson and the *Edinburgh Review*. Before European American writers could form their own national and aesthetic identity, it was necessary for them to become proficient (but formal) in the European mode. However, to produce a literature of the American landscape and character that was both universal and particular, but of content and structure new to Europe, they had to turn to the Americanisms of the oral tradition and to themselves to validate their literary nationhood. Oral tradition for European Americans, then, as for African Americans and other Third World writers, is the sun that illuminates and enlivens the literary planets. Currently, Third World writers recognize oral tradition more consciously as a creative principle and life force.

The spirit of change blows through European works as well. In the resolution of Hermann Hesse's masterwork *The Glass Bead Game*,

Magister Ludi finally rejects mere formalism—the approved, uncreated forms of the old masters—and goes out into the world to improvise his text and discover "an originality in style quite alien to the spirit of Castalia," which is mimetic and "artificially controlled" to recreate and analyze the techniques of classical styles but can "produce no new music themselves." It is oral tradition that allows the African American writers to desert the Castalias of the literary imagination through which they may merely "master [that is, imitate] the Game," and that permits them to "translate . . . sense of inner wholeness . . . into creative activity."[8]

This study has focused mainly on the stylistic strategies suggested by the oral tradition. Beyond style is content, and African American writers in the future may delve more into the content of oral tradition—particularly the magical reality of the stories and the cultural heroes—the sense of surprise and wonder quite equal to the amazing juxtapositions and transformations that one finds in modern literary texts. Guillaume Apollinaire, one of the founders of surrealism and the artistic perspective of the movement has spoken of the element of wonder in literature. In her article "Apollinaire and the Modern Mind," Anna Balakian quotes from the poet on the need for inventiveness in the artistic imagination: "Wonder should be the primary concern of the novelist, we should abandon for a while—long enough to realize what reality is—all this false realism which overwhelms us in most novels of today, and which is only platitude."[9] African American writers such as Ralph Ellison, Ishmael Reed, and Steve Cannon have stepped beyond naturalism to reclaim the imagination and the "conceptual voice,"[10] inspired by individual acts of invention from an oral tradition that offers elements of magic and the supernatural in its experiential range and scope. The examples include the tales of flying Africans, the transformation tales which also dissolve considerations of time and space, the supernatural elements in African epics, the surrealistic juxtapositions in oral poetry and blues, the sense of wonder in boasting and conjuring tales. These and others may be more and more imaginatively explored. The African American artist cannot merely duplicate the African transforming and lycanthropic tales (where, for instance, the elephant turns into grass to escape from the hunter, or Railroad Bill changes form at will to escape pursuit). As with Sherley Williams's improvisations on the texts of the blues, the writers must use the oral tradition as spur, as starting point, as foundation for their own creative expressions, but each work must indicate the versatility, richness, and depth of his or her individual imagination.

When Magister Ludi leaves the controlled world of Castalia where alterations of classical styles were impermissible, he plunges into the chaos of the world, or "plunges outside of [artistic] history," as Ellison would call it. How then does he form a new artistic plan from this chaos? Similarly, how does the African American artist, seeking forms outside the established Western forms for literary excellence, develop his own standards of excellence and make judgments? Is everything permitted so long as it has its source in oral tradition or motif? Questions of literary standards have often been elusive and deceptive. Even E. M. Forster says there are some literary judgments about which critics can be unreasonable: "The story is primitive, it reaches back to the origins of literature, before reading was discovered, and it appeals to something primitive in us. That is why we are so unreasonable over the stories we like, and so ready to bully those who like something else."[11] Attempting to pursue the standards set by the folktale creators in the midst of Western established order continues to be problematic for the African American writer. It is very difficult to become a "master of the game," any literary game; even to imitate well is a very difficult thing to do. Before he could make his break, Magister Ludi first had to become a master; perhaps only then was it possible for him to meet the "toils and dangers and delights" of the world. One wonders in this regard whether American writers ever mastered the European literary game before they developed their New World standards of literary excellence. In fact some Europeans became affected by American writers. Edgar Allan Poe was important to Baudelaire and Rimbaud and was a major influence on French symbolism and movements growing out of it, such as surrealism.[12] But other writers in the European tradition will always criticize certain American literary values, particularly the emphasis on action versus "the interior life."[13]

There are such things as antagonistic or at least antithetical literary standards. For instance, in *Masterpieces of the Orient*, G. L. Anderson speaks of Oriental in contrast to European drama: "To regard the *kabuki*, *joruri*, and *kyogen* as dramatic types approximating Western ones is an oversimplification, but a useful one if it serves to force the reader to regard the *no* as having no Western counterpart, though its poetry and its subtlety have inspired Westerners, especially William Butler Yeats. Indeed, the *no*, in an Aristotelian analysis, might not qualify as drama at all: it lacks a strong plot line, lacks moments of intense passion, and might better be described as the recollection of an action as a state of feeling rather than the imitation of an action." Perhaps it is the revelation of thought/feeling rather than action which is the key to the standard in the idea of Japanese theater. In his discussion of Indian drama Anderson distinguishes Sanskrit dramatic theory from Aristotelian: "Sanskrit theory is that the drama is not the imitation of an action or actions, but the imitation of states of being . . . the Sanskrit play does not offer a linear graph of action."[14]

The writer who looks to techniques from African American and African oral traditions as alternative literary standards should make use of them in a way which will be effective in literature. Some of these oral techniques work only with oral delivery; for instance, characterization in Akan oral tradition:

> One finds that characterisation, the limning of the individual in the round, was notably absent in the traditional Akan literature. This has an explanation in the very conception of society and of the individual. Since society was thought of as comprising individuals with antecedent duties and responsibilities, the three-dimensional individual, completely subsistent, and a distinct atom, was non-existent. Literature did not therefore portray him. The social contract was not merely false of Akan society; with reference to it, it was nonsensical, for, even before a man was born, his spiritual factors belonged to specific ethnic groups. Character types *were therefore more interesting* [my italics] than characters in the round. It is probably this different tradition of type-characterisation, typical of African literature, which has made three-dimensional characterisation by African novelists in English and French so far a failure.[15]

Although this observation may be correct, the oral tradition may offer characterizations more suitable to African Americans in the subtlety and range of roles the characters may play, since Western literary characterizations of Africans and African Americans make continuous reductions of the African American and African type to comedy, villainy, or noble savagery. The quality and range of type might thus be enhanced by the wider compass in oral tradition, but the development and realization of three-dimensional character might retain the standard from Western literature, which has achieved fine delineations in this area (at least in depictions of the Westerners' self-images), and which has grappled longer with the literary percipience of developing character necessary for the novel. Yet even Western characterization could profit by the addition of the contradictory/paradoxical character of blues—comparable to the Western Manichean character exemplified in the Steppenwolf—in the type developed by Ralph Ellison in *Invisible Man*. This type of characterization could offer a supplementary standard for creating character and getting at the African Americans' sense of their "multiform experience"[16] and multidimensionality achieved in jazz. (In support of true cultural autonomy, however, one might argue that if Japanese drama can portray "states of feeling" instead of "imitation of action," African authors could present character in symbolic abstractions suggesting traditional African sculpture, which, though three-dimensional because of the nature of the medium, does not delineate particulars or personalize identity as did Western sculpture before it was influenced by African and pre-Columbian art.)

In writing dialogue, the African American (and African) standard of excellence would not follow Steve McNeil, who asserts that such dialogue need not "sound" but must only "read." The standard of Gaines and others requires that it *sound and read* well. The oral procedures of dialogue-making suit the African American writers, making their dialogues spring to life both on and beyond the pages. In his *Women Writers in Black Africa,* Lloyd W. Brown speaks of Flora Nwapa's use of orally inspired dialogue in a way that could possibly offer a standard for its use in novelistic structure: "These dialogues are fairly representative of Nwapa's skills in developing oral forms into effective narrative devices. They suggest a careful attention, on the novelist's part, to dramatic development and suspense, to a sense of moral and social order, and to a sense of design in both society and her art. They are also the means of integrating the social and moral significance of talk in the community with the novel's structure as a whole: the scrupulously developed sense of design in each dialogue is really a part of the larger design of the novel's total structure. At the same time, the formal or moral order, represented by the dialogue and by the narrative structure as a whole, symbolizes the social relationships and individual experience that her themes describe. The community's perceptions of the woman's personality and the woman's response to the community are all presented through oral experiences (especially dialogue and storytelling)." In *Efuru,* her first novel, Nwapa uses oral techniques of dialogue-making to offer an alternative solution to the problem of characterization discussed in Akan literature: "The analytical commentary that is familiar in the Western novel is often replaced by the narrative formula which is based on general time references rather than specific dates, on elliptical rather than precise narrative detail, and on the archetypal rather than personal identity of some characters."[17]

There may be other instances where the African American writers as well as their African fellows may look to their oral traditions for standards that expand rather than reduce the possibilities of literature, in the way that the depth and vigor of African American music expanded contemporary popular and classical song. And so sure are the musicians of African American musical criteria for excellence that they form their own critical judgments for Western music, as Kimberly Benston does in comparing African American and European American avant-garde music.[18] The latter simply does not meet the standard.

Western literary tradition itself harbors antagonistic standards. Some critics dismiss the "moderns" altogether. When the naturalists appeared on the American literary scene, nothing of their work was ever acceptable to the defenders of ideality, who accused them of "thrusting into sight everywhere the foulnesses that are better ignored." Yet the naturalists triumphed when Sinclair Lewis received the Nobel Prize for Literature.[19]

Certain standards the African American writers will develop from their oral traditions will never be acceptable or will stay antagonistic, as the American action novel is antagonistic to the European contemplative novel. (The same is true if one compares films.) For the land of the "frontier spirit," with its emphasis on adventure, action, movement, anything else seems alien and "sluggish." *Magister Ludi: The Glass Bead Game* will stay philosophy and never true fiction for some critics, while for others it is superior fiction. (Hesse's Nobel Prize was awarded principally for this work.) *Finnegans Wake,* an acknowledged masterpiece by some, would never be successful as fiction for others, but only a literary exercise, though a magnificent one. And jazz will never become "real music" for the Steppenwolf, while for others not only is it real but extends their idea of what music can do and be in the world. For some, African American literature and history will seem unchanged. Nothing an Arabic writer could possibly do would ever meet the standard of the Koran, and to admit there is anything in the world better is to be a terrible blasphemer; this is perhaps the ultimate example of what I'm describing.

People, said Forster, are unreasonable about the stories that they like. Nations of people are often unreasonable about the standards they set. Phillis Wheatley clearly mastered the neoclassical literary standards of her day, yet for Thomas Jefferson, who had contentious attitudes toward Europe, she was considered "beneath criticism."[20] There are clearly extraliterary things at work. And yet he was freer and surer of developing a self-authenticating literary standard than she was. Wheatley, to prove she could master Pope, accepted limitations without gaining possibilities of expression, and actually put herself in the same predicament as the American idealists who "held firmly to a set of standards that allowed them to write only 'ideal' poetry. They did not suspect how completely this literary asceticism had devitalized their imaginative powers and cut them off from the modern world."[21]

Perhaps a measure for standards of excellence is doing what is most difficult to do, which does not necessarily mean that it is more difficult to understand. For instance, in creative writing it is easier to report what happens than to recreate it, so the latter would be the more difficult standard. Oral tradition holds such standards, though orality seems easy from the point of view of literary culture. But Hughes's early blues poems, for instance, do not meet the standards of imagery, magical juxtaposition, and imaginative energy of the folk creators themselves, as George Kent has pointed out. It is easier to get the form of a tradition than the imaginative spirit of it. His poems do point, however, to the standard that must be met when working from oral inspiration. Other African American aurally inspired writers look to standards of excellence set by African American music—even more difficult to meet in literature, but also modifying the standards of literature.

Contemporary Western writers find literary standards being modified by technologies, their literatures competing with their technologies in a way that the African American writer competes with the musicians for his audience: "Storytellers who will be writing for this generation and for generations to follow and who care about being read by more than a select few thousand will have to acknowledge that they are walking around in a world where people's brains are being wired for holograms and sensurround and the competition is not whatever was reviewed in the Sunday Times but what's playing down the block and whatever's on CBS (or WNET) tonight. [This means] there has to be a great streamlining, a stripping, a clean-to-the-bone eloquence projected." It is curious where this effort leads in the (Western) writer's description of his own literary procedures to achieve this "hurrying eloquence" (to make the "print on the paper . . . crackle with life") and the terms he uses for expression: "Plot always comes automatically once I know who my people are. The inevitability of their personalities makes the 'story' a natural projection of what drives them from day to day. In a given scene I may know nothing more than how it's supposed to end, most of the time not even that. *Scenes are improvised* [my italics]. A character does or says something and with as much spontaneity and schizophrenia as I can muster, another character responds. In this way, everything I write is spontaneous chain reaction."[22]

The standard set by African American music seems the highest artistic standard developed within the African American culture, so it is important to continue to discover ways in which it can be translated into words and literature. African American literature seems essentially a literature "of transition and experiment," never fully establishing itself. It is also still vexed by the problem of audience. Ernest Gaines noted the irony of the militant sixties, when most of those who purchased books by black writers were Northern white liberals and radicals, and the only "black books" they wished to buy were ones that dealt with the "black problem." The necessary militance thus became a commercial value for whites and subverted other possibilities of black creative expression. Black audiences themselves would often subvert their literary possibilities, demanding that their black writers all sound like the currently militant fashion. During Ellison's visit to one college campus, it became clear that one group of wrangling students hadn't even read his book. And with the exception of the writers who first published with Dudley Randall's Broadside Press, most black writers often gained visibility with black audiences after the white reading public made them visible. They were then condemned by other Blacks because whites were the source of their visibility. Alice Walker notes that an editor of a leading black journal dismissed her work *without reading it* simply because it had been praised by a white critic, not allowing that a white and a black critic may very well praise a book for different reasons, or discover different values and meanings in it. Standards based solely on antithetical responses to white critical approval or disapproval are not genuine.

Use of oral tradition, then, is not all that is needed in the movement toward literary independence and the freeing of voice. What enabled Americans to gain an autonomy of voice were not literary efforts in a vacuum, set apart from other efforts of the imagination. The writers of one American literary history speak of economic autonomy—another foundation upon which Americans could assert themselves: The "spirit of self-confidence had been fed by other fires: by the material promise of timber, land, and waterway, convertible at a touch into real wealth; and by the technological promise—already apparent—of American mechanical and social invention."[23] Other attainments were complementing and strengthening the security of American literary self-confidence necessary for building and maintaining an independent literary tradition. Ellison may be suggesting this correlation in an interview in *Chant of Saints:* "The other day I had to tell a black student . . . who came up with an easy criticism of George Washington Carver that I didn't like Dr. Carver either, but for a specific and personal reason: At Tuskegee he was always chasing me out of Rockefeller Hall where I'd go to work out my harmonic exercises on the piano. My investigations into the mysteries of harmony interfered with his investigations of the peanut, and to me harmony was more important. But today I realize that not only did a large industry draw upon his experiments but by manipulating strains of peanuts he was growing himself an American President!"[24]

The support of American audiences was also important for the new literary self-trust. The relationship between the black audiences and writers does not offer continuity—while the black musician offers a model for the black writer, the response to the musical endeavor is often quite different from the response to writing. In an earlier chapter I mentioned the encounter of Richard Wright and a white woman to whom he revealed his desire to become a writer; let's look at the response of Wright's black audience. His schoolmates could not believe that he had written a story. "We had never had any instruction in literary matters at school; the literature of the nation or the Negro had never been mentioned. My schoolmates could not understand why anyone would want to write a story; and, above all, they could not understand why I had called it *The Voodoo of Hell's Half-Acre*. The mood out of which a story was written was the most alien thing conceivable to them. They looked at me with new eyes, and a distance, a suspiciousness came between us. . . . At home the effects were no less disturbing." Granny considered writing a made-up story to be lying—"Devil's work," she called it. His mother was worried:

> Suppose the superintendent of schools would ask you to teach here in Jackson, and he found out that you had been writing stories?"
>
> Uncle Tom, though surprised, was highly critical and contemptuous. The story had no point, he said.
>
> In the end I was so angry that I refused to talk about the story. From no quarter, with the exception of the Negro newspaper editor, had there come a single encouraging word.[25]

It seems that the black musician has an easier relationship with his public. There are not the same problems of character; no demands for flattering portraits from audiences that are victims of stereotyping. When Ntozake Shange was asked, "Looking back at 'colored girls,' why do you think the play caused such a ruckus?" she replied: "I don't know. The only thing I can think of is that we're a highly self-conscious culture and therefore it makes it very difficult to rid ourselves of cultural rationalizations. It is not to our liking to reveal these things. It's just not done. I think we're conservative in that sense. We're very Asian in the sense of saving face and maintaining public decorum, which I don't think is healthy. I think it's a defense mechanism that has begun to hurt us as much as it was protecting."[26]

If new standards of excellence are indeed developed from oral heritage, one still wonders if the response of the black audience will be favorable. Jean Toomer comes closest to achieving the standards of literary excellence one finds in the music and is a major influence and celebrated voice among fellow black writers. Yet he is often dismissed by the broader black readership, at least if general student response in recent years to this "mysterious voice" is any indication; one student even advised that the marvelous *Cane* should be omitted from the reading list on student evaluation of the choice of texts. Toomer said that a true artist is "a critic of meanings and values," but many black audiences permit the artist to be a critic if the criticism is directed to whites only; they would not so easily accept a statement like the following, by South African writer Fatima Dike: "but you see—there are things I don't like about my own people, and I will always bring them up in my plays. Violence—I'll always bring whatever qualities I don't like in my people into my plays, so that when they see them they can go back, or go out of the theatre and think about them."[27] The Joyces and Steinbecks would always be rejected (it seems) by their fellow Dubliners or fellow Salinas citizens. Again, the problem is compounded by a history of stereotyping vis-à-vis Western literature. Yet the literary artists themselves have attempted in their various ways to take us to unseen territories, and Alice Walker said the last word—that all (even the black writer) should be free to explore possibilities as our musicians are free to explore. She means the "toils and dangers" as well as the "delights."

But no alternatives to Western standards of excellence (some incorporating, others modifying/amplifying those standards) will last without a successful writer-audience relationship and the confidence of an audience in the particular literary development. English drama developed especially rapidly in the sixteenth century "owing to real demand for their services."[28] Writers must have a demand within a culture, but right now the culture keeps demanding musicians. Still, one wonders how many writers are in their season of "germination" before the flowering. Such writers, I feel, will continue to work with the effects, expressions, and artistic inspiration from oral tradition, its abundant and vital energy. But it is also possible that a new *Cane* would still have a limited audience and some, like Wright's relatives and acquaintances, would want to eliminate it altogether from the choice of texts. It is right also that African Americans, like others, should have competing literary standards. Oral tradition as a foundation grants a formal unity to the substantial diversity. And when one speaks with Shange about the African Americans' concern with saving face, which was even more rampant in the "uplift period," one should also observe that much of the most sophisticated and intricate world literature has not traveled far beyond the early Arabic tribal poetry, whose aim was always to praise one's own tribe and damn all the others. Members of the other tribes were all fools and clowns, while one's own tribe was composed of virtuous, intelligent, and courageous people. Any tribal songster who was misguided enough to turn his scrutiny upon his own tribe—their virtues and their follies—was banished. American popular and media stories, romanticized stories which appeal to the mass white audience, are written in this vein of self-glorification, where Blacks and other aliens are always the Darth Vaders of the imagination. Yet other American writers do give themselves greater variations of self-scrutiny. These writers, to quote Arthur Miller, provide alternative moral views without the "reassurance of foreign models"[29] and reserve their right to say "what is evil in the United States (and in themselves) and what is good, what is confused and what is clear."

In African American artistic endeavor, black musicians may still be the vanguard. Musicians use "collection(s) of sounds to communicate to one another . . . things that language cannot adequately convey . . . feelings and realities"; they can more easily "create possibilities"[30] and transcend audience controversies over definitions of African American reality and character in the New World. And musicians more easily transcend class boundaries, though some would perhaps feel that because of its intellectual base, jazz would have quite different audience appeal than the blues. But both strains have in fact transformed the world's whole idea of music as well as its whole musical history. One cannot yet make the same assertion about African American literature. But the relationship of the African American writer to his oral tradition makes his writing a vital part of world literary history, in which writers mine the rich veins of their oral heritages as they move from imitation to creation, from representation to invention, and from being destroyers of old forms to creators of new ones. Oral traditions provide the terrain through which many writers have searched and wandered until they have been surprised by the blooming orchid, then called out in their own clear voices, as Zora Neale Hurston's Janie might call out, for others to come and see.

Postscript

The preceding chapters, which focus on technique, were completed in 1982, at a time when nearly all African American literary criticism emphasized theme and content. I then left the States for Paris. In the years that followed African American literary criticism dramatically shifted its focus, from theme and content to the texts and to close reading. This shift synthesizes New Criticism with a reaction to or development from earlier African American prescriptive and proscriptive criticism. As one critic puts it, imaginative writers tend to rebel against strictures. I suppose critics do likewise.

The new generation of critics includes Houston Baker, Jr., Henry Louis Gates, Jr., John F. Callahan, Abena P. B. Busia, and others, not all of whom belong to the same generation, however. Some, such as Houston Baker, Jr., have revised their earlier theories in more recent writings that reflect this new approach to the African American texts. They all have begun to look inside the African American tradition and the oral modes themselves—the "virtuoso riffs" (Baker)—to acquire new paradigms for discussing African American imaginative writing. Baker introduces the blues critic as a deft and cogent reader of the tradition, while Gates employs the metaphor and oral mode of "signifying" in his reading of the many intertextual repetitions and reversals (linguistic, formal and thematic) within African American literary texts.

Earlier Black Aesthetic criticism, as part of the Black Arts Movement of the 1960s and early 1970s, proposed a "radical reordering of the Western cultural aesthetic . . . a separate symbolism, mythology, critique and iconology" (Larry Neal) by utilizing musical and verbal strategies from oral tradition in new literary experiments. However, while assaulting racist strictures, these critics often employed new strictures of exclusion and created a new hegemony. Another shortcoming of their vision is that it was rather vague and general and offered no specific analyses of the resonant devices they proposed, except for applauding "kinetic art" to move the listener to revolutionary action. They acknowledged the dilemma of African American literature versus its music and spoke in the language of political ideology, but these were merely hints with no real maps, much less bridges. Yet the Black Aesthetic critics launched the principal attack on the presumptions of Western establishment criticism.

The new works of Robert Steptoe, Dexter Fisher, and others have presented more formal critiques of the African American literary tradition. In the literary-theoretical studies of Gates and Baker, the vernacular is placed up front. Each critique represents a stage toward a truly autonomous criticism from within, offering a freeing of the African American critic's voice which mirrors the development of the African American texts themselves.

Black women critics too are involved in this restoring of the voice. Mary Helen Washington, Valerie Smith, Hortense Spillers, Hazel Carby, Abena P. B. Busia, and Deborah E. McDowell are all black women writers seizing control of their own voices and making of their experiences the "stuff of art." The new black male critics, using strategies from within the tradition, have come to see the women's free(r) voices as complements to male voices. Gates even sees innovations in certain of the women's texts, for example, Zora Neale Hurston's. Formerly, few women writers were admitted into the canon of the Black Aesthetic critics.

One of the failures of insight of the new critics, which I have emphasized, is that the problems of the freed voice apply not only to African American literature and criticism, but to all the world's literatures and criticisms: European versus American, Anglo-American versus Chicano, French Standard versus French Creole, Canadian English versus Canadian French, Russian versus Estonian, and so on. One sees it in the dynamics of every national literature vis-à-vis another. The voices of the less powerful group, "the other," always must free themselves from the frame of the more powerful group, in texts of self-discovery, authority, and wholeness.

To liberate their voices from the often tyrannic frame of another's outlook, many world literatures continue to look to their own folklores and oral modes for forms, themes, tastes, conceptions of symmetry, time, space, detail, and human values.

GLOSSARY

NOTES

INDEX

Glossary

The techniques derived from the oral tradition are to be taken not as standards but as a sort of continuum; their very nature mitigates against standardization in the Western sense. Perhaps "mode" is a better word than "standard," since African American verbal and musical oral traditions are dynamic, fluid, and ever-changing, but still may offer ongoing guidelines for technical exploration and personal/group improvisations. The following terms/modes/forms have been frequently used in the text: *jazz* (America's "classical music") and *blues* (an original American music, a complicated form, though deceptively simple). Oral folktales may be seen to participate in this expressive tradition.

Herein, I also include general terms and key words from literature as they apply specifically to African American literary tradition. I have not included those terms which are already defined in the text, for example "worrying-the-line," double-consciousness, and signifying.

Blues

Ralph Ellison in *Shadow and Act* defined blues as "an impulse to keep the painful details and episodes of a brutal experience alive in one's aching consciousness, to finger its jagged grain, and to transcend it, not by the consolation of philosophy, but by squeezing from it a near-tragic, near-comic lyricism" (pp. 78–79). Traditional blues structure consists of three-lined, twelve-bar stanzas, rhyming aab. Besides repetition, blues forms include worrying-the-line, call-and-response, shouts, "field hollers," and other interjections. These may vary in mood, tone, and structure with each blues singer. As writers from Douglass to Baldwin have noted, outsiders often hear only the surface sounds, the entertainment value, but not the "deep song," its ritual significance and wisdom.

Blues may influence the writer in theme, mood, or structure. The creative writer may adhere closely to the traditional blues form or simply suggest the form in vocabulary, subject matter, worrying the line, repetitions and variations on key lines or phrases, like the blues singer who "won't let a line alone." Without using the rhythms and language of the blues, the writer may simply suggest it through the mood of the texts or even plot resolutions. As in music, blues mode in the literary text can be used to "transform the mood" of the reader. Despite the implications of its name, blues songs travel the whole spectrum of emotions, subject matter, and rhetorical strategy and are not limited to melancholy.

The tempo of a blues text is generally slow. The slow pacing can be seen not only in the syntax and rhythm of the prose but also in the pace of a tale's revelations. The relationship between the text and the audience in a blues text seems direct and immediate. Minor chords—in the sense of structural complications—are more likely to be played than major chords.

Some black writers and critics have rejected the blues. For Ron Karenga blues is bound to the past; it teaches resignation and acceptance of reality. "We have come to change reality," he said. Others reject its redundancies. George Kent found it problematic, because of its unpredictability, instability, and sense of chaos or precariousness. While acknowledging that it is an unstable form in the sense of its variability and flexibility, other critics such as Bernard W. Bell credit the blues with creating a sense of order and coherence through its social ritual. Houston Baker, Jr., has called it the "dream of American Form."

Blues language

The vocabulary, syntax, style, and rhythm in which a blues text is rendered. The language of blues is generally concrete, graphic, imagistic, immediate. It can also include scatological expressions, generally "double-entendre," as in the "Jelly-Roll Blues." (The "blue joke's" challenge to so-called decent language might be compared to this aspect of the blues, though blues language is broader in its experiential range.) Blues has a number of complex rhetorical and expressive strategies, as Houston Baker, Jr., has noted, from parody to irony. Paul Oliver points out that the blues can also be obscure. There are incongruities in language and juxtapositions of moods and images. The Trueblood episode of Ralph Ellison's *Invisible Man* is in blues language, and the experience might be called a blues experience. Blues can also be surreal and lyrical. Says Baker in *Blues, Ideology, and Afro-American Literature,* "blues (is an) affirmation of human identity in the face of dehumanizing circumstances" (p. 190). In this sense its language can be resonant, revivifying.

Call-and-response

Antiphonal back-and-forth pattern which exists in many African American oral traditional forms, from sermon to interjective folktale to blues, jazz and spirituals, and so on. In the sermonic tradition, the preacher calls in fixed or improvised refrains, while the congregation responds, in either fixed and formulaic or spontaneous words and phrases. In oral storytelling the listeners may interject their commentary in a modified call-and-response pattern derived from African musical tradition.

In the literary text both dialogue and plot structure may demonstrate this call-and-response pattern: one scene may serve as a commentary on a previous scene while a later scene becomes a commentary or response to that one. In Ralph Ellison's *Invisible Man,* for example, the prologue might be read as containing numerous "calls" to which the episodes are various "responses."

Coherence

The principle which gives a sense of wholeness, intelligibility, structural or thematic integrity to a work: the parts are related to each other and to the whole. When an African American work draws its principle(s) of coherence from a non-Western system, structure, or mode, it is often perceived as incoherent vis-à-vis a Western standard (as jazz was vis-à-vis Western classical music).

Criticism, descriptive

Criticism which simply describes or details what a work of literature is doing, but does not evaluate. For example, a Western critic might choose to provide a descriptive critique of a No play without offering an evaluation if his only framework of reference is Aristotelian. Literary traditions that have not yet solidified their own criteria for judgment might depend more heavily on descriptive criticisms, like medieval Japanese literature and art before they separated from the Chinese tradition. New or young literary and art traditions often begin with descriptive criticism, first describing themes, techniques, and values, then using the descriptions to formulate autonomous standards. For example, a standard which emerges from descriptive criticism of African American oral and literary traditions is that successful dialogue should both sound and read well, as opposed to merely reading or scanning well.

Criticism, prescriptive

Criticism based on established or traditional rules, requirements, and guidelines. Examples of prescriptive criticism from Western literary tradition are: (1) whatever is promised at the beginning of a story should be delivered; (2) viewpoint should be maintained throughout; (3) consistency of character and language should be maintained; (4) "dramatize, dramatize, dramatize" (Henry James), and so on. Experimental stories often deliberately subvert these prescriptions, and James's admonition might have been seen as a modern addition to the rules of his own time, when events were as likely to be told in narrative summary as shown in dramatic form. And the French neo-novelists as well as the post-modernists often do not "dramatize, dramatize, dramatize."

Criticism, proscriptive

Criticism based on prohibitions. For example, the aesthetic theory in Joyce's *A Portrait of the Artist as a Young Man* prohibits "kinetic art," that is, art that moves the reader/viewer/listener to action rather than merely contemplation. Most Third World literatures, on the other hand, champion kinetic art, some even prescribing it. Most judicial or evaluative critiques are a combination of descriptive, prescriptive, and proscriptive criticisms.

Duality

Either/or; the twofold or dichotomous conception of reality and human nature: for example, in philosophy, mind and matter; in psychology, mind and body; in theology, good and evil. Nondualistic or holistic systems integrate these dichotomous elements in interdependent wholes. In *Blues, Ideology, and Afro-American Literature* Houston Baker, Jr., has noted that "As a driving force the blues matrix thus avoids simple dualities. It perpetually achieves its effects as a fluid and multivalent network" (p. 9). Most African American oral forms tend to avoid simple dualities. Michael Harper has referred to them as "modal." Duality requires yes or no answers. In "Moral Responsibility in Dreaming" Freud asks the question, "Is one morally responsible for a dream sin?" His answer is yes. In *Invisible Man,* Trueblood's answer to the same question is both yes and no. Invisible Man himself is both visible and invisible at the same time.

Framed story

A story contained within or bracketed by another story. Usually—but not always—the story within the frame is written in a variant language, considered subordinate or inferior. Vernacular stories are mostly framed within standard English (or other standard languages), for regional and local color effect. Occasionally, however, framed stories use the same language, such as the vernacular stories framing vernacular stories (Ernest Gaines) or standard tales framing standard tales (Joseph Conrad). As John Wideman has noted, the evolution of African American fiction has been an evolution out of the frame. Framing vernacular stories within vernacular stories might also be seen as an innovative modification of the standard Western tradition in that it uses the frame but does not subordinate one language system to that of another.

Hero and heroine

The principal character in a poem, story, or play; the protagonist. In part, the change of perspective and "controlling of story" in African American literature has involved the selection of particular heroes and heroines and definition of heroic traits. From the point of view of "the other" one group's or nations heroes/heroines are often considered another's villains/rogues. Likewise, the qualities of courage or nobility celebrated in the in-group are often looked upon with suspicion or disfavor when they are the attributes of others. (Feminists have noted this in cross-sexual attributes.) From the European American perspective, the fugitive slave, for example, or the courageous rebel would be villain/criminal/anti-hero, but from the African American perspective the same individual would be hero/heroine. Conversely, whites' positive traits for blacks, such as Dr. Melville's description of Jube Benson, may be negative traits from an African American perspective. Would Melville use the same terms of praise for himself? (Sometimes the blanket rejection of a character by Blacks because whites happen to like him or her can be problematic. Whites might or might not like the African American character for the wrong or inappropriate reasons, but African Americans should select their own terms for value.)

African American writers frequently draw upon archetypes from African and African American mythology, folklore, and history as paradigms for the heroic qualities of their protagonists.

Ironic attitude

Irony implies a contrast between the apparent and real meaning of a figure of speech, character, or situation, the latter being an example of dramatic irony. Ironic attitude is a way of describing the relationship between the author and the author/narrator or author/character. It also keys the reader as to what attitude to take toward the text. The ironic attitude helps the reader distinguish what a character professes to believe or feel from the author's (and also reader's) comprehension. Cues to the ironic attitude lie in choice of descriptive vocabulary, tone, and various forms of verbal and situational incongruity. However, even with these cues, readers often confuse the author (real and implied) with the narrator and the character, as for instance James Joyce and Stephen Daedalus, Gustave Flaubert and Madame Bovary, Henry James and his numerous implied authors/narrators/characters, and in African American tradition James Weldon Johnson and the Ex-Coloured Man.

Jazz

A native American music whose roots are African American and Southern, dating from the turn of the century. There are numerous forms and styles of jazz, depending on region (Chicago, New York, New Orleans) and era (bebop, swing, fusion). In literature jazz can affect the subject matter—the conceptual and symbolic functions of a text, translate directly into the jazz hero, or have stylistic implications.

The writer's attempt to imply or reproduce musical rhythms can take the form of jazz-like flexibility and fluidity in prose rhythms (words, lines, paragraphs, the whole text), such as nonchronological syncopated order, pacing, or tempo. A sense of jazz—the jam session—can also emerge from an interplay of voices improvising on the basic themes or motifs of the text, in key words and phrases. Often seemingly nonlogical and associational, the jazz text is generally more complex and sophisticated than blues text in its harmonies, rhythms, and surface structure (its deep structure can be as complex, but there its intricacies are noticeable). Jazz text is stronger in its accents; its vocabulary and syntax are often more convoluted and ambiguous than blues. It is often more difficult to read than a blues text, tending to abstractions over concreteness of detail. It shares with a blues text a sense of extemporaneity in its fluid rhythmical design and syncopated understructure, its sound and meaning systems, its rejection of duality. Jazz tends to have a faster pace and tempo than a blues text.

African Americans were not alone to experiment with jazz modes in their writing. The Beat Generation has incorporated them in its literature and one might argue for their presence in the nonchronological jazzings or riffs, pacings, inventive flexibility and phrase structures, and associational jumps in modern Western poetry (Eliot's *The Waste Land*), modern jazz fiction (the works of the Beats), and even the syncopated pacing of modern film.

Although there are no strict guidelines regarding setting or milieu, jazz texts tend to be urban while most blues texts tend to be Southern and rural; Wright's *Native Son,* however, might be said to be an urban blues.

It is important to note that in jazz the concepts "improvisational" and "extemporaneity" are only a manner of speaking: jazz is mastery of technique, and a superb jazz text is as exacting a form as its musical counterpart. This technique is not like "automatic writing," because the jazz musician (and writer), as Ellison has noted, improvises upon traditional materials. Again, *Invisible Man* provides the example.

Perspective

The vantage point from which a story is told. Unlike folklore, African American literature was not written from a black perspective and has had to move *toward* it. Early writers were admonished that to be "universal" they had to write from a white perspective. This reached its apogee in the 1950s, when black writers such as James Baldwin, Ann Petry, Willard Motley, and Richard Wright wrote novels in which the main or all characters were whites. Restored perspective involves the return of Blacks to the center of their fictional worlds. Perspective also affects numerous other aspects of the works: significant events and relationships; conceptions of heroic action; significant themes; principles of coherence.

Perspective is not just a function of literature. The recent controversy over films depicting the Civil Rights movement is pertinent here. The films, such as "Mississippi Burning," renewed the assumption that to be objective and significant, "significant events" even in African American history must be told from European American perspective with European American heroes. Blacks could not have authority over their own stories. To tell the history of the Civil Rights Movement from an African American perspective could only be subjective, while from a white (male) perspective it could be objective and significant. The problem of perspective can extend to other art forms as well. The narrator of James Weldon Johnson's *The Autobiography of an Ex-Coloured Man* suggests that even jazz must be rendered from another perspective to be significant!

The literatures of other minority and Third World traditions reveal a comparable movement and perspective shift. As Raymund A. Paredes has noted in distinguishing the perspective in Chicano literature from that of its folklore, "the literary record of Mexican-Americans . . . shows a considerably slower movement toward a distinctly Chicano perspective than does the folklore" (Baker, ed., *Three American Literatures,* p. 45). Asian American literature and colonial literatures also move toward what Asian American writer Lawson Inada calls one's own sense of who one is and where one is, which needs no justification vis-à-vis another. He refers to it as the perspective of the "full self," the self-determining self (Baker, ed., *Three American Literatures,* p. 255).

Significant event

Event that is meaningful, valuable, or has symbolic import for a person, group, or culture. W. E. Abraham in *The Mind of Africa* applies this term to historical events. Their significance, Abraham states, is culturally determined. That is, a historical event that would be significant from the point of view of one culture might be considered trivial from the point of view of another. This idea applies as well to literature.

Skaz

Term Russian Formalists used for texts that resemble oral narration. Coincidentally, it sounds like a combination of "skat" and "jazz," paradigms of African American oral tradition.

Spiritual

Anonymously composed, the spiritual takes its subject matter and imagery from the Bible. It is made up of rhymed or unrhymed stanzas or combinations of both and contains elements of call-and-response. There is a sense of improvisation and spontaneity. During the time of slavery, spirituals often carried coded messages about a planned escape or rebellion.

Spirituals have been incorporated into slave narratives and novels, such as Frederick Douglass' *Narrative,* William Wells Brown's *Clotel,* Jean Toomer's *Cane,* and James Baldwin's *Just Above My Head.* The spiritual may also be present as a thematic or tonal device, informing the whole text's rhythm, language, style, characterizations, conversations, and events. Thematically, Alice Walker's concern with the "survival whole" of Blacks illuminates the dynamics of the spiritual motif in its spiritual and secular dimensions. Spiritual experiences in the works of Walker, Baldwin, Toni Cade Bambara, and Toni Morrison might also be attributed to this oral traditional form.

Transcription technique

The way of writing down a spoken language, especially dialect or vernacular. As Harold Courlander has pointed out, in most early writings only black speech is distorted by orthographic changes while white vernacular often receives its full linguistic value.

How a language is transcribed contributes to the sense of its autonomy as a literary language. From the point of view of British English, all colonial versions would be transcribed with orthographic distortions, but as "nation languages" (Braithwaite's phrase) they are not: one has a sense of them as "wholesome" rather than deviant.

Notes

Introduction

1. Geormbeeyi Adaii-Mortly, "Ewe Poetry," *Introduction to African Literature,* Ulli Beier, ed. (London: Longman, 1979), p. 11.
2. N. Scott Momaday, *House Made of Dawn* (New York: New American Library, 1969), p. 88.
3. James Joyce, *A Portrait of the Artist as a Young Man* (1916, rpt. New York: Modern Library, 1928). Stephen Daedalus in his aesthetic theory denounces "kinetic art," which moves the reader to action. It is the art of contemplation that he champions.
4. Federico García Lorca, *The Selected Poetry of Federico García Lorca,* Donald M. Allen, ed. (New York: New Directions, 1955, 1961), pp. ix–x.
5. On Japanese, Arabic, and Indian literatures see G. L. Anderson, ed., *Masterpieces of the Orient* (New York: Norton, 1977), p. 594; my quotations from pages 595, 368–369, 4, 130–131.
6. James Joyce, *Finnegans Wake* (1939, rpt. New York: Viking Press, 1967), p. 419
7. Clara Thomas, The Manawaka World of Margaret Laurence (Toronto: McClelland and Stewart, 1976), p. 1.
8. Margaret Laurence, *The Diviners* (New York: Knopf, 1974), p. 3.
9. Anne Tibble, ed., *African English Literature* (New York: October House, 1965), pp. 99, 33.
10. William Flint Thrall, Addison Hibbard, and C. Hugh Holman, eds., *A Handbook of Literature* (New York: Odyssey Press, rpt. 1960), p. 12.
11. Ibid., pp. 12–13.
12. Michael S. Harper and Robert B. Steptoe, eds., *Chant of Saints* (Urbana: University of Illinois Press, 1979), p. 466.
13. Robert E. Spiller, Willard Thorp, Thomas H. Johnson, Henry Seidel Canby, Richard M. Ludwig, eds., *Literary History of the United States* (1946, rpt., New York: Macmillan, 1963), pp. 921–922.

14. Ibid., p. 922. Yet, "now and again he yearned for the lusty old ways of medieval speech, 'full of unconscious coarseness and innocent indecencies,' 'good old questionable stories,' as the Connecticut Yankee says" (p. 925).

15. Ishmael Reed, ed., *19 Necromancers from Now* (New York: Anchor Books, 1970), p. xiv.

16. John O'Brien, ed. *Interviews with Black Writers* (New York: Liveright, 1973), p. 173.

17. Robert B. Steptoe, "After Modernism, after Hibernation: Michael Harper, Robert Hayden, and Jay Wright," in *Chant of Saints,* pp. 470–486.

1. From Dialect to Blues and Spirituals

1. James Weldon Johnson, *The Book of American Negro Poetry* (1922, rpt. New York: Harcourt, Brace and World, 1959), p. 4.

2. Dickson D. Bruce, "Jingles in a Broken Tongue," *A Singer in the Dawn,* Jay Martin, ed. (New York: Dodd, Mead, 1975), p. 110–111.

3. Houston Baker, Jr., ed., *Black Literature in America* (New York: McGraw-Hill, 1971), p. 108.

4. Sterling Brown, *Collected Poems,* introduction by Sterling Stuckey (New York: Harper and Row, 1980), p. 9.

5. Arnold Arnoff, ed., *The Poetry of Black America* (New York: Harper and Row, 1973), pp. 10–11. All quotations from the poem are from these pages.

6. John O'Brien, *Interviews with Black Writers* (New York: Liveright, 1973), p. 104.

7. Nikki Giovanni, "My House," in *Giant Talk,* Quincy Troupe and Rainer Schulte, eds. (New York: Vintage, 1975), p. 440.

8. Kimberly Benston, "Late Coltrane: A Re-membering of Orpheus," in *Chant of Saints,* Michael S. Harper and Robert B. Steptoe, eds. (Urbana: University of Illinois Press, 1979), p. 416.

9. Ron Welburn, "Percussions," in *Giant Talk,* p. 237.

10. Myron Simon, "Dunbar and Dialect Poetry," in *A Singer in the Dawn,* p. 130.

11. Ibid.

12. Johnson, *American Negro Poetry,* p. 4.

13. Arnoff, *Poetry of Black America,* pp. 3–4.

14. Langston Hughes, "Blues at Dawn," *Blackamerican Literature,* Ruth Miller, ed. (Mission Hills, Calif.: Glencoe Press, 1971), p. 386. See Nancy B. McGhee's "Langston Hughes: Poet in the Folk Manner" for discussion of Hughes's complex and imaginative jazz poems; his "Blues at Dawn" is more useful in showing the problems of strict adherence to folk form. See also Arthur P. Davis's "Cool Poet." Both articles are in *Langston*

Hughes: Black Genius, Therman B. O'Daniel, ed. (New York: William Morrow, 1971).

15. John F. Matheus, "Langston Hughes as Translator," in *Langston Hughes: Black Genius,* p. 162.

16. Ibid., p. 165. Langston Hughes's translation of "Blades" by Nicolás Guillén is reprinted by permission of Harold Ober Associates; copyright 1948 by Langston Hughes and Ben Carruthers; copyright renewed 1976 by George Houston Bass.

17. *Giant Talk,* p. xl.

18. *Giant Talk,* p. xxxix.

19. George E. Kent, "Langston Hughes and Afro-American Folk and Cultural Tradition," in *Langston Hughes: Black Genius,* pp. 198–199.

20. Ibid., pp. 200–201.

21. Sterling Brown, "Negro Folk Expression: Spirituals, Seculars, Ballads, and Work Songs," *The Making of Black America,* vol. II, August Meier and Elliott Rudwick, eds. (New York: Atheneum, 1974), p. 210.

22. Brown, *The Making of Black America.*

23. See Robert B. Steptoe, *From behind the Veil: A Study of Afro-American Narrative* (Urbana: University of Illinois Press, 1979) for discussion of "authenticating narrative."

2. Folk Speech and Character Revelation

1. Ruth Miller, ed., *Blackamerican Literature* (Mission Hills, Calif.: Glencoe Press, 1971), pp. 218–219.

2. James Weldon Johnson, *The Autobiography of an Ex-Coloured Man* (1912, rpt. New York: Hill and Wang, 1960), p. 56.

3. LeRoi Jones (Imamu Amiri Baraka), "The Screamers," in *American Negro Short Stories,* John Henrik Clarke, ed. (New York: Hill and Wang, 1968).

4. Robert E. Spiller, Willard Thorp, Thomas H. Johnson, Henry Seidel Canby, Richard M. Ludwig, eds., *Literary History of the United States* (New York: Macmillan, 1963), p. 1265.

5. Richard Wright, "I Tried to Be a Communist," in *A Casebook on Ralph Ellison's Invisible Man,* Joseph F. Trimmer, ed. (New York: Thomas Y. Crowell, 1972), p. 56.

6. Johnson, *The Autobiography,* pp. 167–168.

7. Nathan Huggins, *The Harlem Renaissance* (New York: Oxford University Press, 1971).

8. Sterling Brown, *The Negro in American Fiction* (1938, rpt. New York: Atheneum, 1969), p. 149.

9. Erich Auerbach, *Mimesis: the representation of reality in Western literature* (Princeton: Princeton University Press, 1953), p. 521.

10. Leon Damas, "Bargain," in *Giant Talk: An Anthology of Third World Writings,* Quincy Troupe and Rainer Schulte, eds. (New York: Vintage, 1975), p. 347.

11. Aimé Cesaire, "An Introduction to American Negro Poetry," Ellen Conroy Kennedy, trans. *Black Collegian* (Louisiana: April-May 1981), p. 145.

12. See the introduction by Sterling Stuckey, p. 9, in Brown, *The Collected Poems,* where he discusses "individualized portraits revelatory of interior lives."

13. Ramón Menéndez Pidal, *Flor nueva de romances viejos* (Buenos Aires: Espasa-Calpe Argentina, 1939), p. 13.

14. Richard Wright, *Native Son* (1940, rpt. New York: Harper and Row, 1966), p. 149.

15. *Giant Talk,* p. xliii.

16. Brown, *The Collected Poems,* pp. 218–219. All quotations from the poem are taken from these pages.

17. This is from Robert B. Steptoe's article "After Modernism, after Hibernation: Michael Harper, Robert Hayden and Jay Wright," *Chant of Saints,* Michael S. Harper and Robert B. Steptoe, eds. (Urbana: University of Illinois Press, 1979). His phrase is "control his history."

18. Ralph Ellison, *Shadow and Act* (1953, 1964, rpt. New York: Vintage, 1972). See article entitled "Change the Joke and Slip the Yoke," pp. 45–59.

19. Ruth Finnegan, *Oral Literature in Africa* (London: Oxford University Press, 1970), p. 456.

3. Multiple-Voiced Blues

1. Sherley A. Williams, "The Blues Roots of Contemporary Afro-American Poetry," *Chant of Saints,* Michael S. Harper and Robert B. Steptoe, eds. (Urbana: University of Illinois Press, 1979), p. 126.

2. Ibid., p. 135. Robert Hayden, of an earlier generation, is also a master of perspective shifts and multivoiced perspectives, especially in such seminal poems as "Middle Passage" and "Runagate Runagate." Though his poetry might also have been chosen for this type of mobility, since my focus here is on the expansion of the use of dialect as linguistic/poetic material, I have chosen Williams's poetry to display its potential. Sterling Brown's "Cabaret" is also a multivoiced and multileveled poem.

3. Ibid., p. 117. The text of the poem is quoted from this anthology.

4. Ibid., p. 127.

5. Ibid., p. 134.

6. Ibid., p. 130.

7. Carlos Fuentes, *Where the Air Is Clear,* tr. Sam Hileman (New York: Farrar, Straus and Giroux, 1960).

4. Jazz Modalities

1. Michael S. Harper, notes on jacket of John Coltrane's album, a Prestige 24003 recording.

2. Michael S. Harper, "Uplift from a Dark Tower," in *Chant of Saints,* Michael S. Harper and Robert B. Steptoe, eds. (Urbana: University of Illinois Press, 1979), pp. 23–30. All quotations from the poem are taken from these pages; quotations from the poems of Michael Harper appear by permission of the poet.

3. Michael S. Harper, interviewed by James Randall, *Ploughshares,* 7:1 (1981), pp. 17–18.

4. Robert Hayden, "Aunt Jemima of the Ocean Waves," in *The Poetry of Black America,* Arnold Arnoff, ed. (New York: Harper and Row, 1973), pp. 125–127.

5. Michael S. Harper, interviewed by John O'Brien in *Interviews with Black Writers,* John O'Brien, ed. (New York: Liveright, 1973), p. 98.

6. *Ploughshares,* 7:1, p. 24.

7. Kimberly Benston, "Late Coltrane: A Re-membering of Orpheus," *Chant of Saints,* p. 414.

8. Hermann Hesse, *Steppenwolf* (1927; rpt. New York: Bantam, 1970), pp. 34–35. See also pp. 21–43 and pp. 65–67.

9. Robert B. Steptoe, "After Modernism, after Hibernation: Michael Harper, Robert Hayden, and Jay Wright," in *Chant of Saints,* pp. 472–476.

10. *Ploughshares,* 7:1, pp. 22–24.

11. Ibid., p. 19.

12. Prestige 24003.

13. Quoted by Alex Aronson, *Music and the Novel: A Study in Twentieth-Century Fiction* (Totowa, N.J.: Rowman and Littlefield, 1980), p. 10.

5. Breaking out of the Conventions of Dialect

1. Janheinz Jahn, *Neo-African Literature: A History of Black Writing* (New York: Grove Press, 1968), pp. 149–151.

2. Camille Yarbrough, "Black Dance in America," *The Black Collegian,* 11:5 (April/May 1981), pp. 20–21. See also Robert C. Toll's *On With the Show* (New York: Oxford University Press, 1976, ch. 4.

3. Robert Hemenway, *Zora Neale Hurston: A Literary Biography* (Urbana: University of Illinois Press, 1977), p. 241. Also see Richard Wright's review of *Their Eyes Were Watching God,* in *New Masses,* Oct. 5, 1937.

4. James Weldon Johnson, *The Book of American Negro Poetry,* (New York: Harcourt, Brace and World, 1959), p. 4.

5. M. H. Abrams, ed., *The Norton Anthology of English Literature,* 4th ed., vol. II (New York: Norton, 1979), p. 89.

6. Paul Laurence Dunbar, "The Lynching of Jube Benson," *American Negro Short Stories,* John Henrik Clarke, ed. (New York: Hill and Wang, 1966), pp. 1–8. All quotations from the story are taken from this anthology.

7. Robert B. Steptoe, *From behind the Veil: A Study of Afro-American Narrative* (Urbana: University of Illinois Press, 1979), pp. 43–44.

8. Zora Neale Hurston, "The Gilded Six-Bits," *American Negro Short Stories,* pp. 63–74. All quotations from the story are taken from this anthology.

9. Roseann P. Bell, Bettye J. Parker, and Beverly Guy-Sheftall, eds., *Sturdy Black Bridges: Visions of Black Women in Literature* (New York: Anchor, 1979), p. 225.

10. W. E. Abraham, *The Mind of Africa* (Chicago: The University of Chicago Press, 1962), p. 11. Abraham speaks of historical events which "derive their significance from the culture in which they find themselves." His discussion may also raise questions regarding the significance of events in literature and "evaluation of facts and events."

11. Mary Gordon, "The Parable of the Cave or: In Praise of Water Colors," in *The Writer on Her Work,* Janet Sternburg, ed. (New York: Norton, 1980), pp. 28–29.

12. *Sturdy Black Bridges,* pp. 226, 228–229.

13. Lloyd W. Brown, *Women Writers in Black Africa* (Westport, Conn.: Greenwood Press, 1981), p. 140.

14. John Wideman, "Frame and Dialect: The Evolution of the Black Voice," *The American Poetry Review* (Sept.-Oct. 1976), pp. 34–37.

6. Blues Ballad

1. E. M. Forster, *Aspects of the Novel* (New York: Harcourt, Brace, 1927), pp. 64–66.

2. Jean Toomer, "Karintha," *Cane* (1923, rpt. New York: Harper and Row, 1969), p. 1. all quotations from *Cane* are taken from this edition.

3. Sherley A. Williams, "The Blues Roots of Contemporary Afro-American Poetry," *Chant of Saints,* Michael S. Harper and Robert B. Steptoe, eds. (Urbana: University of Illinois Press, 1979), p. 125.

4. George Kent, interviewed by Roseann P. Bell in *Sturdy Black Bridges,* Roseann P. Bell, Bettye J. Parker, and Beverly Guy-Sheftall, eds. (New York: Anchor, 1979), p. 220.

5. Langston Hughes and Arna Bontemps, eds., *Book of Negro Folklore* (New York: Dodd, Mead, 1958), pp. 392–394.

6. César Vallejo, "The anger that breaks the man into children," *Giant Talk: An Anthology of Third World Writings,* Quincy Troupe and Rainer Schulte, eds. (New York: Vintage, 1975), p. 3.

7. Hughes and Bontemps, *Book of Negro Folklore,* p. 345.

8. Michael S. Harper, interviewed by James Randall, *Ploughshares,* 7:1 (1981), p. 19.

9. Quoted by Harper, ibid., p. 27.

10. Ibid., p. 19.

11. Gertrude Stein, *Portraits and Prayers* (New York: Random House, 1934), p. 46.
12. Robert E. Spiller, Willard Thorp, Thomas H. Johnson, Henry Seidel Canby, Richard M. Ludwig, eds., *Literary History of the United States* (New York: Macmillan, 1963).
13. Janheinz Jahn, Neo-African Literature: A History of Black Writing (New York: Grove Press, 1968), p. 173.
14. Ibid., p. 174.
15. Ibid., p. 171.
16. Ibid.
17. *Giant Talk,* Troupe and Schulte, eds., p. xliii.
18. Toomer, *Cane,* quoted from Arna Bontemps's introduction.
19. Jean Toomer, *Essentials* (Chicago: Lakeside Press, 1923).

7. Slang, Theme, and Structure

1. Jean Toomer, "Bloodburning Moon," *Cane* (1923, rpt. New York: Harper and Row, 1969), p. 56.
2. Clyde Taylor, "The Language of Hip: From Africa to What's Happening Now," *First World,* 1:1 (Jan.-Feb. 1977), p. 36.
3. Ibid., p. 32.
4. William Flint Thrall and Addison Hubbard, eds., *Handbook of Literature* (New York: Odyssey Press, 1960), p. 462.
5. Imamu Amiri Baraka, "Ka 'Ba," *New Black Voices,* Abraham Chapman, ed. (New York: New American Library, 1972), p. 208.
6. Quincy Troupe and Rainer Schulte, eds., *Giant Talk: An Anthology of Third World Writings* (New York: Vintage, 1975), pp. xxxiv–xxxv.
7. Edward Albert, *History of English Literature,* 5th ed., revised by J. A. Stone (1923, rpt. London: Harrap, 1979), p. 35.
8. Edmund Wilson, *Axel's Castle* (New York: Charles Scribner's Sons, 1931), p. 94.
9. Ibid., p. 95.
10. Ibid., p. 96.
11. Ibid., p. 98.
12. Ibid., p. 99.
13. Ibid., p. 100.
14. Ernest J. Gaines, "Just Like a Tree," in *Bloodline* (New York: Dial Press, 1967), p. 230.
15. Rudolph Fisher, "The City of Refuge," in *American Negro Short Stories,* John Henrik Clarke, ed. (New York: Hill and Wang, 1966), p. 25. Note here also the Northerner's stereotyping of the Southern black, a frequent theme.

16. Taylor, "The Language of Hip," p. 30.
17. Loyle Hairston, "The Winds of Change," *American Negro Short Stories*, p. 297.
18. Ruth Miller, ed., *Blackamerican Literature* (Mission Hills, Calif.: Glencoe Press, 1971), p. 119.
19. Taylor, "The Language of Hip," p. 28.
20. Ibid., p. 27.
21. John O'Brien, *Interviews with Black Writers* (New York: Liveright, 1973), pp. 173–175.
22. Wilson, *Axel's Castle*, p. 113.
23. Ntozake Shange, *for colored girls who have considered suicide/when the rainbow is enuf* (New York: Bantam, 1977), p. 1.
24. Taylor, "The Language of Hip," p. 32.
25. Houston Baker, Jr., *Black Literature in America* (New York: McGraw-Hill, 1971), p. 18.

8. *Jazz/Blues Structure in Ann Petry's "Solo on the Drums"*

1. Richard Wright, *Black Boy* (1945, rpt. New York: Harper and Row, 1966), pp. 162–163.
2. Houston Baker, Jr., *The Journey Back* (Chicago: The University of Chicago Press, 1980), p. 88.
3. Alex Aronson, *Music and the Novel* (Totowa, N.J.: Rowman and Littlefield, 1980), p. 132.
4. Roseann P. Bell, Bettye J. Parker, and Beverly Guy-Sheftall, eds., *Sturdy Black Bridges: Visions of Black Women in Literature* (New York: Anchor, 1979), p. 237.
5. *Callaloo* 3:1 (1978), p. 46.
6. John O'Brien, ed., *Interviews with Black Writers* (New York: Liveright, 1973), p. 204.
7. Michael S. Harper, *Dear John, Dear Coltrane* (Pittsburgh: University of Pittsburgh Press, 1970), p. 5.
8. Ann Petry, "Solo on the Drums," *American Negro Short Stories*, John Henrik Clarke, ed. (New York: Hill and Wang, 1966), pp. 165–169. All quotations from the story are taken from these pages.
9. See Williams's article in *Chant of Saints*, Michael S. Harper and Robert B. Steptoe, eds. (Urbana: University of Illinois Press, 1979), pp. 123–135.
10. This excerpt is quoted from *Giant Talk*, Quincy Troupe and Rainer Schulte, eds. (New York: Vintage, 1975). The novel was published by Random House in 1973.
11. Ruth Finnegan, *Oral Literature in Africa* (London: Oxford University Press, 1970). See "Drum Language and Literature," pp. 481–482.

12. Toni Cade Bambara's short stories "Medley" and "Witchbird" are influenced by jazz improvisation. See Mary Helen Washington's introduction to her work in the anthology *Midnight Birds,* Mary Helen Washington, ed. (New York: Anchor, 1980), pp. 169–171.

9. Folktale, Character, and Resolution

1. Charles W. Chesnutt, "The Goophered Grapevine," *American Negro Short Stories,* John Henrik Clarke, ed. (New York: Hill and Wang, 1966), pp. 11–20.
2. Ralph Ellison, "Flying Home," *The Best Short Stories by Negro Writers,* Langston Hughes, ed. (Boston: Little, Brown, 1967), pp. 151–170. All quotations from the story are taken from these pages. In *Invisible Man* too it is the voice that clues us to his identity, that makes the central character paradoxically visible in his invisibility. It is his oration of self that finally enables him to know who he is.
3. W. E. B. Du Bois, *The Souls of Black Folk* (1903, rpt. Connecticut: Fawcett, 1961), pp. 16–17.
4. Robert E. Spiller, Willard Thorp, Thomas H. Johnson, Henry Seidel Canby, Richard M. Ludwig, eds., *Literary History of the United States* (New York: Macmillan, 1963), pp. 212–220 and 285.
5. Joanne Harumi Sechi, "Being Japanese-American Doesn't Mean 'Made in Japan,'" *The Third Woman: Minority Women Writers in the United States,* Dexter Fisher, ed. (Boston: Houghton Mifflin, 1980), pp. 445–447.
6. Alan Dundes, *Interpreting Folklore* (Bloomington: Indiana University Press, 1980), p. 23.
7. Ibid., p. 61.
8. Ibid.
9. Ralph Ellison, *Invisible Man* (New York: Random House, 1952), pp. 152–153.
10. It is notable here in the same context that often whenever black audiences disapprove of black portrayals, such portrayals are dismissed as "tales for white folks." It is important to note that this folktale, unlike Chesnutt's, is clearly meant for a black audience. (So is Chesnutt's, indirectly, in that it is probably only the black audience would recognize and share the "joke.")
11. Michael S. Harper, interviewed by James Randall in *Ploughshares,* 7:1, (1981), pp. 24–25.

10. The Freeing of Traditional Forms

1. Edmund Wilson, *Axel's Castle* (New York: Charles Scribner's Sons, 1931), pp. 304–312. See also Anna Balakian, *Surrealism* (New York: Noonday Press, 1959), pp. 112–161.

2. Robert E. Spiller, Willard Thorp, Thomas H. Johnson, Henry Seidel Canby, Richard M. Ludwig, eds., *Literary History of the United States* (New York: Macmillan, 1963), pp. 1413–1414.

3. Albert Camus, *The Rebel* (New York: Vintage, 1956), p. 47.

4. Wilson, *Axel's Castle*, p. 273.

5. Spiller et al., *Literary History of the United States*, p. 273.

6. Donald Gibson, *Introduction to Modern Black Poets* (Englewood Cliffs, N.J.: Prentice Hall, 1973), p. 10.

7. Ishmael Reed, *19 Necromancers from Now* (New York: Doubleday Anchor, 1970), p. 175.

8. Kimberly W. Benston, "Late Coltrane; A Re-membering of Orpheus," *Chant of Saints,* Michael S. Harper and Robert B. Steptoe, eds. (Urbana: University of Illinois Press, 1979). See pp. 414–420.

9. Spiller et al., *Literary History of the United States*, p. 1414.

10. LeRoi Jones (Amiri Baraka), "The Screamers," *American Negro Short Stories,* John Henrik Clarke, ed. (New York: Hill and Wang, 1966), pp. 304–310. All quotations from this story are taken from these pages.

11. Ralph Ellison, *Invisible Man* (New York: Random House, 1952), p. 136.

12. Richard Wright, "Blueprint for Negro Writing," *Richard Wright Reader,* Ellen Wright and Michel Fabre, eds. (New York: Harper and Row, 1978), p. 37.

13. Ibid., p. 38.

14. Frederick Douglass, *Narrative of the Life of Frederick Douglass* (1845, rpt. New York: Signet, 1968), p. 50. Alice Walker, in an interview with John O'Brien *(Interviews with Black Writers),* speaks of a similar incident. When her first novel was published, "a leading black monthly admitted [the editor did] that the book itself was never read but the magazine ran an item stating that a white reviewer had praised the book (which was, in itself, an indication that the book was no good—such went the logic)."

15. Ralph Ellison, *Shadow and Act* (1953, 1964, rpt. New York: Vintage, 1972), p. 25.

16. Alice Walker, "The Child Who Favored Daughter," *In Love and Trouble* (New York: Harcourt Brace Jovanovich, 1973), p. 40; the larger quote is: "In a world where innocence and guilt become further complicated by questions of race and color . . ."

17. Lloyd W. Brown, *Amiri Baraka* (Boston: Twayne Publishers, 1980), p. 56.

18. Michael S. Harper, interviewed by James Randall, *Ploughshares,* 7:1 (1981), p. 15.

19. Ibid.

20. Wilson, *Axel's Castle*, p. 113.

21. Morris Sweetkind, *Getting into Poetry* (Boston: Holbrook Press, 1972), p. 356.

11. Dialect and Narrative

1. William Wells Brown, *Clotel* (1853, rpt. New York: Macmillan, 1970).
2. Robert E. Spiller, Willard Thorp, Thomas H. Johnson, Henry Seidel Canby, Richard M. Ludwig, eds., *Literary History of the United States* (New York: Macmillan, 1963), p. 651.
3. Brown, *Clotel,* p. 98.
4. William York Tindall, *A Reader's Guide to James Joyce* (New York: Noonday Press, 1959), p. 126. Tindall notes Woolf's description of Joyce's *Ulysses* as "illiterate"; however, earlier, when parts of *Ulysses* were still being published by the "little magazines," Woolf had praised its innovations; perhaps she was unaware of the author's social class. Similar interpretative and evaluative shifts take place when critics/readers suddenly discover a writer's true race or sex. For example, a certain European American science fiction writer, a woman who used initials rather than a first name, was thought to be a man earlier in her career. She received numerous science fiction awards until it was discovered she was a woman. The awards dried up. Flaws of technique and substance were suddenly pointed out where there had been none before. One can only speculate how much Charles W. Chesnutt's early having been "mistaken for white" contributed to the early acclaim, favorable reviews, and publication in the prestigious and demanding *Atlantic Monthly.*
5. Martin R. Delany, *Blake or the Huts of America* (1859, rpt. Boston: Beacon Press, 1970), p. 76.
6. Quoted in *Literary History of the United States,* p. 650.
7. Alice Walker, interview, *Interviews with Black Writers,* ed. John O'Brien (New York: Liveright, 1973), pp. 202–203.
8. Rebecca Chalmers Barton, *Witnesses for Freedom* (1948, rpt. New York: Dowling College Press, 1976), p. 276.
9. Mildred Thompson, "Experiences of a Black Artist in Europe and the United States," *Black Art: an international quarterly* (Spring 1977), p. 28.
10. Michael S. Harper, interviewed by James Randall, *Ploughshares,* 7:1 (1981), p. 24.
11. Zora Neale Hurston, *Their Eyes Were Watching God* (1937, rpt. Greenwood Press, Westport, Conn.: 1965). All references to the text and quotations from it are from this edition.
12. John Wideman, "Frame and Dialect: The Evolution of the Black Voice," *The American Poetry Review* (Sept/Oct 1976).
13. Robert B. Steptoe, *From behind the Veil: A Study of Afro-American Narrative* (Urbana: University of Illinois Press, 1979), p. 166.
14. Robert Hemenway, *Zora Neale Hurston: A Literary Biography* (Urbana: University of Illinois Press, 1977), pp. 238–239.

15. Delany, *Blake,* p. 17.
16. James Bennett, *Prose Style* (California: Chandler Publishing, 1972), p. 174.
17. Ralph Ellison, *Shadow and Act* (1953, 1964, rpt. New York: Vintage, 1972), p. 55.

12. *Riddle*

1. Ralph Ellison, *Shadow and Act* (1953, 1964, rpt. New York: Vintage, 1972), pp. 103–105.
2. Ibid., pp. 105–106.
3. Ralph Ellison, *Invisible Man* (New York: Random House, 1952), p. 11. All quotations from the book are taken from this edition.
4. Ibid., p. 106.
5. John M. Reilley, "Introduction," *Twentieth Century Interpretations of Invisible Man* (Englewood Cliffs, N.J.: Prentice Hall, 1970), p. 8.
6. Ralph Ellison, "The Art of Romare Bearden," *Chant of Saints,* Michael S. Harper and Robert B. Steptoe, eds. (Urbana: University of Illinois Press, 1970), pp. 163–165.
7. Michael Harper, interviewed by Abraham Chapman, *Arts and Society,* 2:3 (1975), p. 464.
8. Ruth Finnegan, "Riddles," *Oral Literature in Africa* (London: Oxford University Press, 1970), pp. 426–427.
9. Ellison, *Shadow and Act,* p. 54.
10. Ellison, *Invisible Man,* p. 43.
11. Selma Fraiberg, "Two Modern Incest Heroes," *Twentieth Century Interpretations of Invisible Man,* p. 77.
12. Alan Dundes, *Interpreting Folklore* (Bloomington: Indiana University Press, 1980), p. 25.
13. Ellison, *Shadow and Act,* p. 53.
14. Finnegan, "Riddles."
15. Sterling Brown, *The Negro in American Fiction* (New York: Atheneum, 1969), p. 149.
16. John O'Brien, *Interviews with Black Writers* (New York: Liveright, 1973), p. 204.
17. Toni Cade Bambara, "What It Is I Think I'm Doing Anyhow," *The Writer on Her Work,* Janet Sternburg, ed. (New York: Norton, 1980), pp. 156–157.
18. Ellison, *Shadow and Act,* p. 53.
19. Ibid., p. 58.
20. Ibid., p. 49.
21. William York Tindall, *A Reader's Guide to James Joyce* (New York: Noonday Press, 1959), p. 275.

22. Ellison, *Shadow and Act,* p. 25.
23. Ibid., p. 55.
24. Richard Wright, "I Tried to Be a Communist," *A Casebook on Ralph Ellison's Invisible Man,* Joseph F. Trimmer, ed. (New York: Thomas Y. Crowell, 1972), pp. 55–56.
25. Ellison, "The Art of Romare Bearden," p. 163.
26. *Shadow and Act,* pp. 229–230.
27. Anna Balakian, *Surrealism: the Road to the Absolute* (New York: Noonday Press, 1959), pp. 123–124.
28. Ellison, *Shadow and Act,* pp. 56–57.
29. Miguel de Cervantes Saavedra, *Don Quijote de la Mancha* (1605–1615, rpt. New York: Las Americas, 1967). All quotations from the book are taken from this edition. See page 1056.
30. Ellison, *Shadow and Act,* p. 57.

13. Blues and Spirituals

1. Alice Walker, *The Third Life of Grange Copeland* (New York: Harcourt Brace Jovanovich, 1970). All quotations are taken from this edition.
2. Michael S. Harper, *Images of Kin* (Urbana: University of Illinois Press, 1977), pp. 46–47.
3. Etheridge Knight, quoted by Addison Gayle, Jr., "Blueprint for Black Criticism," *First World,* 1:1 (January 1977), p. 42.
4. James Baldwin, *Just above My Head* (London: Michael Joseph, 1979), pp. 308–309.
5. Octavio Paz, *Labyrinth of Solitude* (New York: Grove Press, 1961), p. 330.
6. Richard Wright, *Native Son* (1940, rpt., New York: Harper and Row, 1966), pp. 13–14.
7. Alice Walker, "The Child Who Favored Daughter," *In Love and Trouble* (New York: Harcourt Brace Jovanovich, 1973), p. 40.
8. Alice Walker, interviewed by John O'Brien, ed., *Interviews with Black Writers* (New York: Liveright, 1973), p. 192.
9. Carlos Fuentes, *Where the Air Is Clear* (New York: Farrar, Straus and Giroux, 1960), p. 47.
10. Floyd Horowitz, "Ralph Ellison's Modern Version of Brer Bear and Brer Rabbit," *Twentieth Century Interpretations of Invisible Man* (Englewood Cliffs, N.J.: Prentice Hall, 1970), pp. 32–38.
11. Alan Dundes, *Interpreting Folklore* (Bloomington: Indiana University Press, 1980), p. 25.
12. Wright, *Native Son,* p. 110.

13. Sharon Spencer, *Space, Time and Structure in the Modern Novel* (New York: New York University Press, 1971), pp. 197–198.
14. Robert E. Spiller, Willard Thorp, Thomas H. Johnson, Henry Seidel Canby, Richard M. Ludwig, eds., *Literary History of the United States* (New York: Macmillan, 1963).

14. Freeing the Voice

1. Ernest Gaines, *The Autobiography of Miss Jane Pittman* (New York: Dial Press, 1971). All quotations from the book are taken from this edition.
2. Robert B. Steptoe, *From behind the Veil: A Study of Afro-American Narrative* (Urbana: University of Illinois Press, 1979), p. 166.
3. Barry Beckham, "Jane Pittman and Oral Tradition," *Callaloo*, 1:3 (1978).
4. N. Scott Momaday, *House Made of Dawn* (New York: New American Library, 1968), p. 88.
5. Ernest Gaines, "Miss Jane and I," *Callaloo*, pp. 37–38.
6. Lorna Dee Cervantes, "Para un Revolucionario," *The Third Woman: Minority Women Writers of the United States,* Dexter Fisher, ed. (Boston: Houghton Mifflin, 1980), p. 382.
7. Gerald Moore, "Discovery," *Modern Black Novelists*, M. G. Cooke, ed. (Englewood Cliffs, N.J.: Prentice Hall, 1971), pp. 148–149.
8. Quoted in Robert E. Spiller, Willard Thorp, Thomas H. Johnson, Henry Seidel Canby, Richard M. Ludwig, eds., *Literary History of the United States* (New York: Macmillan, 1963), p. 291.
9. Quoted in ibid., p. 151.
10. Ibid., p. 161.
11. Ibid., p. 345.
12. Richard Bridgman, "From Hawthorne to Hemingway," *Prose Style,* James R. Bennett, ed. (California: Chandler Publishing, 1971), p. 174.
13. Eudora Welty, "Why I Live at the P.O.," *Short Story Masterpieces,* Robert Penn Warren and Albert Erskine, eds. (New York: Dell Press, 1954), p. 537.
14. John F. Callahan, "The Historical Frequencies of Ralph Waldo Ellison," *Chant of Saints,* Michael S. Harper and Robert B. Steptoe, eds. (Urbana: University of Illinois Press, 1970), p. 35.
15. Ernest Gaines, interviewed by Charles H. Rowell, *Callaloo*, 1:3 (1978), p. 41.
16. Steve McNeil, "Dialogue Tells the Story," *The Writer's Handbook*, A. S. Burack, ed. (Boston: The Writer, 1964).
17. *Callaloo*, 1:3, p. 41.
18. Amos Tutuola, *The Palm-Wine Drinkard* (New York: Grove Press, 1953), p. 50.

15. Motives of Folktale

1. Richard Bridgman, "From Hawthorne to Hemingway," *Prose Style,* James R. Bennett, ed. (California: Chandler Publishing, 1971), pp. 172–174.
2. Toni Morrison, *Song of Solomon* (New York: Knopf, 1977). All quotations from the book are taken from this edition.
3. Lloyd W. Brown, *Women Writers in Black Africa* (Westport, Conn.: Greenwood Press, 1981), p. 80.
4. See Ulli Beier, ed., *African Poetry: An Anthology of Traditional African Poems* (New York: Cambridge University Press, 1966), p. 56.
5. Harold Courlander, *A Treasury of Afro-American Folklore* (New York: Crown Publishers, 1976), p. 286.
6. Bridgman, "From Hawthorne to Hemingway."
7. Gerald Moore, "Tchikaya U Tam'si: Surrealism and Negritude in His Poetry," *Introduction to African Literature,* p. 117.
8. Amos Tutuola, *The Palm-Wine Drinkard* (New York: Grove Press, 1953), p. 83.
9. Bridgman, "From Hawthorne to Hemingway," p. 174.
10. Carlos Fuentes, *Where the Air Is Clear* (New York: Farrar, Straus and Giroux, 1960), p. 44.
11. Octavio Paz, *Labyrinth of Solitude* (New York: Grove Press, 1961), p. 30.
12. Fuentes, *Where the Air Is Clear,* p. 249.

Conclusion

1. N. Scott Momaday, *House Made of Dawn* (New York: New American Library, 1968), p. 88.
2. Elizabeth Cook-Lynn, Laureen Mars, Diana Chang, Jessica Hagedorn, Lorna Dee Cervantes, and Marcela Lucero-Trujilla in *The Third Woman: Minority Women Writers of the United States,* Dexter Fisher, ed. (Boston: Houghton Mifflin, 1980), p. 105.
3. This point is made in the introduction to *Giant Talk,* Quincy Troupe and Rainer Schulte, eds. (New York: Vintage, 1975), p. xxiv.
4. Ibid., p. xxl.
5. Lloyd W. Brown, *Women Writers in Black Africa* (Westport, Conn.: Greenwood Press, 1981), p. 80.
6. Richard Bridgman, "From Hawthorne to Hemingway," *Prose Style,* James R. Bennett, ed. (California: Chandler Publishing, 1971), p. 174. It should be noted that much African American oral literature is not merely naturalistic, but also enters the arena of supernatural, metaphysical, and spiritual conflicts.
7. Brown, *Women Writers in Black Africa,* p. 99.

8. Alex Aronson, *Music and the Novel* (Totowa, N.J.: Rowman and Little-field, 1980), pp. 173–174.

9. Anna Balakian, *Surrealism: The Road to the Absolute* (New York: Noonday Press, 1959), p. 55.

10. *Giant Talk*, p. xliii. The authors use "conceptual voyage." The African oral epics are also relevant here, especially as regards their supernatural elements. Ruth Finnegan has argued that there are no epics in Africa, but see Isidore Okpewho's *The Epic in Africa* (New York: Columbia University Press, 1979).

11. E. M. Forster, *Aspects of the Novel* (New York: Harcourt, Brace, 1927), p. 66.

12. *Literary History of the United States,* pp. 340–341.

13. See Albert Camus's discussion of "the American novel" in *The Rebel* (New York: Knopf, 1956), pp. 265–266, albeit he is referring to "the 'tough' novel of the thirties and forties and not the admirable American efflorescence of the nineteenth century."

14. G. L. Anderson, ed., *Masterpieces of the Orient,* (New York: Norton, 1961), pp. 703, 232.

15. W. E. Abraham, *The Mind of Africa* (Chicago: The University of Chicago Press, 1962), pp. 96–97. See also Ruth Finnegan's discussion of African oral characterization in *Oral Literature in Africa* (London: Oxford University Press, 1970), pp. 383–384.

16. *Literary History of the United States,* p. 902. In African tradition, Isidore Okpewho has referred to "the ambivalence of the heroic image." It contributes to the complexity of characterization found in African oral epics, such as the Mwindo epic.

17. Brown, *Women Writers in Black Africa,* p. 141.

18. See Kimberly Benston's "Late Coltrane: A Re-membering of Orpheus," *Chant of Saints,* Michael S. Harper and Robert B. Steptoe, eds. (Urbana: University of Illinois Press, 1979), pp. 421–422.

19. *Literary History of the United States,* p. 820.

20. Geneva Cobb Moore, "Metamorphosis: The Shaping of Phillis Wheatley and Her Poetry" (Ph.D. diss., University of Michigan, 1981).

21. *Literary History of the United States,* p. 825.

22. Richard Price, "Aim for the Throat," quoted by Kit Reed in *Story First: The Writer as Insider* (Englewood Cliffs, N.J.: Prentice Hall, 1982), pp. 139–140.

23. *Literary History of the United States,* pp. 345–346.

24. *Chant of Saints,* p. 466.

25. Richard Wright, *Black Boy* (1942, rpt. New York: Harper and Row, 1966), pp. 184–186.

26. Ntozake Shange, interviewed by Robert Fleming in *Encore,* June 1980, p. 36.

27. Fatima Dike, interview, *Callaloo,* 3:1–3.
28. Edward Albert, *History of English Literature* (1923, rpt. London: Harrap, 1979), p. 49.
29. Arthur Miller, "The American Writer: The American Theatre," *Michigan Quarterly Review,* 21:1 (Winter 1982), pp. 4–20.
30. Shange in *Encore,* June 1980, p. 36.

Index